THE NEW GROVE

WAGNER

THE NEW GROVE
DICTIONARY OF MUSIC AND MUSICIANS
Editor: Stanley Sadie

The Composer Biography Series

THE NEW GROVE

WAGNER

John Deathridge
Carl Dahlhaus

I.C.C. LIBRARY

W. W. NORTON & COMPANY

NEW YORK   LONDON

75188

Chapters 4 and 5 first published in
The New Grove Dictionary of Music and Musicians,
edited by Stanley Sadie, 1980

First published in UK in paperback 1984 by
PAPERMAC
a division of Macmillan Publishers Limited
London and Basingstoke

ISBN 0 333 36065 6

First published in UK in hardback 1984 by
MACMILLAN LONDON LIMITED
4 Little Essex Street London WC2R 3LF
and Basingstoke

ISBN 0 333 36184 9

First American edition in book form 1984 by
W.W. NORTON & COMPANY
New York and London

ISBN 0-393-30092-7 (paperback)
ISBN 0-393-01688-9 (hardback)

Printed in Great Britain

Contents

List of illustrations

Illustration acknowledgments

We are grateful to the following for permission to reproduce illustrative material: Library of Congress, Washington (fig.14); Mary Evans Picture Library, London (fig.12); Nationalarchiv der Richard-Wagner-Stiftung/Richard-Wagner-Gedenkstätte, Bayreuth (cover, figs.1–3, 5–11, 13, 15, 16); Pierpont Morgan Library, New York (fig.4).

General abbreviations

arr.	arrangement, arranged by/for	op.	opus
aut.	autumn	orch	orchestra, orchestral
		orchd	orchestrated (by)
		orig.	original(ly)
B	bass [voice]	ov.	overture
Bar	baritone [voice]		
		perf.	performance, performed (by)
c	circa [about]		
cf	confer [compare]	pf	piano
chap.	chapter	prol	prologue
cl	clarinet	pseud.	pseudonym
cond.	conductor, conducted by	pubd	published
		pubn	publication
ded.	dedication, dedicated to		
diss.	dissertation	qnt	quintet
		qt	quartet
ed.	editor, edited (by)		
edn.	edition	R	photographic reprint
Eng.	English	repr.	reprinted
		rev.	revision, revised (by/for)
facs.	facsimile		
Fr.	French	S	Santa [Saint]; soprano
frag.	fragment	ser.	series
		spr.	spring
Ger.	German	str	string(s)
gui	guitar	sum.	summer
		suppl.	suplement, supplementary
inc.	incomplete		
incl.	includes, including		
inst	instrument, instrumental	T	tenor [voice]
		trans.	translation, translated by
Jb	Jahrbuch [yearbook]		
Jg.	Jahrgang [year of publication/volume]	transcr.	transcription, transcribed by/for
lib	libretto	U.	University
movt	movement	v, vv	voice, voices
		vn	violin
no.	number	vol.	volume
n.p.	no place of publication		
nr.	near	wint.	winter

Symbols for the library sources of works, printed in *italic*, correspond to those used in *Répertoire international des sources musicales*, Ser. A.

Bibliographical abbreviations

AMf	Archiv für Musikforschung
AMw	Archiv für Musikwissenschaft
AMZ	Allgemeine musikalische Zeitung
AnMc	Analecta musicologica
BMw	Beiträge zur Musikwissenschaft
DJbM	Deutsches Jahrbuch der Musikwissenschaft
GfMKB	Gesellschaft für Musikforschung Kongressbericht
IMSCR	International Musicological Society Congress Report
JAMS	Journal of the American Musicological Society
Mf	Die Musikforschung
ML	Music and Letters
MQ	The Musical Quarterly
MR	The Music Review
MT	The Musical Times
NZM	Neue Zeitschrift für Musik
ÖMz	Österreichische Musikzeitschrift
PRMA	Proceedings of the Royal Musical Association
RdM	Revue de Musicologie
ReM	La revue musicale
SMz	Schweizerische Musikzeitung/Revue musicale suisse
ZfM	Zeitschrift für Musik
ZMw	Zeitschrift für Musikwissenschaft

Preface

This volume is one of a series of short biographies derived from *The New Grove Dictionary of Music and Musicians* (London, 1980). *The New Grove Dictionary* was written in the mid-1970s and finalized at the end of that decade. Research on Richard Wagner, however, has moved fast over the last few years; it was accordingly decided to invite John Deathridge to replace the biographical material, originally contributed by the late Curt von Westernhagen, and to invite Professor Carl Dahlhaus, who contributed the section on Wagner's aesthetics and music in *The New Grove Dictionary*, to replace the original contributions on Wagner's critical, theoretical and autobiographical writings. The work-list has been prepared anew by John Deathridge in the light of the work done by himself, Martin Geck and Egon Voss towards the preparation of a comprehensive thematic catalogue of Wagner's musical works. John Deathridge has also extended the list of Wagner's writings. The bibliography was initially prepared by Robert Bailey and has been revised and brought up to date by Professor Dahlhaus and Dr Deathridge.

The fact that the texts of the books in the series are in the first place designed as dictionary articles inevitably gives them a character somewhat different from that of books conceived as such. They are intended to accommodate a very great deal of information in a manner that makes reference quick and easy. Their first concern is with fact rather than opinion, and this leads to a larger than usual proportion of the texts being devoted to biography than to critical discussion. The nature of a reference work gives it a particular obligation to convey received knowledge and to treat of composers' lives and works in an encyclopedic fashion, with proper acknowledgment of sources and due care to reflect different standpoints, rather than to embody imaginative or speculative writing about a composer's character or his music. It is hoped that the comprehensive work-lists and extended bibliographies, indicative of the origins of the books in a reference work, will be valuable to the reader who is eager for full and accurate reference information and who may not have ready access to *The New Grove Dictionary* or who may prefer to have it in this more compact form.

S.S.

CHAPTER ONE

Life

I Early years: 1813–32

Wilhelm Richard Wagner was born in Leipzig on 22
May 1813. He was the legal son of a police actuary,
(Carl) Friedrich (Wilhelm) Wagner (*b* Leipzig, 18
June 1770; *d* Leipzig, 23 Nov 1813), and his wife
Johanna (Rosine), née Pätz (*b* Weissenfels, 19 Sept
1774; *d* Leipzig, 9 Jan 1848), the daughter of a baker.
On Goethe's 65th birthday (28 August 1814), nine
months after the death of Friedrich Wagner, Johanna
married Ludwig (Heinrich Christian) Geyer (*b* Eis-
leben, 21 Jan 1779; *d* Dresden, 30 Sept 1821), a
portrait painter, actor and poet.

The famous and unanswerable question of
Wagner's paternity is less important than Wagner's
thoughts about it. According to Cosima's diaries (26
Dec 1868) he 'did not believe' that Ludwig Geyer was
his real father. At the same time he attributed a
supposed resemblance, noticed by Cosima, between
his son Siegfried and Geyer to 'elective affinities'
(*Wahlverwandtschaften*) – a suggestive quotation
possibly alluding to Geyer's cordial relations with
Goethe, but sufficiently ambiguous to cloud permanently the most definitive statement.

Wagner was also unsure – or less sure than he
probably would have admitted – about his birth and

1

baptism. In his first diary, the so-called 'Red Pocket-Book' (*die Rote Brieftasche*, begun mid-August 1835), the day of his birth has been changed from '12' to '22' – a small and perhaps insignificant mistake that undermines the theatrical self-assurance of the diary's opening. (Wagner's full name, date and place of birth at the beginning of the diary look more like the start of an article in a dictionary of music than a private *aide mémoire*.) In addition, his autobiography *Mein Leben* begins with the incorrect statement that his baptism in the Thomaskirche in Leipzig took place two days after his birth. He was actually baptized three months later, on 16 August 1813. The apparent cause of the delay, about which a great fuss has been made, was a journey undertaken by Johanna in the previous month to Teplitz (now Tepliče), Bohemia, where Geyer had an engagement as an actor. Despite a thorough investigation of Wagner's origins by Strobel, Reihlen and Rauschenberger (undertaken not surprisingly during the Nazi years) the journey only deepens the mystery since its purpose remains unclear.

The one certainty about Wagner's paternity, then, is that Wagner himself was uncertain about it. This may explain the almost cosmic significance he attached to each of his birthdays in later years. And it was probably the reason he adopted Nietzsche's suggestion for the crest that adorns the title-pages of each section of the first edition of *Mein Leben*. The crest shows a vulture (*Geier*) with a shield on which are emblazoned the seven stars of the Great Bear or the Plough (*der Wagen*). The vulture could be seen as an ironic allusion to the crests of German aristocratic

1. *The opening of Wagner's diary, the so-called 'Red Pocket-Book', begun in Frankfurt in the summer of 1835*

families that used the similar form of the eagle as a symbol of power. (Unlike Beethoven, Wagner had no illusions about his middle-class origins.) But it is more likely that the combination of *der Wagen* with the *Geier* symbol refers to Wagner's 'dual' paternity, as he probably saw it, and perhaps to the emotional void left by the premature deaths of both his 'fathers' (see fig. 3).

It is tempting to interpret the course of Wagner's life in terms of its less than stable beginning. Certainly, there are signs of what Erik Erikson would call an 'identity crisis' in the young Wagner that was caused by (among other things) the absence of a strong father figure and the simple fact that he was called Richard Geyer until his entry on 21 January 1828 into the Leipzig Nicolaischule at the age of almost fifteen. (Later manuscripts on which Wagner has written 'Wagner' not once but several times sug-

3

2. A self-portrait of Ludwig Geyer, c1806; no portrait of Friedrich Wagner has survived

gest that he was even unsure of his name.) It is also obvious that Wagner's deep-seated existential doubts (often confessed privately in letters to friends) had much to do with his overbearing egotism and the ten-dentious dramaturgy of *Mein Leben*. His autobiogra-phical writings, however, present the biographer with a more immediate problem. If Wagner's need to record, interpret and reinterpret his life in detail was a lasting symptom of his 'identity crisis', it is the muddle this has caused, rather than the crisis itself, that must be clarified first.

To judge by the surviving documents, Wagner's early life was intellectually more gregarious and trau-matic than the entertaining opening pages of *Mein Leben* suggest. Wagner numbed his birth pangs as an artist by turning them into a joke. Ludwig II 'laughed heartily' when he heard Wagner recite from the first part of his autobiography; and Nietzsche confessed that he could hardly suppress a smile when he re-membered Wagner's rendering from *Mein Leben* of his youthful escapades. Wagner's early compositions and letters, however, reveal a hard-working, vulner-able and at the same time surprisingly business-like individual unlike the autobiographical image of reck-less genius 'almost without actual learning'. Alone the quantity and variety of his early compositions prove that his early musical and literary tastes were wider and more cosmopolitan than he later admitted. His letters, too, show a willingness to conform to every shade of prevailing fashion that contrasts strikingly with the openly aggressive reformism of the mature artist.

The main facts of Wagner's education are as follows. After the Wagner family had moved with Ludwig Geyer to Dresden, Wagner was sent to the school of the Vizehofkantor Carl Friedrich Schmidt there in 1817. He entered the Kreuzschule in Dresden on 2 December 1822 where he took a few piano lessons. The Wagner/Geyer family moved to Prague in 1826, but Richard stayed in Dresden and became increasingly obsessed with Ancient Greece, translating the songs of the *Odyssey*, and trying in vain to write an epic poem *Die Schlacht am Parnassus*. After moving to the Nicolaischule in Leipzig in 1828, he finished his first extant work *Leubald* (an unintentionally surrealist amalgam of Shakespeare, Kleist and Goethe) which, in order to provide it with music, prompted him to study Johann Bernhard Logier's theory of composition and Beethoven's music for *Egmont*. (An early copy of part of the *Egmont* music in Wagner's hand has survived.) In the autumn of

3. Wagner's crest from the title-page of the first private edition of 'Mein Leben' (1870)

1828 he began secret lessons in the theory of harmony with Christian Gottlieb Müller, a local composer and conductor, and on 16 June 1830 entered the Thomasschule in Leipzig where he took violin lessons for a short time with a member of the Gewandhaus Orchestra, Robert Sipp. He soon discovered Beethoven, completing a piano score of the Ninth Symphony by Easter 1831. He enrolled at Leipzig University to study music on 23 February 1831, and in autumn of the same year became a pupil of the Thomaskantor Christian Theodor Weinlig with whom (according to *Mein Leben*) he studied counterpoint for six months.

Wagner's statement in *Mein Leben* that he heard Wilhelmine Schröder-Devrient sing Fidelio in Leipzig in 1829 is untrue. The performance is not mentioned in his diary, the Red Pocket-Book, and there is no trace of it in the theatre records of the period. (Whether or not he heard her sing Emmy in the first performance of Marschner's *Der Vampyr* in Leipzig in 1828 is an open question.) The available evidence suggests that it was Schröder-Devrient's famous portrayal of Romeo in Bellini's *I Capuleti e i Montecchi* that really influenced him, probably during the Leipzig performances of March 1834. Wagner seems to have backdated the experience, changing both work and composer, in order to make his supposed inheritance of Beethoven's legacy, and with it his destiny as the creator of a specifically German music drama, seem inevitable from the outset.

Wagner's composition lessons were also not quite as perfunctory as *Mein Leben* says they were. Entries in the Red Pocket-Book and a recently discovered letter to his first teacher Müller (now in the Pierpont Morgan Library, New York) show that he was dependent on Müller for far longer than the unflattering account in his autobiography implies. Moreover, we only have Wagner's word for it that his lessons with Weinlig lasted merely half a year. His extant contrapuntal exercises are undated. And his assertion in *Mein Leben* that he renounced composition in order to concentrate on counterpoint is untrue since a series of dated manuscripts, including the second version of the Overture in D minor (wwv20) and the Fantasie in F♯ minor (wwv22), prove that he was busy with non-contrapuntal works for at least part of his supposedly six-month study. The dedication to Weinlig of Wagner's first published work, the Piano Sonata in B♭ (wwv21), is a sign, too, that Weinlig's lessons were wider in scope than Wagner suggests, extending perhaps beyond fugue and canon to classical sonata forms.

The large grains of truth in *Mein Leben* make its deceptions all the more subtle. It is true that the young Wagner was profoundly influenced by Beethoven. Apart from lessons in composition, he trained himself by making careful copies of the full scores of the Fifth and Ninth Symphonies (now in the Bayreuth Archives), and many of his first instrumental works are influenced by Beethovenian models. The constant implication in *Mein Leben*, however, that the spirit of music drama already began to take flight on the wings of Beethoven's symphonic music at the beginning of his career is a distortion of the

4. Part of an autograph letter from Wagner to his first composition teacher, Christian Gottlieb Müller, probably written on Christmas eve 1830

more modest truth that he began as a composer of works in several, predominantly instrumental, genres in the classical mould. According to the Red Pocket-Book he studied Mozart's symphonies as well as Beethoven's. He made a piano arrangement of Haydn's Symphony no.103 in E♭ and a copy in his hand of Symphony no.104 in D still exists. (It is preserved in the Huntingdon Library, San Marino, California.) But it was Beethoven who dominated his early sonatas, overtures and incidental music. Ironically, when he finally began to write operas, Beethoven's musical influence on him rapidly lost its former intensity.

II First operas and first marriage: 1832–6

Apart from an early *Schäferoper* (wwv6) that was never completed, Wagner made his first attempt at a full-scale opera in October and November 1832 while visiting the house of Count Pachta in Pravonin near Prague. (The year 1832 is also notable for what was probably Wagner's first appearance as a conductor in the Leipzig music society 'Euterpe' in March when he directed the first performance of his Concert Overture in C.) Like many significant developments in Wagner's life, his beginnings as an opera composer were marked by a false start. At first he wanted to adapt Johann Büsching's *Ritterzeit und Ritterwesen* as a novelette, but then decided to expand it into an opera libretto. He called the opera *Die Hochzeit* and began drafting music for it on 5 December 1832. However, his sister Rosalie disliked the text. Without her approval (she was a well-known actress with good connections in the Royal Court Theatre in Leipzig) he probably saw no chance of having the work performed, and in a letter dated 3 January 1833 announced that he had 'torn up' the libretto. Possibly because Weinlig approved of what little his pupil had already composed (at least according to *Mein Leben*), the music of the opening scene has survived.

Meanwhile, Wagner's career as a late classical composer of instrumental music reached its peak in November 1832 with the first performance in Prague of his Symphony in C. It was performed again on 15 December 1832 in the Euterpe in Leipzig and yet again on 10 January 1833 in the Gewandhaus. The work was warmly received by Heinrich Laube in the *Zeitung für die elegante Welt*; but after another performance in Würzburg on 27 August 1833 under the composer's direction, it was not played again until Wagner revived and revised it for a private performance in the Teatro Fenice in Venice on 25 December 1882. (It was the last work he conducted.)

Having destroyed most of *Die Hochzeit*, Wagner immediately set to work on another opera, *Die Feen*, retaining some names of the characters from the rejected work. The libretto was based on Carlo Gozzi's play *La donna serpente* and completed by the end of February 1833. As it happened, the beginning of work on Wagner's first complete opera coincided with his first job in an opera house. With the help of his brother, the singer Albert Wagner, he became a 'rehearser of the chorus' (*Choreinstudierer*) at the city theatre of Würzburg. As a fledgling, not to say eminently practical, composer of operas with a strong

11

instinct for survival, he probably made the move not only in order to acquaint himself with the inner workings of the theatre but also to escape military service in Saxony.

While in Würzburg, Wagner composed the text and music to a new concluding allegro for Aubry's aria (no.15) in Marschner's *Der Vampyr* (wwv33). The impression given in *Mein Leben*, however, that this was a present for his brother Albert, and an atonement for an unsuccessful instrumentation of a cavatina from Bellini's *Il pirata* (wwv34) that Albert had previously commissioned from him, is another piece of autobiographical jiggery-pokery which is intended to praise the German composer at the expense of the Italian. In fact, Wagner must have orchestrated Bellini's cavatina well after 29 September 1833 when his addition to *Der Vampyr* was first performed. The Würzburg theatre programme shows that the performance of Bellini's *La straniera*, for which the cavatina from *Il pirata* was intended as an additional aria, did not take place until 5 December 1833. When Wagner implied in *Mein Leben* that his imitation of Marschner had eradicated the memory of Bellini's 'thin' music, he forgot to add that he had reversed the order of events.

Wagner wrote the entire score of *Die Feen* in Würzburg, completing it on 6 January 1834. His autobiography, however, makes no mention of the fact that he revised parts of it after his return to Leipzig on 21 January. The guest performances of Schröder-Devrient in Bellini's *I Capuleti e i Montecchi* during March clearly inspired him to rewrite not only the music but also the dramatic content of Ada's aria in Act 2. Further, surviving documents prove that he introduced new spoken dialogue in place of many scenes, probably in order to placate the theatre authorities in Leipzig who complained that the opera was 'through-composed' (*durchkomponiert*). Despite the intervention of his sister Rosalie and brother-in-law Friedrich Brockhaus, the opera was not accepted and did not receive its (posthumous) first performance until 29 June 1888 in Munich.

In Leipzig Wagner became increasingly involved in the so-called 'Young German' movement – a loose conglomerate of intellectuals, including Heinrich Laube and Theodor Mundt, whose views were directed against Germany's feudal structure in favour of a rapidly emerging 'liberal' middle-class. (Young Germany's enthusiasm for Schröder-Devrient as an artistic symbol of its ideals undoubtedly influenced Wagner at this time.) Wagner's first published essay, 'Die deutsche Oper', appeared on 10 June 1834 in Laube's *Zeitung für die elegante Welt*; and in Teplitz he turned Shakespeare's *Measure for Measure* into a 'grand comic opera' which glorifies Italian sensuality at the expense of German small-mindedness. (Wagner changed the location of the piece from Vienna to Palermo to reinforce the point.) He became music director to Heinrich Bethmann's theatrical company at the end of July 1834, and on 2 August, perhaps in keeping with his new philosophy, made his début as an opera conductor in Lauchstädt (Thuringia) with Mozart's *Don Giovanni*.

During the summer of 1834 Wagner made his last

attempt to write a classical symphony. According to *Mein Leben*, the Symphony in E (wwv35) was based on Beethoven's Seventh and Eighth Symphonies. He drafted the first and part of the second movement in Lauchstädt and Rudolstadt, but suddenly announced to his friend Theodor Apel, in a letter dated 13 September 1834, that there was 'no way' he could finish it. Except for incipits communicated by Wilhelm Tappert, the fragment (including an orchestration of it made by Felix Mottl in July 1887) is now lost.

Wagner's waning interest in Beethoven as a model for purely instrumental compositions was matched by a growing enthusiasm for France and Italy. His activities as a conductor in Magdeburg, where he was appointed music director of Bethmann's company in October 1834, brought him into contact with operas by Auber, Bellini, Boieldieu, Cherubini and Paisiello. He made his first contribution – an essay entitled 'Pasticcio' – to Robert Schumann's *Neue Zeitschrift für Musik* in November, and finished the libretto of his new 'grand comic opera' a month later. After conducting his opera in Magdeburg on 29 March 1836, he wrote an anonymous report for Schumann's paper in which he described his own work as 'containing much that I like . . . there is music and melody in it, and that's something we have a pretty hard time finding in our German operas'.

The new opera was called *Das Liebesverbot* ('The Ban on Love'). Before directing its first performance, Wagner tried to have it accepted by theatres in Leipzig, Berlin and even the Opéra-Comique in Paris. Well aware that Bethmann was approaching bankruptcy, however, he decided to perform it while the Magdeburg company was still in existence. His instinct proved correct: the second performance on 30 March 1836 had to be cancelled because of fist-fights among the cast and, soon after, the company was disbanded. Wagner's statement in *Mein Leben*, incidentally, that he had to change the title of the opera on police orders is not true. The authorities showed not the slightest objection, as an officially stamped document in the Bayreuth Archives proves. Wagner publicly called the opera *Die Novize von Palermo* ('The Novice of Palermo') and changed the genre to 'grand' instead of 'grand comic' opera probably for the simple reason that he was forced through pressure of time to conduct the work in Easter Week.

Apart from the composition of *Das Liebesverbot*, the two overtures *Columbus* (wwv37) and *Polonia* (wwv39), and scenarios for an opera *Die hohe Braut* (wwv40), the most important event in Wagner's life in this period was his love affair with the actress Christine Wilhelmine ('Minna') Planer (*b* Oderan, 5 Sept 1809; *d* Dresden, 25 Jan 1866). He first met her in Lauchstädt in the summer of 1834. From the start he was plagued by jealousy, as he freely admits in *Mein Leben*. The impression conveyed by Wagner, however, that he was attracted merely by her freshness and motherly instincts was a half-truth intended for the ears of his second wife, Cosima. (Cosima wrote down the text of *Mein Leben* at Wagner's dictation.) In fact, his early letters to Minna show that he was deeply in love and desperately afraid of losing her. He followed her to Magdeburg and then to

Königsberg on 7 July 1836 where she had accepted an acting engagement. They were eventually married in a church in Königsberg-Tragheim on 24 November of the same year.

III Königsberg, Riga, Paris: 1837–42

Wagner's first marriage was dogged from the start by insecurity. At first he was without a job in Königsberg. And two months after he was appointed music director at the city theatre (1 April 1837), Minna left him. On 31 May she secretly departed for Dresden with a prosperous businessman called Dietrich. Wagner followed her; but despite a brief reconciliation she left him again and did not rejoin him until the following October. The situation was not helped by Minna's decision to allow her illegitimate daughter Natalie (*b* 22 Feb 1826) to continue living with her under the pretence that she was her sister. (Natalie, who withheld from Wagner and his heirs some important documents that had been in Minna's possession, later became a key, if highly unreliable, source for the collector Mary Burrell.) Matters were not improved either by Wagner's jealousy and the tendency particularly noticeable in his letters to talk his partner into submission (his *Suada* or 'persuasive garrulousness' as Minna aptly called it). Wagner seriously considered divorce, but seems to have been dissuaded from taking this step by his sister Ottilie and her husband, the orientalist Hermann Brockhaus.

The difficult start of Wagner's marriage was reflected by his low productivity. Apart from some incidental music to J. Singer's romantic historical play *Die letzte Heidenverschwörung* (wwv41) and the bombastic overture *Rule Britannia* (wwv42), he composed and conducted little. He admits in his autobiography that this inactivity was 'wounding' to his pride, particularly as his wife was better known and more successful at the time. But he tried to cover up this vulnerable moment in his life with a false impression of his creative activity. His claim in *Mein Leben* that he sketched out the text of a 'comic opera', *Männerlist grösser als Frauenlist* (wwv48), in Königsberg in early 1837 is probably untrue. The Red Pocket-Book and his earlier autobiographical writings give the date as summer 1838 when Wagner was already in Riga. The later date is also more likely because the lighter *Singspiel* character of the text (the story is taken from the 194th of the 1001 Nights) was in keeping with the tastes of the director of the theatre in Riga, Karl von Holtei.

Wagner was engaged as music director in Riga in June 1837. While waiting to take up his appointment, he read Edward Bulwer Lytton's novel *Rienzi, the Last of the Roman Tribunes* in Blasewitz near Dresden. According to *Mein Leben*, he was immediately attracted by the idea of creating something grand and utopian in order to escape the sordid reality of his life. It is almost certain, however, that the idea of making a 'grand heroic opera' out of *Rienzi* originated with his friend Theodor Apel at least a year earlier in 1836, as a letter to Apel dated 20 September 1840 and Wagner's 'Autobiographische Skizze' (1843) suggest.

Wagner made his début in Riga simultaneously as conductor and composer on 1 September 1837 with a performance of Carl Blum's comic opera *Mary, Max und Michel*, for which he wrote an additional bass aria (wwv43). He composed a 'Hymn of the People', *Nicolay* (wwv44), in honour of Emperor Nicolay Pavlovich and conducted several operas, some of which he provided with extra music or partially reorchestrated (Weigl's *Die Schweizerfamilie*, Bellini's *Norma*, and Meyerbeer's *Robert le diable*). Besides arranging music for numerous plays and vaudevilles, he began a series of subscription concerts on 15 November 1838 in which he conducted the *Columbus* and *Rule Britannia* overtures, his orchestration of a duet from Rossini's *Les soirées musicales*, his arrangement of the Hunting Chorus from Weber's *Euryanthe*, and works by Beethoven (Symphonies nos.3–8, Overture *Leonore* no.3), Cherubini, Mendelssohn (*Calm Sea and Prosperous Voyage* Overture), Mozart and Weber.

Wagner's intense activity and his plans for reforming orchestra and theatre hardly made him popular with the talented but lightweight director von Holtei. Consequently his contract with the theatre for the 1838–9 season was not renewed. Having started serious work on the libretto and music of *Rienzi* in the summer of 1838, he therefore decided to learn French and to make for Paris, where he hoped his opera would be accepted in French translation. (He also thought of offering it to Berlin; the idea that he originally intended *Rienzi* only for production in Paris is a myth.) Accordingly he set out with Minna to cross the Russian border into East Prussia. On 19 July 1839 they boarded the schooner *Thetis* in Pillau (now Baltiysk, USSR) and after a rough journey via the coast of Norway they arrived in London on 12 August. On 20 August they crossed the English Channel to France (where Wagner met Meyerbeer for the first time in Boulogne-sur-mer) and arrived in Paris on 17 September.

The account in *Mein Leben* of Wagner's first Paris sojourn – his 'years of starvation' as sympathetic Wagnerites are wont to call it – is one of his cleverest, and unfortunately most tendentious, autobiographical *coups de théâtre*. For one thing, he rearranged the chronology of his works to make it appear that he was the victim and not the beneficiary of alien influence. An additional aria for Bellini's *Norma* (wwv52) written for the singer Luigi Lablache, for example, was not composed after the song *Mignonne* (wwv57) as a last resort to catch the attention of influential people in Paris, as Wagner suggests: we know from a letter to Gottfried Engelbert Anders dated 13 October 1839 that it must have been one of the first things he composed when he arrived in the city. A chorus he wrote for the Paris vaudeville, *Descendons gaiment la courtille* (wwv65), was not composed in the early part of 1840, as Wagner and most work-lists tell us, but a year later when, according to *Mein Leben*, he had supposedly given up Paris as a lost cause in order to devote himself to true German art. His work for Paris publishers in arranging other composers' music, too, was more extensive and spread over a longer period than is generally realized. The making of piano scores, duets and string quartet arrangements of Donizetti, Herz, Auber and Halévy (see wwv62*A–F*) was not forced on him by the Jewish publisher Maurice Schlesinger, as *Mein Leben* suggests. He worked for other publishers too; and there is evidence that it was he himself who took the initiative.

Wagner also had to redate and reinterpret one of his key artistic experiences: his alleged rediscovery of Beethoven's Ninth Symphony in a rehearsal of the first three movements by the Paris Conservatoire orchestra under Habeneck. According to *Mein Leben*, the work again opened his eyes to the glories of German art. Despite the allegedly wilful aloofness of influential Jews like Meyerbeer and Schlesinger (Wagner's depiction of Meyerbeer in *Mein Leben* constantly verges on libel), it inspired him to write a profoundly 'German' work, the *Faust* Overture (wwv59). Unfortunately, however, there is no evidence that Wagner heard Beethoven's Ninth when he said he did. On the contrary, the dating of Wagner's sketches suggests that it was Berlioz's dramatic symphony *Roméo et Juliette* that really influenced him (the Ninth Symphony was rehearsed and performed a few months after the *Faust* Overture was composed). Wagner attended either the first or the second performance of *Roméo et Juliette*, conducted by Berlioz in the Paris Conservatoire on 24 November and 1 December 1839. Already by 13 December he had completed the first draft of the *Faust* Overture. The score of the original version, which was completed on 12 January 1840, contains French directions and the use of four bassoons (reduced to three in the revised published version) is characteristic of Berlioz's orchestration. In later years, Wagner admitted privately to the London critic Edward Dannreuther that he had made a 'minute study' of Berlioz's instrumentation 'as early as 1840'.

If Berlioz rather than Beethoven opened new musical vistas for Wagner, it was Meyerbeer who, at first, provided the model for his career as an opera composer. (This is not to say that Wagner was influenced technically by Meyerbeer.) At Meyerbeer's suggestion, he tried to have his 'grand comic opera' *Das Liebesverbot* accepted by the smaller Théâtre de la Renaissance before attempting something more ambitious with the Opéra. He translated the libretto into French and arranged some numbers for an audition. But there is no evidence that he received a firm offer, and none that he was ignorant of the theatre's disastrous finances, as he states in *Mein Leben*. The implication that Meyerbeer played him false by concealing the facts of the theatre's affairs is probably untrue. Surviving documents, including Meyerbeer's diaries, show that Wagner was actually the better informed of the two composers: in a letter dated 3 May 1840, Wagner himself told Meyerbeer that the Théâtre de la Renaissance was heading for bankruptcy.

At the beginning of May 1840 Wagner sent Meyerbeer's principal librettist, Eugène Scribe, a prose draft of a new opera called *Der fliegende Holländer* and asked him to consider turning it into a libretto. Wagner hoped to receive a commission from the

21

Opéra to write the music and composed three numbers for a special audition, providing them with verse
himself in a French translation by Marion Dumersan
(not Emile Deschamps as Wagner says in *Mein
Leben*). Wagner informed Meyerbeer on 26 July 1840
that the three numbers – Senta's Ballad and the songs
of the Norwegian sailors and the Dutchman's crew –
were 'ready'. (His later claim that Senta's Ballad was
the first number of the opera to be composed is not
borne out by a close study of the sources.) Neither
the audition nor the commission materialized, however, and Wagner cut his losses by selling the French
prose draft of the opera for 500 francs to Léon Pillet,
the director of the Opéra, on 2 July 1841. (The draft
was converted into a libretto by P. Foucher and
B. H. Révoil, and set to music as *Le Vaisseau-
Fantôme* by Pierre Louis Philippe Dietsch, the future
conductor of the Paris *Tannhäuser*.)

Wagner did not follow Meyerbeer's suggestion in
the summer of 1840 that he should collaborate with
another composer on some ballet music for the Opéra.
Instead, he continued working on *Rienzi* and
managed to finish the full score on 19 November
1840. With the help of friends (including Schröder-
Devrient) and a strong recommendation from Meyerbeer, he succeeded in having the work accepted in
June 1841 for performance at the Royal Court
Theatre in Dresden. The success spurred him on to
write the rest of *Der fliegende Holländer*. He began
by composing the remaining two of the five songs
central to the opera: the Steersman's Song in Act 1
and the Spinning Chorus in Act 2. The full score was

5. *Wagner in his late twenties in Paris: pencil drawing by Ernst Benedikt Kietz (begun January 1840, completed June 1842)*

finished by November and, again with Meyerbeer's strong support, was accepted in March 1842 for performance at the Berlin Hofoper.

When Berlioz later recalled Wagner's first stay in Paris in his memoirs, he commented that Wagner had failed to make his name there as a composer. (A performance of the *Columbus* Overture on 4 February 1841 in Berlioz's presence and the *Liebesverbot* audition in May of the previous year had been failures.) But Berlioz did remember Wagner's success as an author, particularly with some frothy pieces in the style of Heine and E. T. A. Hoffmann written for the *Revue et Gazette musicale*. The years 1840–42, however, were also notable for the appearance of some of the first of Wagner's more serious essays (e.g. *Über die Ouvertüre* and three articles on Halévy and his opera *La reine de Chypre*) which touch on historical and theoretical issues that were to preoccupy the mature artist. Wagner was a skilled journalist, too, and his numerous reports to German newspapers about musical life in the French capital are still worth reading.

IV Royal Kapellmeister: 1843–9

On 7 April 1842 Wagner left Paris for Germany, where he arrived in Dresden with Minna on 12 April to help with rehearsals for *Rienzi*. In June he took a holiday in Teplitz during which he wrote two prose drafts for his next opera, *Tannhäuser* (or *Der Venusberg*, as it was then still called). He returned to Dresden and found the town full of enthusiastic rumours about the forthcoming production of *Rienzi*. The first performance on 20 October 1842 was an overwhelming success and an immediate decision was made to produce Wagner's next opera, *Der fliegende Holländer*. A few days after the *Rienzi* première, on 28 October, the death was announced of the royal Kapellmeister Francesco Morlacchi and all eyes turned to Wagner as his most likely successor. At first Wagner hesitated, pleading that he needed more time to work out *Tannhäuser* and other projects, possibly *Die Sarazenin* (wwv66) and *Die Bergwerke zu Falun* (wwv67) for which he had drafted scenarios in Paris. He soon relented, however, and on 2 February 1843 was installed as royal Kapellmeister for life at a salary of 1500 thalers.

On 7 February 1843 Wagner directed a performance of *Der fliegende Holländer*. (The première had taken place in Dresden on 2 January.) It was his first appearance as royal Kapellmeister and the start of a long and bitter campaign against the musical and political establishment of the Dresden court that was to end with his exile from Germany. At first, it was merely Wagner's original talent as a conductor that caused trouble with singers and members of the orchestra. (The originality and influence of Wagner as a performer, incidentally, still require systematic investigation.) His interpretation of Mozart was particularly controversial, although his revival of Gluck's *Armide* on 5 March 1843 and a thorough revision and reorchestration of the same composer's *Iphigénie en Aulide*, which he first conducted on 24 February 1847, were more successful. Wagner's plan to perform Beethoven's Ninth Symphony on Palm Sunday, 5

April 1846, met with furious resistance from the orchestra and the Intendant of the Court Theatre, von Lüttichau. But his novel reading carried the day (complete with quotations from Goethe's *Faust* in the programme notes) and the performance had to be repeated on Palm Sunday the following year.

A day after Wagner's début as royal Kapellmeister, Heinrich Laube published the second instalment of Wagner's 'Autobiographische Skizze' on 8 February 1843 in the *Zeitung für die elegante Welt*. It contains the earliest account of his sea voyage via the Norwegian coast to London in 1839, and the famous and highly influential suggestion that the journey through the Norwegian reefs had been a decisive influence on the 'distinctive' colouring of *Der fliegende Holländer*. What Wagner did not say was that he had moved the location of his opera to Norway only a few weeks before its première, as the autograph score and numerous changes in the Dresden parts prove. Like Marschner's *Der Vampyr*, the original version of the opera is set in Scotland with Scottish names for some of the characters. The chance of publishing an essay about himself in a prominent periodical seems to have tempted Wagner into heightening the aura of the opera by deliberately providing it with a suggestive autobiographical image. He never referred to the change in his writings, nor indeed to the many other alterations he made to the work in the 1840s and 1850s. According to Cosima's diaries, he was still contemplating a thorough revision of the opera as late as 9 April 1880.

Wagner wrote in *Mein Leben* that the sight of the

6. *Part of the autograph MS of 'Der fliegende Holländer', showing the substitution (bottom right) of 'Holystrand', the bay sighted in scene i of the Scottish version, for 'Sandwike', the name of the Norwegian coastal town visited by Wagner during his voyage to London*

historic Wartburg in Thuringia on his way back from
Paris in 1842 had 'warmed' him inwardly against
'wind', 'weather' and 'Jews', and had furthermore
given him the scenic idea for Act 3 of *Tannhäuser*.
Once again he was stirring a rich brew of autobiographical associations that have tended to obscure his
difficulties with *Tannhäuser* and the important fact
that he revised it more thoroughly than any of his
other major works. The original title *Der Venusberg*
was dropped soon after completion of the libretto on
22 May 1843 – not two years later at the suggestion
of his publisher Meser, as Wagner says in *Mein Leben*.
(There is no evidence either for Curt von Westernhagen's assertion that 'the most important themes' were
already sketched in Teplitz in June–July 1842.) The
composition of the music was begun in summer 1843
and the full score finished on 13 April 1845. The initially
lukewarm response to the première of *Tannhäuser* on
19 October 1845, and its steadily increasing popularity after its third performance several days later,
were due less to the intellectual torpor of the audience, as Wagner and the Wagnerites later suggested,
than to the fact that cuts and revisions were made
after the first performance in order to close the gap
between Wagner's more daring dramatic innovations
and the inadequacy of their technical realization. (The
alterations included a shortening of the finales of the
first and second acts, and a new version of the prelude
to Act 3.) Almost two years later Wagner composed
a new ending to the opera, with the reappearance of
Venus and without the chorus of the Young Pilgrims;
it was first performed in Dresden on 1 August 1847.

7. Title-page of the autograph 'Tannhäuser' libretto, showing Wagner's alteration of the original title 'Der Venusberg'; in a letter to his brother Albert, dated 14 June 1843, Wagner called the opera 'Tannhäuser', suggesting that he had already altered the title

The post of royal Kapellmeister was a prominent and politically sensitive one that gave Wagner some insight into outside institutions and events connected with the Court Opera. In November 1844 he helped to organize the transfer of Weber's remains from London to Dresden – a large-scale public occasion for which he composed the chorus *An Webers Grabe* (wwv72) and the *Trauermusik* for wind instruments (wwv73) on themes from *Euryanthe*. Over a year before he had played a key role, too, in organizing a huge choir festival for which he wrote the 'biblical scene' *Das Liebesmahl der Apostel* (wwv69) for male-voice choirs and large orchestra. He conducted the first performance on 6 July 1843 in the Frauenkirche in Dresden with an ensemble of no less than 1200 singers from choral societies all over Saxony and an orchestra of 100 players. The work had been composed, copied and rehearsed in less than two months – a virtuoso feat of administrative coordination that was astonishing even for Wagner. Indeed, a close study of his sketches for *Liebesmahl* (parts were already being copied and put into rehearsal before he had finished composing it) would reveal a classic example *in nuce* of his ability to dovetail creativity and management – one of the many talents to which we owe the existence of Bayreuth.

Between 1844 and 1849 Wagner met several influential figures and drafted or completed some of his most important works. In the autumn of 1844 he invited Spontini on behalf of the Dresden Court Theatre to conduct a new production of his famous opera *La vestale*. (The account of this in *Mein Leben*

30

is more caricature than fact, as the extant correspondence between the two composers shows.) On 16 July 1845 in Marienbad he completed the first prose draft of *Die Meistersinger* and then on 3 August a detailed scenario of *Lohengrin*. He read the libretto to colleagues, including Ferdinand Hiller and Robert Schumann, in the Engelklub in Dresden on 17 December 1845 (not 17 November, as is usually stated). It is not true, as some prominent Wagnerians have maintained, that Wagner began the music of *Lohengrin* by composing the third act. Apart from the prelude, the first complete draft was written through from beginning to end and completed in Gross-Graupe on 30 July 1846. On account of revisions in the libretto, however, Wagner did begin with the third act when he started detailed work on the second complete draft of the music. After a number of interruptions he finished the full score on 28 April 1848 and conducted the finale of Act 1 in a concert celebrating the 300th anniversary of the Dresden Royal Court Orchestra on 22 September of the same year.

On 1 March 1846 Wagner finished an essay on the reform of the Royal Court Orchestra. Over two years later on 11 May 1848 he completed a detailed plan 'On the Organization of a German National Theatre for the Kingdom of Saxony'. His artistic interests were merging rapidly with open political activity: he saw the theatre as a mirror of a reactionary society that had first to be changed if he was to realize his artistic aims. The more his plans for reform of the theatre were rejected (he also tried in vain to interest Franz Grillparzer and Eduard Hanslick in Vienna), the more he became involved in subversive politics. Through his friend August Röckel he met the famous Russian anarchist Michael Bakunin in the summer of 1848 and soon began to publish anonymous articles celebrating revolution and anarchy while at the same time pleading for the retention of the monarchy. The ambiguity of his position allowed him to retain his public office; but it became increasingly obvious that Wagner, despite his monarchist leanings, was agitating for the abolition of the royal court. In the early months of 1849 the political situation worsened rapidly and at the beginning of May a breach of the constitution by the King of Saxony led to open revolution; this marked the end of Wagner's career as royal Kapellmeister.

V Exile, partial amnesty: 1849–60

Just how much Wagner was implicated in the Dresden Revolution of 1849 is still not clear. He was involved in the ordering of grenades and it is certain that he distributed placards exhorting the population to take sides with the rebels against the Prussian troops that had been brought in to stop the fighting. A warrant for his arrest was issued on 16 May 1849. With the help of Franz Liszt he managed to escape on 24 May to Switzerland where he arrived four days later. For the next 11 years he was banned from Germany.

In the months preceding the Revolution, the influence of Jakob Grimm's book *Deutsche Mythologie*, which Wagner had first read in the summer of 1843, made itself felt in a number of ways. The last months of 1848 had been devoted to the creation of *Siegfrieds*

Tod (later entitled *Götterdämmerung*), the libretto of which was finished on 28 November. And in December Wagner changed his handwriting radically by following Grimm's suggestion for lower-case lettering for nouns and using Latin instead of German script. But his interests were not entirely directed towards myth: as the Revolution approached he lost interest in *Siegfrieds Tod* in favour of an older project, *Friedrich I* (wwv76), which he expanded into a complex essay, *Die Wibelungen*. In his autobiography and the second volume of his collected writings, however, he has reversed the chronology of *Siegfrieds Tod* and *Die Wibelungen* to make it appear that his interest in history was merely a foil for his more meaningful preoccupation with myth. A close scrutiny of the sources and the diary of Eduard Devrient, the actor and producer who saw Wagner frequently at this time, suggest that his interest in *Friedrich I* and another project in keeping with his 'Vormärz' philosophy, *Jesus von Nazareth* (wwv80), was stronger than he later admitted. It was only two years later, in 1851, after some fruitless experimenting with the music of *Siegfrieds Tod* and consideration of at least two other projects, *Achilleus* (wwv81) and *Wieland der Schmied* (wwv82), that Wagner decided definitely to compose the *Ring*.

On the advice of Liszt and with the support of Minna, who had joined her husband in Switzerland at the beginning of September 1849, Wagner decided once again to try his luck in Paris. He left for the French capital on 29 January 1850. At first he had difficulty in deciding which of the operatic projects he had on hand would be suitable for French taste. He eventually chose *Wieland der Schmied*, but had little success in convincing others. His fortunes then took an unexpected turn: he met and apparently fell in love with Jessie Laussot, a distant acquaintance from his Dresden years. The affair lasted from March until May when their plans to elope to Greece and Asia Minor were thwarted by Jessie's husband Eugène, a rich wine merchant in Bordeaux. After some ugly recriminations, Wagner returned to Minna in Zurich on 3 July. Four days later he wrote to his old friend, the painter, Ernst Benedikt Kietz, in Paris that his plans to travel East were at an end, adding humorously that he had arrived back in Zurich 'without the horse's tail and turban' – the Turkish symbols of marital authority.

Wagner's bitter experiences in Paris and particularly the success there of Meyerbeer's *Le prophète* were probably the moving forces behind his most notorious essay 'Das Judentum in der Musik'. He finished it on 24 August 1850 and it was published soon after in the *Neue Zeitschrift für Musik* under the pseudonym K. Freigedank. (It was published again in 1869 under his real name with an explanatory foreword justifying its content.) The first performance of *Lohengrin* in Weimar on 28 August 1850 under Liszt's direction was a disappointment and confirmed his lack of faith in the conventional theatre. Reports on the production from friends were dispiriting and for the first time in a letter to E. B. Kietz dated 14 September 1850 he mentioned the idea of a festival theatre built by himself according

8. *Ernst Benedikt Kietz's reply to Wagner's letter of 7 July 1850, showing Wagner with the Turkish symbols of marital authority*

to his own design in which he would be sure of ideal performances.

Wagner finished his central theoretical work *Oper und Drama* on 10 January 1851. In May and June of the same year he wrote the prose draft and libretto of *Der junge Siegfried* (later called *Siegfried*). Most of his time in July and August was spent on a highly influential foreword to an edition of the librettos of his early operas. It was a virtuoso essay in the art of self-profile, 'Eine Mitteilung an meine Freunde' ('A Communication to my Friends'), his most important autobiographical statement before *Mein Leben*. The text of the remaining part of the *Ring* was committed to paper in the ensuing 18 months: Wagner wrote the prose sketches of *Das Rheingold* and *Die Walküre* (in that order) while taking a water-cure at Albisbrunn near Zurich in November and completed the librettos (in the reverse order) during the following year. The two Siegfried dramas then had to be thoroughly revised and in some places rewritten. (*Siegfrieds Tod*, for example, was provided with a new ending influenced by the philosopher Ludwig Feuerbach.) Apart from fair copies, the text of the entire *Ring* was completed by 15 December 1852.

In Zurich Wagner quickly attracted friends who were willing to support him financially. The most important of them was the silk merchant Otto Wesendonck. He first made Wagner's acquaintance in February 1852 and soon began to supplement the income of 800 thalers yearly that had been bestowed on Wagner by the latter's Dresden friend Julie Ritter. After two years Wesendonck was helping to extricate

Wagner from serious financial crises caused by mounting debts. Matters were made more complex by Wagner's famous infatuation with Wesendonck's wife, Mathilde. The true extent of their relationship will probably never be known: apart from the tantalizingly few documents that escaped the grasp of Wagner's heirs, the originals of his published letters to Mathilde have been destroyed except for the musical quotations, which were carefully cut out and preserved in an envelope that is still in the Bayreuth Archives.

Wagner's difficulties in beginning the composition of the *Ring*, as he admitted in 'Eine Mitteilung an meine Freunde', had a great deal to do with the fact that he had still not heard *Lohengrin* except for the finale of the first act which he had conducted in Dresden. On 18, 20 and 22 May 1853 he organized a series of concerts in Zurich which included (along with excerpts from *Rienzi, Holländer* and *Tannhäuser*) the prelude, choral sections from Act 2, and the Introduction and Bridal Chorus from Act 3. He provided the *Lohengrin* excerpts with new transitions and endings (most of which are lost) and guided the audience's appreciation with elaborate programme notes that became a model for many future concerts in which he was to introduce new and usually unperformed works with his own arrangement of salient extracts. The May concerts, incidentally, were only one high point of his activities as a performer in Zurich. Apart from regular performances of Beethoven's symphonies, other notable occasions were his arrangement of Mozart's *Don Giovanni* (wwv83) on

37

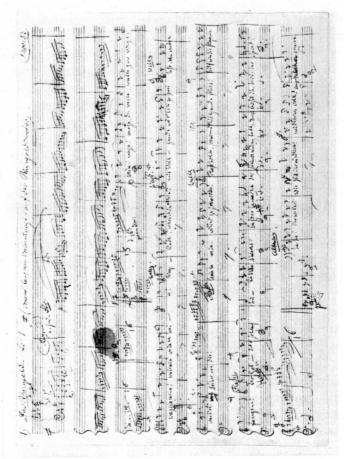

9. Autograph MS
of the beginning
of the first
complete draft of
'Das Rheingold',
dated 1 November
1853

38

8 November 1850, a new ending to the overture of Gluck's *Iphigénie en Aulide* (wwv87) which he conducted on 7 March 1854, and the first performance of the revised version of the *Faust* Overture (wwv59) on 23 January 1855.

The famous description in *Mein Leben* of Wagner's so-called 'vision' of the prelude to *Das Rheingold* in La Spezia on 5 September 1853 is to be treated with some scepticism. Wagner's letters immediately after this date make no mention of the experience. The first extant draft of the prelude dated 1 November 1853, too, was written much later, and is far less definitive, than the account in *Mein Leben* suggests. (The first draft of the prelude in its final form is in full score and dated 1 February 1854.) Moreover, the earliest reference to the La Spezia 'vision' is in a letter to Emilie Ritter written over a year later, on 29 December 1854 (not 25 December, as is usually stated). Shortly before, in the autumn of 1854, the poet Georg Herwegh had introduced Wagner to two books by Schopenhauer, *Die Welt als Wille und Vorstellung* ('The World as Will and Idea') and *Parerga und Paralipomena*. In the second work Wagner found a chapter entitled 'On the Seeing of Spirits and Related Matter' containing an explanation of clairvoyance and the phenomenon of dreams that clearly influenced his description of the La Spezia experience. (We know from a letter postmarked 29 October 1854 to Hans von Bülow that Wagner read both books Herwegh recommended.) Whether Wagner felt 'flowing water' and heard the 'pure triad' of E♭ major in his 'somnolent state' cannot be said for certain. It seems more likely, as his sketches and correspondence tend to suggest, that he was back-dating a musical idea and combining it with an experience of some other kind in order to heighten the aura of the work – once again – with a powerful autobiographical image.

Wagner completed the full score of *Das Rheingold* on 26 September 1854. The composition of *Die Wal-küre* was already well under way: he had begun the first draft on 28 June and managed to complete the full score by 23 March 1856. The only major inter-ruption was an engagement with the Philharmonic Society in London to conduct eight concerts from March to June 1855. Wagner saw the offer as a chance of silencing the most blatant recurring motif in his life: the problem of his debts. The concerts yielded far less than expected; but they did give him a chance to meet Queen Victoria and to make friends with one of his most valuable future colleagues, the pianist Karl Klindworth. A concentrated study of Wagner's first stay in London would offer a good example of how his reputation and writings (translated extracts from *Oper und Drama* appeared in the *Mus-ical World*) prejudiced the reception of his music. Many critics were against him from the start. But at least one more original soul had to confess that he found the extracts from *Lohengrin* disappointingly conservative.

It is not clear when Wagner had the idea of writing *Tristan und Isolde*. He first mentioned it in a letter to Liszt dated 16 December 1854. Some of his undated prose sketches for *Tristan*, however, could be earlier.

Before deciding definitely to compose *Tristan*, he made a prose sketch on 16 May 1856 for a drama based on a Buddhist legend, *Die Sieger* (wwv89). And as a further result of his reading of Indian literature he sketched out another new ending for the *Ring* influenced by Buddhist philosophy. It is not strictly true that he changed the titles of *Der junge Siegfried* and *Siegfrieds Tod* in 1856; although he indicated the more familiar *Siegfried* and *Götterdämmerung* in a letter to Franz Müller dated 22 June 1856, this was not intended as definitive. In letters to friends and publishers Wagner continued to use the old titles until the appearance of the second edition of the *Ring* poem in 1863.

Wagner's statement in *Mein Leben* that he wrote the first prose sketch of *Parsifal* on Good Friday 1857 (10 April) is not true. He later confessed as much to Cosima who quoted him in her diaries as saying: 'In fact it is all as far-fetched as my love affairs, for it was not a Good Friday at all – just a pleasant mood in Nature which made me think, "This is how a Good Friday ought to be"' (22 April 1879). Wagner did not move into the 'Asyl', the cottage near Zurich provided by Otto Wesendonck where the *Parsifal* sketch was supposed to have been written, until 28 April 1857. It was there that on 9 August he broke off work on *Siegfried*, at the end of the second complete draft of Act 2, in order to devote himself to *Tristan*, the prose draft of which was begun on 20 August. Apart from his love affair with Mathilde Wesendonck and the need to 'drive himself to the brink' musically, there were two more mundane reasons for writing the work: his debts and the refusal of Breitkopf & Härtel to publish the *Ring*. Breitkopf eventually agreed to *Tristan* after Wagner's assurances that it would be manageable for most German theatres. In a letter dated 4 January 1858 he demanded a fee of 600 louis d'or or 12,000 francs, which was to be paid in cash in three instalments (4000 francs after the delivery of each act). For the first time in his life he found himself in a situation where the printing of one of his works began before he had finished composing it. (He sent each act to the printer on completion before going on to compose the next.) With a remarkable feat of precision planning that contrasts strikingly with the subjective aura of the work, Wagner and Breitkopf between them were able to finish engraving, proof-reading and finally publishing the highly complex score on 13 January 1860, only five months after the autograph had been completed.

Between November 1857 and May 1858 Wagner set five of Mathilde Wesendonck's poems to music (wwv91*A–E*), two of which, *Träume* and *Im Treibhaus*, he later described as 'studies' for *Tristan*. His wife Minna's interception of a letter addressed to Mathilde (one of the few and most wildly interpreted documents to have escaped the grasp of Wagner's heirs) precipitated on 7 April 1858 a catastrophe that eventually led to his departure from the 'Asyl' (17 August). He went to Venice and there, in the Palazzo Giustinian, finished the full score of Act 2 of *Tristan* on 18 March 1859. The Saxon police intervened to limit his stay in Venice, and on 24 March he moved, first to Lucerne, where he completed *Tristan*, and then to Paris where he arrived in September with the intention of persuading the Opéra to produce *Tannhäuser*.

The plan to have *Tannhäuser* performed in Paris dates from the autumn of 1857, as a letter (presumably to the impresario Leopold Amat) written on 23 November of that year proves. Three successful concerts in Paris on 25 January, 1 and 8 February 1860, for which Wagner wrote new endings for the overture to *Der fliegende Holländer* and the prelude to *Tristan*, paved the way for a series of diplomatic moves that culminated on 11 March with an order from Napoleon III for the production of *Tannhäuser* at the Opéra. Wagner's diplomatic friends, including the Saxon ambassador in Paris, Baron von Seebach, immediately took him under their protection and began manoeuvring towards an amnesty for the one German composer now favoured by the highest powers in France. They succeeded. On 15 July 1860 Seebach received a letter from Baron von Beust, the President of the Saxon Council and Minister for Foreign Affairs, allowing Wagner free access to Germany with the exception of Saxony.

VI Paris, Vienna, Biebrich: 1860–64

For most of 1860 and the early months of 1861, Wagner spent his time rewriting the first two scenes of *Tannhäuser*, preparing the French libretto, and making numerous changes of detail in the score. He wrote one of his best essays (with the ironic title 'Zukunftsmusik') as a foreword to a French prose translation by Paul Challemel-Lacour of *Der fliegende Holländer*, *Tannhäuser*, *Lohengrin* and *Tristan*. (The performing version of the *Tannhäuser* text was translated, with Wagner's assistance, by Charles Nuitter.) The new versions of the Bacchanale and Venusberg scenes were completed on 28 January 1861 and Wagner continued making changes to the rest of the score until the first performance on 13 March, largely because of difficulties with the orchestra and its conductor Pierre Louis Philippe Dietsch. In addition, the famous tenor Albert Niemann, in the role of the protagonist, caused trouble by his refusal to comply with revisions in the Tournament of Song in Act 2. The scandal of the première, too, prompted Wagner to make further, sometimes radical, changes for the subsequent performances on 18 and 24 March.

The famous furore of the Paris *Tannhäuser* performances was brought about not only by the conservative tastes of the Jockey Club, but also by people of influence who wanted to use the occasion as a veiled political protest against the pro-Austrian policies of Napoleon III. (Wagner's patron Princess Metternich, who played an important role in having *Tannhäuser* accepted by the Opéra, was the wife of the Austrian ambassador in Paris.) The work was withdrawn after the third performance and Wagner left Paris soon after for Karlsruhe, expressly to discuss with the young Grand Duke Friedrich of Baden the possibility of producing *Tristan* there. After returning to Paris for a short time, he travelled to Vienna in order to look for singers. The Vienna Court Opera took such a keen interest, however, that he began negotiations with the Intendant, Count Lanck-oronski, as well. He heard *Lohengrin* on stage complete for the first time in a rehearsal at the Vienna Opera on 11 May 1861. The leading role was sung by Aloys Ander and Wagner immediately chose him to sing Tristan. Various sources suggest that Wagner was prepared to make extraordinary compromises with extensive cuts and revisions of the vocal part when he realized that Ander was not equal to the task. The situation was complicated by intrigues, and in March 1864 the project was eventually abandoned.

On 30 October 1861 Wagner suggested to the publisher Franz Schott the idea of a 'grand comic opera', *Die Meistersinger von Nürnberg*, for which he could receive some advance payment in order to reduce his accumulating debts. The suggestion in *Mein Leben* that he decided to compose *Die Meistersinger* later after seeing in Venice Titian's famous painting *The Assumption* (now in the church of S Maria dei Frari) is therefore to be regarded with some caution. In a letter dated 21 December 1861 to Mathilde Wesen-donck, who with her husband had invited Wagner to Venice in November 1861, he apologized for his lack of interest in the paintings of the Great Masters. He made no exceptions. As the same letter is also an enthusiastic account of progress with *Die Meister-singer*, his failure to mention Titian raises the suspicion that the later description in his autobiography is an invention. There is no evidence either for his statement that he saw the opera 'musically' before he wrote the text, or that he conceived the 'main part' of the prelude in his head on the train from Venice back to Vienna.

On 2 December 1862 Wagner read the draft of *Die Meistersinger* to Franz Schott in Mainz, who agreed to advance him 10,000 francs. He then went to Paris and rented a room in the Hotel Voltaire. There was no piano, he wrote to Minna on 8 December, because he wanted to write the verses of his libretto there, and not to compose. He finished the libretto on 25 January 1862 and soon left Paris to read it to his publisher in Mainz. Intensive work on the music was begun in an apartment Wagner had rented in Bie-brich, a village on the Rhine. The full score of the prelude was finished in June or July; but the composition of the first act was discontinued in the summer of the same year, largely because of a quarrel with Schott over another hoped-for advance.

Minna visited Wagner in Biebrich and stayed for ten painful days after which they separated for ever. On medical advice Minna settled down in Dresden, and on 25 March 1862 Wagner applied for a full amnesty to the King of Saxony, appending a long medical certificate from Pusinelli, an old Dresden friend, which traced the history of Minna's health. He was granted his request on 28 March.

Wagner spent the next two years of his life mainly indulging in a number of passing 'love affairs' and travelling to conduct performances of his own music. He conducted *Lohengrin* for the first time on 12 September 1862 in Frankfurt, and on 1 November directed the first performance of the prelude to *Die Meistersinger* in the Gewandhaus in Leipzig. Three important concerts took place in Vienna on 26 December 1862, 1 January and 11 January 1863 in which he conducted his own arrangements of extracts from the *Ring* and of parts of *Die Meistersinger* already in existence. The concerts, for which he enlisted the help of Peter Cornelius and the pianist Carl Tausig (Brahms assisted in the copying of the music), included parts of *Das Rheingold* and the first performance of the 'Ride of the Valkyries'. He gave similar concerts in Prague, Budapest, Karlsruhe and Breslau. But the only undertaking to bring him real financial gain was a series of concerts in St Petersburg and Moscow from February to April 1863. It was the hope of repeating this success that led him to set up an extravagant home in Penzing, near Vienna. The 12,000 marks profit from his Russian tour soon dissolved, however, and the debts he incurred brought with them a serious threat of imprisonment. Since unrest in Poland made another trip to Russia impossible, he left Vienna in a hurry on 25 March 1864 for Mariafeld, near Zurich, and then Stuttgart, where he planned to retire to the Swabian mountains to finish *Die Meistersinger*. On 3 May of the same year he was summoned to Munich by Ludwig II, the new King of Bavaria.

VII Munich, Tribschen: 1864–72

The first meeting between Wagner and Ludwig II took place on 4 May 1864 in the Residenz in Munich. Ludwig, who had succeeded his father Max II to the Bavarian throne at the age of 18 in March of the same year, agreed to settle Wagner's debts and granted him a generous allowance. During the course of their friendship (despite scandal and political intrigue it lasted until Wagner's death), Ludwig gave Wagner a total of over 500,000 marks and supported the Bayreuth festival scheme with a credit of 400,000 marks that was paid back by Wagner's heirs with fees from royalties. In return Wagner presented Ludwig with several manuscripts, including the composition draft of *Der fliegende Holländer* and the full scores of *Die Feen*, *Das Liebesverbot*, *Rienzi*, *Das Rheingold*, *Die Walküre*, *Die Meistersinger* and the *Huldigungsmarsch* (wwv97). Except for *Die Meistersinger* and the *Huldigungsmarsch*, the draft and scores are lost; they were in the possession of Adolf Hitler and were presumably destroyed in 1945.

The sheer volume of the published correspondence between Wagner and Ludwig is proof that they rarely met. The theatrical language of the letters, too, is a constant reminder that their 'friendship' existed solely in this stylized literary form. The king remained faithful to Wagner's vision; but he ignored Wagner's person when it suited him and sometimes overruled Wagner in artistic matters as well. Wagner's protestations of undying gratitude to the king disguised considerable exasperation at Ludwig's aloofness and frequent misunderstandings. Although he was often tempted to break with the king, he was too dependent on his benefactor to challenge him openly. On receiving the news of Wagner's death in 1883, Ludwig (according to a note in the Bavarian State Library by the pro-Wagnerian Court Secretary Ludwig von Bürkel) is said to have exclaimed: 'Ah! Actually I'm sorry, but then again not really. There was something I didn't quite like about him.'

It is not clear when Wagner began intimate relations with Cosima (*b* Como, 2 Dec 1837; *d* Bayreuth, 1 April 1930), the daughter of Franz Liszt and wife of the conductor and pianist Hans von Bülow. According to *Mein Leben*, Cosima and Wagner swore eternal fidelity to one another as early as November 1863 when Wagner was visiting the Bülows in Berlin. It is more likely, however, that their relationship began in June or July 1864 when, during the absence of King Ludwig, Cosima visited Wagner in the Villa Pellet on Lake Starnberg for a week without her husband. With the arrival in Starnberg of Hans von Bülow on 7 July the most famous musical *ménage à trois* began. It provided food for scandal and caricature. Among biographers it has produced no end of imaginative reconstruction and even a mythical piece of music, the so-called Starnberg Quartet. (Despite superficially persuasive hypotheses by Ernest Newman and the published 'version' by Gerald Abraham, there is no evidence that the quartet ever existed. See commentary to wwv103.) Wagner's first child, Isolde, was born on 10 April 1865, the day on which Hans von Bülow conducted the first orchestral rehearsal of *Tristan*. She was registered as the legitimate daughter of Hans and Cosima von Bülow, and even in later years Cosima refused to recognize her officially as Wagner's child. Because of public opinion and the fear of jeopardizing Ludwig's good will, the illusion of legality was so important for Wagner that at Isolde's baptism he could bring himself to act as godfather to his own daughter.

On 7 October 1864 Ludwig agreed to give Wagner a contract to finish the *Ring*. The latter was to receive 15,000 florins immediately and the same amount on completion of the project. In the same month Wagner moved to a new and notoriously luxurious house in the Briennerstrasse in Munich that was to become the object of indignation in the local press. At Wagner's suggestion Hans von Bülow was appointed to the royal court as a 'Vorspieler des Königs' at a salary of 2000 florins. Ostensibly Bülow's function was to initiate Ludwig 'in the right way into good musical literature', as Wagner put it; but it soon became clear that the post was merely a ruse to bring Bülow (and of course Cosima) to Munich, several steps nearer the key post that Wagner had envisaged for him at the Hoftheater. Plans were also laid for the building of a festival theatre to be designed by Gottfried Semper. This activity, combined with the intellectual arrogance of Wagner's entourage towards the Bavarians, soon alarmed people of influence in Munich. The stage was set for an unpleasant public wrangle which, inflamed by Wagner's extravagance and rumours of his adultery with Cosima, forced him to leave Munich on 10 December 1865.

During his short-lived residence in Munich, Wagner began making sketches for the third act of *Siegfried*. He also directed preparations for the première of *Tristan und Isolde* on 10 June 1865 in the Munich Hoftheater. Three weeks after the fourth performance, the tenor Ludwig Schnorr von Carolsfeld, who had sung Tristan, died suddenly on 21

July. While it is impossible to ascertain the real cause of his death today, it is clear that the role and the superhuman effort it requires were widely regarded as the chief culprits. Before the first performance three years later in Munich of *Die Meistersinger*, Wagner wrote and published his essay 'Meine Erinnerungen an Ludwig Schnorr von Carolsfeld' expressly with the intention of correcting the by now widespread impression that the tenor had been killed by *Tristan*. Matters had not been helped by Malvina, the tenor's wife who sang Isolde in the première of the work, and who, guided by allegedly 'spiritual' forces, had threatened to reveal the truth of the Wagner–Cosima–Bülow triangle to King Ludwig if Wagner did not mend his artistic ways. Although Malvina's threats were less dangerous than they appeared, Wagner and Cosima descended to what Ernest Newman has rightly called 'depths of subterfuge, shabbiness and malice' in order to save themselves from the threat of exposure.

While still in Munich Wagner began the dictation of his autobiography *Mein Leben* in July 1865 at the request of King Ludwig. He also wrote the first full prose draft of *Parsifal* in August – another project that was to occupy him until almost the end of his life. (After many interruptions, he was to finish the dictation of *Mein Leben* in 1880.) When he left Munich he moved to a house ('Les artichauts') near Geneva in order to resume work on *Die Meistersinger*. He continued to look for a larger house in the south of France where he could settle with Cosima. Quite unexpectedly in January 1866, news reached him

51

in Marseilles that his wife Minna had died in Dresden.

Wagner completed the full score of the first act of *Die Meistersinger* on 23 March 1866 and soon after, on 15 April, moved into Tribschen, a house in Switzerland overlooking the lake near Lucerne where he was to spend the next six years. He finished *Die Meistersinger* in Tribschen on 24 October 1867 and on 21 June 1868 it was given its first performance in Munich.

On 25 October 1866, Wagner wrote to his old friend August Röckel about his undignified dependence on royal patronage: 'If there were a trace of German Spirit in Germany . . . there wouldn't be any need of such artificial roundabout ways of positioning a man like me between sovereign and people'. At the première of *Die Meistersinger* almost two years later King Ludwig took the unprecedented step of allowing Wagner to sit with him in the royal box – a symbolic gesture the significance of which was not lost on Wagner's former political friends. Heinrich Laube, whose negative article on *Die Meistersinger* in the Vienna newspaper *Neue Freie Presse* was hardly, as is often supposed, a mere act of spiteful revenge, knew perhaps better than anyone that Wagner was exchanging his former progressive views for a reactionary vision of *Deutschtum* and German supremacy. Wagner's view of himself as a mediator between opposing political interests through his art had become chauvinistic in the extreme. He had made this clear in the half-official newspaper *Süddeutsche Presse* in 1867 with a series of anonymous articles on 'German Art and German Politics' that can also be interpreted, at least in part, as a commentary on *Die Meistersinger*. This murky brew of aesthetics and revisionist political philosophy proved too strong even for Ludwig who ordered the suppression of the last two articles. Wagner published his text complete in book form in 1868.

Wagner first made the acquaintance of the philologist and philosopher Friedrich Nietzsche on 8 November 1868 in Leipzig at the house of Wagner's brother-in-law Hermann Brockhaus. Nietzsche had been overwhelmed by performances of *Tristan* and *Die Meistersinger* and was already an ardent Wagnerian. In May 1869, after his appointment to a professorship in Basle, he made the first of 23 visits to Tribschen. Wagner and Cosima soon came to regard Nietzsche as an intimate disciple who could be trusted with organization of the printing of the first volumes of *Mein Leben* and whose intellectual development they followed with the keenest interest. Nietzsche's first major publication, *Die Geburt der Tragödie aus dem Geist der Musik*, was not only discussed during these visits, it was directly influenced by Wagner who, after Nietzsche had read it to him in April 1871, suggested alterations and the extension of certain passages. Relations between Wagner and Nietzsche seemed unclouded until the Bayreuth festival in 1876. (Sketches for the fourth of Nietzsche's *Unzeitgemässe Betrachtungen* 'Richard Wagner in Bayreuth', however, reveal clear signs of a breach before this date.) There has been much speculation about the cause of the rift between the two men. Newman's famous attack on the scholarly methods of Nietzsche's sister,

Elisabeth Förster-Nietzsche, is a piece of virtuoso flannelling that merely disguises the uncomfortable truth that we do not really know what brought about the separation. Nietzsche's objections to the first Bayreuth festival and to *Parsifal*, the first prose draft of which he had read in 1869, are too clouded with ambiguity to count as the sole reasons for the estrangement. Nor is it likely that Wagner's unwelcome concern with Nietzsche's sexual life was the cause of the break. When Nietzsche eventually found out that Wagner, behind his back, had written to his doctor Otto Eiser to find out the most intimate details of his 'malady', it simply confirmed a negative view of Wagner that he had held for some time.

In March 1868 Ludwig II broke off negotiations with Gottfried Semper concerning plans for a Wagner festival theatre in Munich. Well aware that the prospect of performing the *Ring* in Munich under ideal conditions was rapidly becoming an illusion, Wagner began the composition of the third act of *Siegfried* on 1 March 1869 in the knowledge that he would have to look elsewhere for a realization of his ideal. In the following May he was elected as a foreign member of the Prussian Academy of Arts in Berlin and two years later delivered a lecture to the Academy on 28 April 1871 entitled 'On the Destiny of Opera'. To outside observers unaware of political subtleties in the organization of the arts in Germany, Wagner's connection with the Academy appears to be something of a self-indulgence. But it was an important part of his strategy in gaining a foothold in

Berlin that could enhance his prospects of directing his festival plans away from Munich. In August and September 1869, an open breach between King Ludwig and Wagner seemed imminent: against Wagner's wishes, Ludwig ordered the first performance of *Das Rheingold* which, despite the composer's attempts to thwart it, took place on 22 September in the Hoftheater in Munich. In the following year, once more against Wagner's wishes, *Die Walküre* received its first performance in the same theatre, on 26 June. The royal order to produce *Siegfried* in Munich was given in March 1871 and in the following September Perfall, the Intendant of the theatre, reported that plans for the scenery and rehearsals with piano were under way but that further progress was impossible without the full score. Although Wagner assured Ludwig in a long letter dated 1 March 1871 that he could not bring himself to finish the scoring of *Siegfried*, the full score of the third act had already been completed in Tribschen shortly before, on 5 February. Munich never received the manuscript and the projected première of *Siegfried* was cancelled.

Wagner's utopian vision of German unity and the merging of Prussia and Bavaria was one reason for his choice of Bayreuth as the site of his festival performances of the *Ring*. The town, which had once belonged to Prussia, was halfway between Munich and Berlin and it possessed an opera house with one of the largest stages in Germany. The idea of Bayreuth came to Wagner on 5 March 1870 assisted by an article on the town in Brockhaus's *Konversationslexikon*. On closer inspection, however, the stage of the opera house proved to be inadequate and a decision was made on 16 April 1871 to build a new theatre. On 1 February 1872 an executive committee consisting of Muncker (the Mayor of Bayreuth), the banker Friedrich Feustel and a lawyer called Käfferlein was founded to supervise the organization of the Bayreuth Festival. Wagner said his last goodbye to Tribschen on 22 April 1872 and arrived in Bayreuth two days later to begin the arduous task of placing his festival idea on a sound artistic and financial footing.

Even the shortest account of Tribschen cannot fail to mention Cosima Wagner. She first visited the house in May 1866 and moved there permanently on 16 November 1868. She gave birth in Tribschen to Wagner's two remaining children, Eva (*b* 17 Feb 1867) and Siegfried (*b* 6 June 1869). Soon after her divorce from Hans von Bülow she married Wagner on 25 August 1870 in the Protestant Hofkirche near Lucerne. It was in Tribschen, too, that she began her famous diaries on 1 January 1869. Although they were intended for her children as an account of 'every hour' of her life, the nearly one million words they contain are surprisingly reticent about her own feelings. Indeed, the gap of more than a week from 21 November to 3 December 1874 when she was 'too upset' to write is in many ways more eloquent than the rest of the diaries put together. 'You know that I always refrain from expressing any opinion as against the Master', she had written to the editor Julius Fröbel in 1867; 'his ideas about art have become our faith'.

VIII Towards the first Bayreuth Festival: 1872–6

Two weeks before his arrival in Bayreuth, Wagner had completed the composition of *Götterdämmerung* in first draft on 10 April 1872. The stage was now set for four of the most active years of his life. Not only did he supervise the building of the Festspielhaus and his house Wahnfried, the first and only home he ever owned, he also toured Germany and Austria looking for singers and technicians as well as giving concerts to raise money for the Bayreuth project. Another huge and time-consuming task was the copying, proof-reading and publication of the four full scores of the *Ring*. The orchestral parts had to be copied, too, and for these and other tasks Wagner gathered together a group of young musicians he envisaged as the future coaches and conductors of his music. The group, known affectionately as the 'Nibelungen-kanzlei' ('the Nibelung Chancellery'), consisted of Hermann Zumpe, Anton Seidl the conductor, the pianist Joseph Rubinstein (who enjoyed special status) and Demetrius Lalas from Macedonia.

As always, Wagner's main problem was finance. Already in 1871 the pianist Carl Tausig had conceived an association of Patrons who would each buy a certificate or *Patronatschein* for 300 thaler entitling them to seats at the festival performances. The scheme was amplified by Emil Heckel, a music dealer in Mannheim, who created the idea of local Wagner societies for people of modest means who could club together for one or more certificates and share the festival performances among them. But these ideas proved to be inadequate. At the beginning of 1875

10. *Richard, Cosima and Siegfried Wagner at Bayreuth, c1873*

when only 490 out of a total of 1300 certificates had been sold, Wagner had to admit that the scheme was virtually a failure. He had tried to interest Bismarck in the Bayreuth project as early as June 1873 (the gesture found few friends in Munich) but received no reply. After King Ludwig had come to the rescue on 20 February 1874 with a loan of 216,152 marks, Wagner still found it expedient in October 1875 to apply for financial support in Berlin. This time he appealed to Emperor Wilhelm I himself. But Rudolf von Delbrück, the president of the Imperial Exchequer, was against the idea and made the polite but impractical suggestion that Wagner should make a public application to the Reichstag.

Wagner laid the foundation stone of the Festspielhaus on 22 May 1872, his 59th birthday. To celebrate the occasion he conducted Beethoven's Ninth Symphony in the Markgräfliches Opernhaus. On 2 August 1873 a party or Hebefest was given to mark the highest point reached in the building of the new theatre. In the following year on 28 April Wagner moved from the Hotel Fantaisie into his new house Wahnfried (an etymological derivation of Wanfried, the name of a town in Hessen) which had been designed by himself, built by Carl Wölfel, and paid for by King Ludwig with a gift of 25,000 thalers.

If the name of Wagner's home suggested peace (*Frieden*) for his illusions (*Wahn*), it is ironic that it was built at a time when the realization of his ideals was still by no means certain. It was only on 21 November 1874 that he at last finished the full score of *Götterdämmerung*, 26 years after he began creating the *Ring* in 1848. Apart from financial crises and sceptical, not to say downright hostile, comments from the press, Wagner had to cope with the organization of rehearsals and further fund-raising concerts in Vienna, Budapest and Berlin that were a considerable drain on his energy. (His conducting fees covered most of the costs of the orchestra and stage rehearsals held during the summer of 1875.) Wagner first heard the orchestra in the Festspielhaus on 2 August 1875 and was delighted that his ideas for the sunken orchestra (incorporated into Semper's Munich theatre plan and modified for Bayreuth by the Leipzig architect Otto Brückwald) had produced such good acoustical results. The first public performances of the *Ring* as a cycle took place a year later between 13 and 30 August 1876. Because of a wish to hear the *Ring* in private, King Ludwig attended the dress rehearsals (performances in all but name) held between 6 and 9 August. He had not seen Wagner for eight years.

IX The first Bayreuth Festival and after: 1876–83
Besides Ludwig, the Bayreuth Festival in 1876 was attended by two other heads of state, Wilhelm I of Prussia and Dom Pedro II of Brazil, as well as many other distinguished members of the aristocracy. 'In former times,' Wagner announced in a speech after the first *Ring* cycle, 'the artist used to dance attendance on emperors and princes: now, for the first time, the emperors and princes had come to the artist.' Despite these proud words, however, Wagner's his-

toric fight for equal status of artist and (aristocratic) patron was almost lost. The first Bayreuth Festival showed a deficit of 150,000 marks which brought the undertaking to the verge of legal bankruptcy. After a four-month holiday in Italy, Wagner agreed to conduct (with the assistance of Hans Richter) a series of eight concerts in May 1877 at the Albert Hall in London with generous excerpts from all his major works. But the profits amounted to a mere £700. He then seriously entertained the idea of selling Wahnfried and emigrating to the USA. (He confided to friends that the best thing about the *Festival March* he had written for the American centenary of the Declaration of Independence in 1876 was the 5000 dollars he had received for it.) Wagner's negative report to his executive director Friedrich Feustel on 14 June 1877 is also tinged with thoughts of America: 'It is not my works that stand condemned but – Bayreuth . . . I can only blame the town to the extent that I chose it myself. Yet I did so with a great idea: with the support of the nation I wanted to create something thoroughly independent that would make the town important – a sort of Washington of Art' (*eine Art Kunst-Washington*).

When all seemed lost, the Munich Treasury signed a contract with Wagner on 31 March 1878 that stipulated, among other things, the liquidation of the outstanding debt of 98,634 marks, 65 pfennigs from the 1876 festival and the right of the Munich Hoftheater to perform *Parsifal* free of charge after its Bayreuth première. (Two years later the latter condition was withdrawn.) This last-minute rescue, however, did little to change the eternal paradox of Wagner's last years: the founding of the reactionary journal *Bayreuther Blätter* in January 1878 on the one hand and the creation of his most sublime work, *Parsifal*, on the other.

For modern sensibilities the connection between *Parsifal* and the tone of Wagner's last anti-semitic and anti-modernist essays is a delicate one, to say the least. There is little question that Wagner's disappointment with the lack of national 'support' at the first Bayreuth Festival nourished ideas on race and regeneration that were a major influence at the beginning of the 20th century on the proto-Nazi philosophy of Houston Stewart Chamberlain and others. But it is equally true that *Parsifal* is a masterly culmination of a lifetime rich in musical experience and reformist zeal in the world of opera which still retains much of its power. If Wagner regarded his aesthetics as a replica of his philosophical ideas, as he certainly tended to do, critics have been all too ready to reject *Parsifal* by unwittingly adopting Wagner's own and highly problematical analogy. The connection between *Parsifal* and Wagner's anti-semitism, however, is too diffuse and – after Hitler – too emotionalized for rational argument and easy analogy to make much sense. A way out of the predicament is difficult and probably impossible. The centenary of the first performance of *Parsifal* in 1982 at least showed that some artists – notably H. J. Syberberg and Ruth Berghaus – were prepared to introduce the moral and historical quandary felt by many into the aesthetic aura of the work itself.

In the minds of most biographers the genesis of *Parsifal* is inseparable from its creator's 'love affair' with Judith Gautier (1846–1917). She was the daughter of the writer Théophile Gautier and in 1868 married a friend of Wagner's, the writer Catulle Mendès. Wagner first met her on 16 July 1869 in Lucerne. He seems to have been attracted to her from the first, although it was only during the Bayreuth Festival of 1876, after she had been divorced from Mendès, that she began to exert an erotic fascination on him. Their correspondence during the early stages of the creation of *Parsifal* is incomplete. And it is impossible to say whether Wagner's passionate remonstrances in the letters – the 'embraces' and 'kisses' that are supposed to have taken place during his secret meetings with Judith in Bayreuth – were real or merely wishful thinking. Judith publicly denied that she had ever been Wagner's mistress, although in private she was more ambiguous about it. She turned down Wagner's invitation to meet him in London in May 1877 and had little contact with him afterwards. To describe her as the muse of *Parsifal*, as many biographers have done, is therefore something of an exaggeration.

In September 1877 Wagner announced to delegates of the Patronatsverein his plan for a music school in Bayreuth that would train musicians in the true 'German style' of performing German music and make possible a performance of all his works from *Der fliegende Holländer* to *Parsifal* in the Festspielhaus between 1878 and 1883. The plan came to nothing. Wagner's rapidly declining health forced him to concentrate all his energy on the creation of *Parsifal* and to spend much of his time away from Bayreuth in the more congenial climate of Italy. During a long stay from 4 January to 30 October 1880 he discovered the model for Klingsor's magic garden in the garden of the Palazzo Rufolo in Ravello on the gulf of Salerno. (Wagner wrote in the visitors' book on 26 May 1880 that 'Klingsor's magic garden has been found!') And during a stay in Siena from August to September of the same year, he asked the Russian painter Paul von Joukowsky, who was to design the scenery and costumes for *Parsifal*, to model the temple of the Holy Grail in Acts 1 and 3 on Siena Cathedral.

On 10 November 1880 Wagner met King Ludwig for the last time. Two days later he conducted the *Parsifal* prelude with the orchestra of the Munich Hoftheater for Ludwig, who sat in the royal box. (Wagner had orchestrated the prelude in advance of the rest of the score, initially in order to have it performed in Wahnfried with a small orchestra for Cosima's 41st birthday, on 25 December 1878.) For the king's guidance Wagner wrote the now famous description of the prelude in which he traced three themes of 'Love', 'Faith' and 'Hope?' The king arrived late for the performance and asked for a repeat of the prelude. According to the painter Franz Lenbach, who was present, Wagner regarded this as a 'profanation' and became really exasperated when the king, for the sake of comparison, asked for the prelude to *Lohengrin*. Wagner turned over the baton to Hermann Levi (the principal Kapellmeister in Munich, later the first conductor of *Parsifal*) and walked away. Even allowing for the possibility that Lenbach's account may be more anecdote than fact, Ernest Newman's surprise that Wagner made no mention of his displeasure in his ensuing correspondence with the king is a little ingenuous. Like Wagner's 'love affair' with Judith Gautier, the 'friendship' with King Ludwig existed to the end less in reality than in the heavily stylized form of Wagner's letters and the future imaginations of his biographers.

At the beginning of May 1881 Wagner attended the first *Ring* performance organized by Angelo Neumann at the Viktoriatheater in Berlin. He also saw, with Comte Gobineau, the fourth cycle at the end of the month. Neumann played a key role in the spread of Wagner's reputation in the last quarter of the 19th century with a touring company that performed the *Ring* in most major European towns. The precise nature of his influence on the reception of Wagner's works, and in particular on styles of production, has yet to be investigated.

After the first 16 performances of *Parsifal* in the Festspielhaus between 26 July and 29 August 1882, for which King Ludwig had placed the chorus and orchestra of the Munich Hoftheater at the disposal of the Bayreuth Festival, Wagner again returned to Italy where he took up residence in the Palazzo Vendramin-Calergi in Venice. The 1882 festival made an unexpected profit of 135,600 marks, which encouraged Wagner to announce further performances for 1883. (He had abolished the patronage system and opened all performances after the second to the general public, who paid directly for their seats.) Hermann

Levi arrived in Venice in February 1883 to discuss the next festival with Wagner. And on 9 February Cosima wrote in her diary: 'he [Wagner] tells me that he will still do his article about masculine and feminine ['Über das Weibliche im Menschlichen'], then write symphonies'. Apart from the *Siegfried Idyll*, which was written in Tribschen in 1870 for Cosima and originally entitled 'Symphony', Wagner's later sketches for symphonic works, some of which are still extant, never progressed beyond disparate fragments. It is highly probable that the one movement form of the *Siegfried Idyll* would have been the model for the programmatic symphonies he wanted to write. But these and other projects (including the completion of his autobiography *Mein Leben*, which had only reached 1864 and the summons to Munich by King Ludwig) were cut short by Wagner's sudden death after a heart attack on 13 February 1883. His doctor in Venice, the resident German physician Dr Friedrich Keppler, later wrote: 'It is self-evident that the innumerable psychical agitations to which Wagner was daily disposed by his peculiar mental constitution and disposition, his sharply defined attitude towards a number of burning questions of art, science and politics, and his remarkable social position did much to hasten his unfortunate end.'

Wagner's death mask was made by Augusto Benvenuti on 14 February 1883 and his body transported to Bayreuth where it was laid to rest in a grave near Wahnfried four days later.

11. Wagner at Tribschen, 1867

CHAPTER TWO

Theoretical writings

'My works as an author were testimonies to my lack
of freedom as an artistic human being', Wagner wrote
to August Röckel on 12 September 1852. 'It was only
under the greatest compulsion that I wrote them, and
the last thing I had in mind was the writing of books;
if that had been the case, you would probably not
have had so many complaints to make about my
style.' Wagner nearly always complained when he felt
compelled to write articles, treatises or books, instead
of operas or musical dramas; yet he left an astonish-
ingly comprehensive corpus of prose writings, running to a total of thousands of pages. (To compare
him with Berlioz, who earned part of his living by his
writing, or with Liszt, whose authorship is disputed,
would be misleading.) Further, the reasons why
Wagner wrote are as various as the subjects he chose
– or which forced themselves upon him – and the
stylistic postures he adopted.

As yet there has been no scholarly analysis and
interpretation of Wagner's writings, although there is
any amount of literature pertaining to the Wagnerian
Weltanschauung. Such a study would have to take due
account of the unreliability of the textual foundations:
there has never yet been an authentic edition of the
writings, and discussion of the importance that should

be attached to their various versions – assessment, that is, of what the terms 'original text' and 'definitive edition' (*Urtext* and *Ausgabe letzter Hand*) mean in Wagner's case – has not even begun.

In the Paris essays of 1840–42 that Wagner contributed, in the guise of fiction, to Schlesinger's *Gazette musicale*, he proved to be a brilliant stylist, modelling himself on E. T. A. Hoffmann and Heinrich Heine. But around 1850, in the writings of the revolutionary period, he adopted a prose style which became almost unendurable by the time of his contributions to *Bayreuther Blätter* from 1878 onwards. It is a style in which magisterial presumption is blended with remnants of the leftist Hegelian dialectics which, in the 'Vormärz', the period before the start of the German revolution in March 1848, belonged to the intellectual fashions in which Wagner dabbled, although he quickly abandoned his attempt to read Hegel at first hand: he was an insatiable and enthusiastic reader, but his fund of patience was small.

The difficulty of a general survey of Wagner's writings lies in establishing a proper vantage point from which to view them. In the preface he wrote in Tribschen in 1871 for his *Gesammelte Schriften und Dichtungen*, he described his 'miscellaneous writings on art' as 'a kind of diary'; the reader had to do 'not with the collected works of an author, but with the record of an artist's activity throughout his life'. That is why he chose to arrange the contents of the edition of 1871–3 (vol.10 appeared in 1883) in chronological order rather than according to subject matter. Autobiography, the dramatic poems, art theory, cultural and political comment, are printed one after the other as the 'documents of a life'. (And the innumerable contradictions that run like crevasses across Wagner's theories are never explained or even mentioned, as if they are only to be expected in a collection of writings that, far from representing a system, amount to no more than 'a kind of diary'.)

On the other hand, the four periods in which Wagner turned to authorship, however unwillingly, are well delineated: the time of acute poverty in Paris (1840–42), the revolutionary years (1849–51), the period in which he resumed work on the *Ring* after interrupting it for the composition of *Tristan* and *Die Meistersinger* (1869–72), and the last years in Bayreuth (1878–83). In Paris Wagner was driven to write by sheer necessity, which makes the outcome all the more astonishing: a miscellany of masterpieces, half-fiction, half-essay, such as *Eine Pilgerfahrt zu Beethoven*, *Ein Ende in Paris* and *Ein glücklicher Abend*, and of occasional journalism which he decided not to include in the eventual collected edition. (The relation between artistic earnest and financial pressure is more complex in Wagner than appears in the all-too-simple dichotomy of what was inspired by an ideal and what was forced out by material need.) In the Zurich years – during which, after the failure of the revolution, Wagner at first still thought of himself as a revolutionary – he felt the need (as he told Theodor Uhlig in a letter of 27 December 1849) to assist by literary means in the overthrow of society before the 'artwork of the future' could come into being. 'That artwork cannot be created at the present time, but only prepared – by a process of revolutionizing, of destroying and smashing everything that is worth destroying and smashing. That is our work, and only then will totally different people from us become the true creative artists.' By the time he returned to the score of *Siegfried*, various experiences – the composition of *Tristan*, his discovery of Schopenhauer in 1854 and the repeated reading of his work thereafter, as well as the need to continue a work that had been interrupted 12 years before – challenged, indeed forced, him to reflect once again on the concept of musical drama. Many of the ideas he had developed in *Oper und Drama* (1851) were taken further and defined more precisely in the writings of this third period, while others were withdrawn (without Wagner's being ready to admit that he had changed his mind). Of the articles on art theory which he wrote in 1879 for *Bayreuther Blätter* ('Über das Dichten und Komponieren', 'Über das Opern-Dichten und Komponieren im Besonderen', 'Über die Anwendung der Musik auf das Drama'), Ernest Newman rightly said: 'In these admirable works we have the ripest fruits of a lifetime of experience.' On the other hand 'Heldentum und Christentum', inspired by Comte Gobineau's theory of race, and 'Religion und Kunst', belong to the corpus of 'Weltanschauungsliteratur' which gave rise to the Bayreuth ideology in the worst sense of the word.

Though it is a course that Wagner himself rejected, it is both possible and useful to make a quasi-systematic arrangement of his writings, as follows: dramatic

71

poems and fragments; autobiography; art theory and projects for theatrical reform; commentaries on his own compositions and those of others; and pronouncements on cultural and political matters. Inevitably, there are problems of categorization: thus the essay in celebration of Beethoven's centenary in 1870 is devoted less to the composer whose example made a composer of Wagner himself than to prolix excursuses testifying to the effect of Wagner's assimilation of Schopenhauer (it should, however, be understood that the orientation by the example of Beethoven, the adoption of Schopenhauer's aesthetic theory – which is essentially a metaphysics of absolute music – and Wagner's unacknowledged 'symphonic ambition', as Egon Voss has called it, were all different facets of one and the same thing).

It is a rule of hermeneutics that an author's statements about his own creations belong not to the premises but to the material on which the interpreter must work. This applies particularly in Wagner's case. What he said in 'Eine Mitteilung an meine Freunde' (1851) about *Der fliegende Holländer* and the development of an entire work out of a central thematic substance relates, strictly speaking, not to the work he had written a decade earlier but to *Der Ring des Nibelungen*. At that date the musical conception of his tetralogy was still an urgent problem for which he had not yet devised the solution, and it was thus the object of a process of reflection that left him no peace, to the extent that it involuntarily obtruded on his account of the earlier operas. What Wagner claims to have done in *Der fliegende Holländer* was in fact his waking dream for the realization of the *Ring*. It is broadly true to say that even when Wagner appeared to be writing about something remote he was secretly discussing his immediate artistic preoccupation as poet and as composer. Thus it was surely no simple coincidence that his first reading of Schopenhauer, in 1854, had on him the effect of sudden illumination precisely at the moment when he was working on the scene of Wotan's despairing outburst in Act 2 of *Die Walküre*. (And while he was composing *Tristan* he outlined in a letter to Mathilde Wesendonck a 'revision' of Schopenhauer's metaphysics – instead of redeeming the 'will' by means of aesthetic contemplation it should now be possible to achieve the same end by means of love, and sexual love at that: the naivety of which would have provoked the philosopher to nothing more than a shrug.) Furthermore, of all the aesthetic ideas put forward by Wagner, it is precisely those which provided the slogans both of Bayreuth orthodoxy and of hostile critics, and thus dominated both apologia and polemic alike, which are concerned with the thorniest and most debatable subjects. If producers take the concept of the *Gesamtkunstwerk* seriously – if, that is, they do not to some degree ignore the postulate that the musical, the verbal and the scenic elements must constantly be intermingled – they are confronted with almost insoluble problems arising from the fact that Wagner's visual, scenic conceptions often lagged far behind the modernity of his musical ideas (while nevertheless leaving their traces in the music), and that dramatic groundplans of genius were often filled in with unspeakable verbal details (which Wagner nevertheless 'composed out'). The inherent weakness of the *Gesamtkunstwerk* is the need for 'simultaneity of the unsimultaneous' (the concept is a precarious one, weakened by the disproportions between the 'component arts'). Alternatively, the example of an expression such as 'unendliche Melodie' – which actually occurs only once in Wagner's writings, in 'Zukunftsmusik' (1860) – shows that enormous importance can become attached to a term, which can even be adopted as a metaphor in the theory of other arts, simply as the result of misunderstanding. Some people have misinterpreted the term, taking it to mean the avoidance of caesura and cadence: an intolerable trivialization. Others, having grasped Wagner's postulate, which was that every note should be 'melodic' in the sense of 'expressively significant', were then forced to accept the aesthetic premise that a 'melody', if worthy of the name, had to be motivated dramatically; this premise has moved so far from the colloquial sense of 'melody' that of the two words making up the term, 'infinite' and 'melody', it is the latter that is more in need of explanation (something that has escaped the exegetes, who have concentrated on 'infinite').

Regardless of the date at which he was writing, or his thesis, Wagner's method of presenting his arguments always remained that of the leftist Hegelian dialectics of the 'Vormärz' period – an era which left on his way of thinking a stamp that any changes in his aesthetic or political convictions never expunged. His philosophical dilemma in 'Zukunftsmusik' (1860) is characteristic. He begins by setting up the idea of opposition between 'Romance form', which imparts well-defined outlines to a national spirit, and German formlessness, which represents an 'obvious disadvantage'. But here dialectics, with their capacity for turning things upside down, come into play. For the other face of 'formlessness' is 'liveliness', or spontaneity; it thus has the potential to restore the 'purely human' which 'Romance form' has suppressed. Wagner might have got away with this argument if he had not been led astray by the assumption (for which the Winckelmann legend put about by Wilhelm von Humboldt was responsible) that the 'German art-form', which he postulated as the higher potential to be achieved by 'formlessness', represented a return of Greek form. If one further notes that Wagner was always intent on preventing the fluidity and constant alteration of life from petrifying in fixed forms, then the configuration of mimetic-cum-improvisatory 'liveliness' and the 'purely human' – that is, of one thing that is always changing and another that is always the same – can be seen, like the configuration of German formlessness and 'classical art-form', to be something of a conceptual riddle.

The problem is complicated further – and again leftist Hegelianism is behind it – by a philosophy of history which assumed that an alleged decline of literary drama on the one hand and of absolute music on the other created a situation where musical drama was needed to come to the rescue (*Oper und Drama*, 1851). As Cosima's diaries make clear, Wagner by no means regarded himself as a greater poet than Shakespeare or a greater composer than Beethoven; on the contrary, he was a great hero-worshipper ('ein grosser Bewunderer', as Thomas Mann put it). But at the stage history had reached in the 19th century the 'world spirit', whose agent Wagner felt himself to be, condemned both absolute music and literary drama as without substance, a condition from which they could be redeemed by musical drama alone (he had a penchant for religious metaphors). In other words, when Wagner acclaimed the *Gesamtkunstwerk* as the 'art work of the future' (*Oper und Drama*), as a typical Hegelian he did so in the belief that, far from making a subjective aesthetic judgment, he was obeying an edict of the 'objective spirit'. Psychologically this may look like arrogance, but to the historian of ideas it is the inheritance of the 'Vormärz'.

The way in which Wagner appropriated and modified the dialectical tradition becomes clearer if one considers what he understood by a drama. The main thesis of *Oper und Drama* – that drama is or should be 'the end', but music merely a 'means of expression' – remains obscure because Wagner allows the concept of drama and the term itself to remain ambivalent. This may be good dialectics; but it is also confusing. (Of course, the dramatic element is not the same thing as the verbal and, accordingly, the mutual relationship of words and music should not be the primary object of operatic analysis; language, like music, is for Wagner a means, serving the end of the drama.) Wagner's conception of drama is not the Brechtian one of a fable, in the representation and exposition of which language, music and spectacle have specific, distinct functions. He was more inclined, on the one hand, to make the mimetic element (the expression of 'liveliness') central to the drama. In his 'self-sacrifice' for the actor, 'the poet fulfils himself'. In 'Beethoven' (1870) Wagner wrote: 'We know that the verses of poets, even those of a Goethe or a Schiller, cannot determine music; only drama may do that, and by drama I mean not the dramatic poem or text but the drama we see taking its course before our eyes, the visible counterpart of the music.' But when, in 1854, he started to read Schopenhauer, Wagner came to think that the essential drama was expressed through the music and that what passed on the stage was nothing but an 'act of music made visible' ('Über die Benennung "Musikdrama"', 1872); 'thus we would not be mistaken if we perceived that man's *a priori* capacity to shape drama at all is in music' ('Beethoven').

Wagner's belief that he was the restitutor of 'classical art-form' is not enough in itself to explain how the mimetic and the musical foundations of drama were to harmonize. Either music, as a means serving the purpose of the scenic element – the 'mimetic-cum-improvisatory element' ('das Mimisch-Improvisatorische', as Wagner said, to gain emphasis) – would appear to surrender its independence, or the audience, immersed in the metaphysical essence of the drama expressed in the music, forgets about the visible enactment. Wagner foresaw both these possibilities; once, in despair, he yearned to obliterate

77

the reality of the stage and to match his invention of the 'invisible orchestra' with that of 'invisible staging'.

The difficulty is most readily resolved, or at least made comprehensible, if one starts with the compositional problem around which Wagner forever circled in his thinking, as in his works: the problem of symphonic opera. Like every true opera composer, he was fully aware that the decisive aesthetic element in opera is the momentary: the scenic and musical present moment. He once expressed the fundamental insight which he shared with his musical antipode, Verdi, as a theory of mimesis: 'An improviser such as an actor must belong entirely to the present moment, and never think of what is to come, indeed not even know it, as it were' (Cosima Wagner's diary, 1 September 1871). At the same time he was in thrall to the creative necessity of 'large form' such as he found realized in the tragedies of Aeschylus, one of the greatest of his heroes. But the integrity of the whole, the restitution of the 'classical art-form' out of the German spirit, was to be sealed (and here is the nub of his argument) through music, specifically a music of symphonic aspirations modelled on Beethoven. (In terms of dramatic structure, *Der Ring des Nibelungen* can lay no claim to 'classical art-form', for all its grecianization of Germanic myths; it suffers from the very weakness with which Wagner, fortified by Aristotle's *Poetics*, reproached Shakespeare's histories and tragedies: 'epic profusion of plot'.)

The dialectical antithesis which continued to preoccupy Wagner in all his theoretical writings was that between the 'mimetic-improvisatory element', guaranteeing 'liveliness', and the 'large form' which is the basis of the artistic character of works for the stage. The solution he found, in spite of all his theories of a *Gesamtkunstwerk*, was primarily musical: the technique of leitmotif, though its significance has to be unravelled in terms of dramatic structure. On the one hand a leitmotif (singular) operates in isolation, and often is linked only loosely with what has already happened and what is to come: in keeping with Wagner's concept of the mimetic element, it accentuates the scenic and musical present moment. On the other hand, the leitmotifs (plural), as a system of musical dramaturgy, constitute a form which embraces the entire work. Thus the leitmotif is both 'operatic' (inseparable from the momentary, which is why Nietzsche called Wagner a 'musical miniaturist') and 'symphonic' (essential to the constitution of large forms which span a wide area: the factor Thomas Mann called 'the magic of associations'). What is missing, for the most part, are forms of intermediate size; Alfred Lorenz's efforts to establish their existence were a failure.

Fluctuating between dialectics and confusion, the mixture of autobiography, art theory, philosophy of history, political polemic and cultural criticism in Wagner's prose writings is well exemplified by the aspect which has done most damage to his reputation: the anti-semitism. His anti-semitism is devastatingly corroborated in Cosima Wagner's diaries, but there remains a question, unexamined at the time of writing, as to the extent to which the views expressed

79

there accurately convey Richard's opinions or, through selection and stylization, rather reflect Cosima's own. In cultivated bourgeois circles in mid-19th-century Germany, anti-semitism was a personal matter, not one that was aired in public, and it did not prevent friendships with individual Jews – such as Wagner himself enjoyed, notably with Samuel Lehrs and Carl Tausig (his relationship with Hermann Levi was more complex). Thus, when he did not scruple to give vent to the offensively drastic expression of a personal idiosyncrasy in 'Das Judentum in der Musik' (1850), it was a vulgar infringement of the rules laid down by the bourgeois attitude of the time. On the other hand, when a newer form of anti-semitism became rife in the 1870s, publicly proclaimed and with a militant political thrust to it, Wagner kept his distance from it, and from the zealots who propagated it (which unfortunately did not become a Bayreuth tradition). His hatred for Meyerbeer, who he wrongly believed had abandoned him to his fate – or had even engineered it – in his early Parisian struggles, was essentially a personal affair, but it was entangled in one of those numerous operatic feuds that were carried on with such astonishing ferocity in the 18th and 19th centuries. It was typical of Wagner that he took up the aesthetic difference – between 'grand opera', with historical subject matter and made up of closed numbers, and 'music drama', with mythological subject matter and constructed from a web of 'melody in dialogue form' sustained by the leitmotifs – and forced it, or reinterpreted it, to assume the shape of a contrast in the light of Hegelian

philosophy of history, according to which the principle he was opposed to was not so much worse aesthetically (which could be disputed) as overcome (left
behind by the 'world spirit', against whose verdict
there could be no appeal). Wagner's animosity towards Mendelssohn was the outcome of the continual
conflict between his publicly proclaimed thesis that
music needed a verbal and/or scenic formal motive (a
justification or raison d'être) and his private and personal symphonic ambition (Egon Voss); in Mendelssohn, Wagner detected a naturalness and effort-
lessness of purely musical logic of which he often felt
the lack in himself. In terms of the history of ideas,
however, the decisive characteristic of Wagner's (as
of Karl Marx's) anti-semitism was the habit, for
which 'Vormärz' Hegelianism was to blame, of thinking of real people as symbolic figures representing
some objective historical phenomenon: the Jew (the
very use of the singular is a fatal depersonalization)
became a kind of allegory or a convenient simplifica-
tion of the causes of the social damage wrought by
the early industrial age, which in reality were far more
difficult to account for. The subjective dislike, with
its personal origins, and the aesthetic controversy,
which should have been debated as such, assumed
the mask of an objective verdict pronounced by history (another questionable depersonalization).

Silence was hard for Wagner, and it is easy to form
the impression that he aired his opinions on every
conceivable subject: art and religion, politics and the
state of contemporary civilization, vivisection (which
he opposed on Schopenhauerian and Buddhist prin-

ciples) and vegetarianism. But any such impression is deceptive; however often he may have spoken of drama as a *Gesamtkunstwerk* – a 'total artwork' or a 'synthesis of all the arts', as the term has variously been translated – he was correspondingly sparing with specific statements on the subject of music. The orthodox explanation of this curious state of affairs would be that, being a 'component art', it could not be spoken of in isolation. It was only rarely that he discussed questions of compositional technique or musical form: in some passages of *Oper und Drama* (1851), in his open letter 'Über Franz Liszts symphonische Dichtungen' (1857) and in the essay 'Über die Anwendung der Musik auf das Drama' (1879). It is as if he fought shy of utterances about the thing on which, in the last analysis, all else depended. 'Über das Dirigieren' (1869) – which with its thesis of tempo modification did as much harm in the history of interpretation as, initially, it did good in an age of mere time-beaters – is the only example from his pen of the kind of publication that one might expect from a musician.

Further, the extent to which he took issue with the musical environment in which he lived, or was forced to live, grew steadily less. The early works, *Die Feen*, *Das Liebesverbot* and *Rienzi*, were each paired with discussions of contemporary German, Italian and French opera. (It often happened that an originally apologetic stance, like the defence of Italian opera at the time of *Das Liebesverbot*, was abandoned the more vehemently for one of attack some years later when Wagner decided that he had gone beyond that particular stage of development.) When it came to his official chief work, *Der Ring des Nibelungen*, Wagner produced nothing less than an entire historico-philosophical construction on the grandest scale, centring on the challenging thesis that both Shakespearean 'literary drama' and the Beethovenian symphony (which had finally transformed itself into vocal music, with the 'Ode to Joy') were subsumed in musical drama, the 'artwork of the future' (he used the participle 'aufgehoben', in the Hegelian sense of simultaneously preserved and annulled, by reason of being raised up on to a higher level). But after the middle of the century, except in his act of friendship in standing up for Liszt's symphonic poems (1857), he ceased to pay serious attention to the history of music, so that in the end he seems to regard himself as the only composer of his time. The fact that he allowed Bruckner to dedicate the Third Symphony to him, in spite of his thesis of the end of the symphony, which was not so wrong-headed around 1850 as it appeared to be after 1870, and that he radiated a little ill-feeling in the direction of Brahms, bears no comparison with the passionate arguments he advanced in earlier days, whether for or against, on the subjects of Weber, Meyerbeer or Berlioz.

The response to Wagner's own writing has brought into being an immense literature, much of it belonging to the least happy chapters of German intellectual history, and the whole frequently marred by a dismaying ignorance of, or alienation from, art. (Even Nietzsche, with his deep understanding of music, had not the least comprehension of the theatre, which he

despised.) Wagner's philosophical theses have been
incessantly paraphrased, and combined with biographical data or psychological surmise, without due
attention to their relevance (or lack of it) to his musical
drama – that is, with no grasp of the fact that in
Wagner's case ideas are a function of the dramatic
works rather than the other way round. (The ending
of *Parsifal*, the declaration of 'redemption to the re-
deemer', is not the quintessence of the work but a
single component in a structure rich in paradoxes
which is a drama simply because it is not a simul-
taneous equation with a solution.) All Wagner's
works, from *Der fliegende Holländer* to *Parsifal*,
return to the idea of 'redemption': the truly fundamental dramatic motive, with which any interpretation must begin, is not, however, the redemption that
Wagner sought and longed for but the entanglement
that he felt reality to be. Reality was oppressive and
painful, and the sense of being trapped in it was the
fundamental emotion that made a dramatic, rather
than a lyric or an epic, creative artist of him. In
Wagner's work – the prose as well as the dramas –
redemption is always precarious and under threat,
and because his genius lay in the tying (the *nouement*,
so to speak) of the dramatic knot and not in its un-
tying (the *dénouement*), there is hardly an ending in his
dramas that is not ambivalent. The endings always
provided his biggest dramaturgical problem, and the
fact that he changed them (*Tannhäuser*), left them
open to interpretation (the *Ring*), considered and then
rejected modification (*Lohengrin*), meddled with the
musical style (which is a dramaturgical factor: *Der*

fliegende Holländer) or sought refuge in a cryptic formula (*Parsifal*), is one of the characteristics of his creative process. Only after analysis and interpretation of that phenomenon will it be possible to determine the meaning of redemption in Wagner.

In Wagner's thinking the divergent traditions and trends of the 19th century either intermingle or directly contradict each other. Though he constantly rebelled against his time, he represented it more completely than did any other single figure. This is nowhere clearer than in the implications of an idea which gradually grew to become the centre of his interpretation of his own oeuvre: the idea of 'Kunstreligion' (the religion of art). 'Religion und Kunst' (1880), the philosophical pendant to *Parsifal*, begins with the proposition of the thesis that the substance of religion has become petrified in the various confessions and is now preserved alive only in art.

It could be said that at the point where religion becomes artificial, it is reserved to art to salvage the kernel of religion, inasmuch as the mythical images which religion would wish to be believed as true are apprehended in art for their symbolic value, and through ideal representation of those symbols art reveals the concealed deep truth within them. While the priest bends every effort to get the allegories of religion regarded as literal truths, the artist has no interest in anything of the kind, for he frankly and freely makes his work known as his own invention.

In other words, it is the free invention that contains the concealed deep truth. It is possible to extract from these two sentences almost all the ideas most characteristic of the century: that music, as an 'organon of philosophy' (Schelling) or 'opus metaphysicum'

85

(Nietzsche), contained in its sounds an apprehension of the absolute which was at first transmitted in absolute instrumental music (E. T. A. Hoffmann on Beethoven) but transferred to musical drama when the latter assumed the substance of the symphony (Wagner); that myths – words or images, that is – are merely external appearances projected by that inner essence of the world which is expressed by music (Schopenhauer); that religion is nothing other than a world of fables 'believed as true' and transposed to a transcendental sphere, while its 'concealed truth' is something that man must recognize as being himself, in his corporeal reality (Feuerbach); that art, the 'invention of the artist', is one of the ways by which to reach the 'deep truth' of religion, which is a truth of the intuition (Schleiermacher); that religion – symbolic representation – is a step by way of which the spirit may progress towards philosophy (Hegel) or art (Wagner). (The order in which the steps are placed is secondary to the fact that Wagner, testifying yet again to the Hegelian inheritance, constructed a series of steps at all.)

The tiresome fact that all these interpretative possibilities remain open is the consequence of an ambiguity characteristic of Wagner's writings. It is less important to seek out the partialities and make exegetical hay with them than to recognize that these are statements in which a composer who was also an intellectual formed in the 'Vormärz' period summoned almost the entire intellectual inheritance of his age and forced it into service to justify his conceptions of musical drama. This process involved some drastic reinterpretation of the philosophies upon which it drew; yet the conceptions they were supposed to serve stood in no need of justification. Further, the nature of the conceptions is anyway such that they are not likely to be more easily understood by apostrophes to musical drama as a philosophy expressed in sound, or by the assembly of fragmentary formulations of that philosophy culled from the composer's prose writings. Wagner varied the philosophical, aesthetic and political theories he proclaimed in his writings entirely for the sake of his musical dramas, which in the last analysis were the only thing that truly possessed him. The works are the key to the writings, not vice versa.

CHAPTER THREE

Letters, diaries, autobiography

In 1967 the first volume was published in an edition of Wagner's letters, in chronological order, which attempts to establish an authentic text. It is hardly possible to predict when the undertaking will end, for the editorial principles are uncertain in the early volumes, the quantity of material is immense, and any estimate of how much may still be undiscovered would be sheer guesswork.

The character of the correspondence is varied, and it is sometimes hard to see where the line should be drawn between letters and other forms of literary expression. Some of the letters to August Röckel, Theodor Uhlig and Franz Liszt bear so close a relationship to the 'reform' writings of around 1850, and to the conception of the *Ring*, that any distinction between them and the essays – in which Wagner also writes of his own works, even when wearing the mask of the general theoretician of the arts – is minimal. There was good reason for publishing the 'Tagebuch seit meiner Flucht aus dem Asyl', the diary he kept in Venice in 1858–9 after his precipitate departure from Zurich, with his letters to Mathilde Wesendonck: the style of the letters is indistinguishable from that of the diary. On the other hand, his letters to King

Ludwig II are not so much a personal correspondence as the documentary evidence of an act of psychological calculation, showing how, when his back was to the wall, Wagner did not shrink from any means, however subtle or however crude, to keep hold of the help he needed – primarily for his work, only secondarily for himself. The most genuine letters, surprisingly enough, are those to Minna Planer (Wagner) because, with alienation accepted between them, he could write to her on the basis of a matter-of-fact stability that he knew with hardly any other person. Peripheral correspondences, like the series of 'letters to a milliner', published out of spite by Daniel Spitzer, created a sensation based on a general failure of understanding: what an artist needs to stimulate his creative powers, whether it be brocade or the smell of rotten apples, is his business and his alone.

It was because Wagner's real life consisted exclusively of an oeuvre which he planned during the 1840s and, with a tenacity that compels admiration, brought to its conclusion in 1882, that he became his own biographer. Unlike Rousseau, he did not write 'confessions' with the intention of anticipating the Last Judgment (as it were), but turned to autobiography in order to give a reckoning of a life sacrificed to his work and in which all the upheavals and questionable aspects were accordingly justified.

The 'Autobiographische Skizze' (1842) was written for Heinrich Laube's fashionable journal *Zeitung für die elegante Welt* at a time when Wagner had just become a local celebrity. In 'Eine Mitteilung an meine Freunde' the exile looked back over his creative past, compelled to do so by the uncertainty of the creative future that lay before him. He first began to assemble biographical notes in 1835, well before there was any prospect of publication; the so-called 'Annals', written down in the *Brown Book*, cover the years 1846–68, thus going beyond the point at which *Mein Leben* breaks off (his summons to Munich in 1864). In 1869 Cosima Wagner began to keep a diary, intended in the first place for their son Siegfried but essentially a continuation of the *Brown Book*. (Publication of both documents was delayed until a legal judgment in 1974 overruled the last objections.)

Wagner's actual autobiography, *Mein Leben*, was for nearly a century the object of unwarranted, scandalous rumours; for some, Wagner and his heirs were to blame, but some, without foundation, were put about by a hostile press. That an autobiography which was put together in the first instance for the private reading of King Ludwig II, which was dictated between 1865 and 1880 to Cosima von Bülow (Wagner), of which the first three parts (in print runs of 15 to 18 copies) were distributed to friends who had to return them after Wagner's death, which was first published commercially in 1911 with cuts intended to put certain personal matters in a different light, and of which an authentic edition was not published until 1963: that a book of that nature gave rise to rumours that did Wagner's image more harm than could ever have been done by the parts of the content it was thought necessary to retouch is something that occurred to Wagner's heirs at all too late a date. *Mein Leben* provides a paradigm of the historical and textual difficulties that Wagner's work always presents. One should not forget the identity of either the prospective reader or the amanuensis when we attempt to distinguish the 'poetry' from the 'truth'. Further, we are confronted with the effect the book had, beginning long after it was written and (following in the wake of the rumours) soon diverted into the wrong channels where the historical truth frequently threatened to disappear in the thicket of the controversy between myth-making and denunciation. When a serious interpretation of *Mein Leben* is undertaken – as yet the surface has merely been scratched – it will have to take account of the fact that the 'poetic truth' of some passages, such as the description of the Wartburg Valley or the (intentionally misdated) 'Good Friday Magic', can sometimes be more instructive for our understanding of the dramatic works than sober, empirical exactitude would have been. Understanding the paths along which Wagner's imagination set off is more important than correcting conscious or unconscious inaccuracies. Yet editorial meticulousness is not to be despised: it is only against the background of empirical truth that the 'poetic truth' can be recognized for what it is – another truth and not a distortion that the exegete is at liberty to dismiss.

CHAPTER FOUR

Aesthetics

In December 1884 Verdi wrote to Clarina Maffei:

I am convinced that this art, so artificial and so elaborately designed, is not compatible with our nature. We are matter-of-fact people and to a large degree sceptics. We are little inclined to blind faith and in the long run we cannot sustain belief in all the fantastications of this foreign art which lacks naturalness and simplicity.

Verdi's admiration for Wagner was as great as the distance that he preferred to keep between them. He was making, and hoped to preserve, a distinction between German music, which he thought of as primarily instrumental, and Italian opera; at the same time he indirectly highlighted some of Wagner's difficulties in attempting to realize, within the conventions of the German musical tradition, a type of musical drama that would be successful in the theatre. (It is significant that works produced in the 1840s, at the same time as Wagner's 'Romantic operas' and proceeding from similar premises, like Schumann's *Genoveva* and Spohr's *Kreuzfahrer*, failed.) 'Fantastications' is a reminder of the labour Wagner had to interest a public accustomed to subjects from Shakespeare, Hugo and Dumas, in Germanic myth, a misty Nordic world about which it knew nothing and cared even less. After the failure of revolution in 1848–9 and the collapse of Hegelianism, the scepticism Verdi felt to be peculiarly Italian became in Germany, too, the stamp of an age of positivism in the natural sciences and of *Realpolitik*. The 'neo-Romanticism' of Wagner and Liszt might well be defined as the musical survival of Romanticism in a positivist epoch. Finally the artificiality, which Verdi thought opera could not assimilate, is, in a more positive light, an artistic claim Wagner advanced on behalf of musical drama with an insistence unprecedented even in the annals of German and French opera, let alone Italian. Absurd as Wagner's thesis of the 'redemption' of the symphony by music drama might be, the driving aesthetic factor (apart from the technical factor of the treatment of themes and motifs) in the idea of linking the two genres was undoubtedly that Wagner sought and obtained the same integrity of artistic character in musical drama as Beethoven had achieved in the symphony and the string quartet. What the Symbolists in France were later to admire in Wagner's work was not only his music, which they scarcely knew, but above all the complete absence of compromise in his elevation of opera – which to Parisian audiences meant just the music – to a work of art by the standards of the Classic-Romantic aesthetic, or what Thomas Mann called the 'lofty and serious concept of art'. Wagner's work, which penetrated the consciousness of the German educated class in the 1850s, gained European recognition with Baudelaire's panegyric of 1861 and reached the peak of its influence around 1900, is representative of an age characterized by contradictory factors maintaining a curious and precarious co-existence: scepticism in philosophy, and enterprise and optimism in technology (the 1850s were already as much a period of business promotion in Germany as in France), Schopenhauerian pessimism and Bismarckian *Realpolitik*, the consignment of art (after the 'end of the age of art' diagnosed by Heine) to a peripheral existence and the simultaneously despairing and ecstatic conviction that art is the sole justification for life. The idea of 'music drama', of the *Gesamtkunstwerk*, is Romantic in origin, but, unlike other Romantic pipe-dreams that remained sketched or fragmentary, it was realized with the dogged, hard-headed persistence of any contemporary business entrepreneur. Bayreuth was the creation of a musical *Real*-politician who yet recognized in Schopenhauer's metaphysics of resignation the key to his own life. And Wagner's life-style, the object of so much righteous indignation, can be understood only if it is realized that nothing counted for him except his work, which he anticipated in its totality in the ideas he formed in the 1840s, and which he completed in the labour of 40 years. He told Liszt in a letter of November 1852:

I know nothing of the real enjoyment of life: for me the 'enjoyment of life and love' is something I have only imagined, not experienced. So my heart has had to move into my head and my living become artificial; it is only as the 'artist' that I can live, as 'man' I have been completely absorbed into him.

The core of Wagner's aesthetic was a rigorous artistic morality in the name of which he condemned Italian opera as a 'trollop' and French as a 'coquette

with a cold smile'. The principle of aesthetic autonomy, that art must take precedence over institutions
in the theatre and not the other way round, gave him
an aversion for the operatic establishment such as
would have been unthinkable for Verdi in spite of his
drudgery of the 'galley years'. Wagner's constant in-
vocation of the theatre of Aeschylus and its rapt
audiences was only a cover for the extremely up-to-
date idea of art for art's sake, the idea that the
audiences were the servants of the work of art, thus
ceasing to be 'audiences' and instead becoming 'con-
gregations'. The concept of art as religion changed its
meaning on its way from Hegel to Wagner: in the
'phenomenology of mind' Hegel defined a religion
that manifested itself in art – in ancient sculpture a
god is not merely represented but present – but for
Wagner art usurped the place of religion.

Political convictions meant nothing to Wagner
except in relation to the idea of musical drama, the
measure of all things for him. He became a revolutionary at a time when he saw social upheaval as the
only means of bringing art to the forefront in the
theatre, in place of the priority given to entertainment
and prestige; he appealed – in 1862, in the preface to
the text of the *Ring* – to a 'prince' to come to his
rescue, at a time when he despaired of the middle
class's will to take art seriously; and he represented
music drama as a national work of art at a time when
he hoped to garner support from the national pride
that burgeoned with the foundation of the German
Empire in 1871. But the actual work for whose sake
he adopted and altered his political creeds was neither

revolutionary, nor feudal, nor national. Art was the only idea in which Wagner believed; and so (as Nietzsche failed to understand) there is no sense in which *Parsifal* refuted the *Ring*.

Anyone who makes malicious comparisons between the image of the 'people' (*Volk*) depicted in the third act of *Die Meistersinger* and the actual phenomenon of Bayreuth, from which Nietzsche recoiled in disillusion, should remember that the 'people' Wagner had in mind in his apostrophes were by no means the German nation as it actually was. (The final words of *Die Meistersinger* are not chauvinist: they plead the cause of art and testify indifference towards the state.) The idea of the people rallying to the cry of art is a utopian image that Wagner was able to delineate simply because art and its 'need to be' was the only constant he knew. The ideas for reform he espoused were a function of the aesthetic autonomy that he postulated for musical drama, after the model of the Beethovenian symphony; he related social philosophy to art, not art to social philosophy. Instead of bringing himself into life with an audience and a form of society, he aspired to subvert the audience and alter the form of society – for art's sake.

If therefore music drama is seen (leaving aside the characteristics of the compositional technique) as the operatic consequence of the principle of aesthetic autonomy, then while it stands athwart the history of the genre it is by no means an isolated phenomenon in the history of music in the 19th century as a whole. The modern symphony concert – in which the symphony is the essential feature and not just the excuse for virtuosity, in which, that is, the claims of art predominate, and not the desire to entertain – was not established as a norm until around 1850 and thus provides an analogy to music drama chronologically as well as in essence, in the aesthetic justification. It followed in the wake of the music festivals built round Handel's oratorios and Beethoven's symphonies, which are also an integral part of the prehistory of Bayreuth. Even in Italy operas took longer to compose after the mid-century than previously, as composers took the demands of art more seriously. What Verdi accomplished for himself – and others – after his triumphs in 1853, was already the rule in French opera half a century earlier, as with Cherubini and Spontini.

In compositional technique, the correlative of the aesthetic claims of the principle of autonomy and art for art's sake is a complex of classical and romantic characteristics which can be summarized as 'musical logic' (a late 18th-century term). The two elements of musical logic, tonal harmony and thematic–motivic working, interact to create musical forms as differentiated in shape as they are in scale, providing the technical justification of music's aesthetic claim to be heard for its own sake: the immanent logic of music presents a discourse in sounds which is significant enough in itself, without fulfilling any extramusical function, to be as satisfactory an object of aesthetic contemplation as poems or works of visual art. Wagner's polemic (in *Oper und Drama*) against 'absolute music' – he coined the term by analogy with

97

Feuerbach's 'absolute philosophy' to mean music bereft of its origins in speech and dance, and growing, as it were, aerial roots – should not obscure the fact that the same technical categories that make possible 'absolute music' also provide the basis of Wagnerian music drama: thematic–motivic working or 'developing variation' (Schoenberg) and tonal harmony, deployed in a reciprocal relationship. The technique of weaving a dense network of relationships that extends over a whole movement or work from the repetition, variation and regrouping of themes and motifs is essentially symphonic (and alien to opera, in contradistinction to music drama). Whether the 'orchestral melodies', as Wagner called them, exist in their own right as instrumental music or are linked to dramatic actions – which should be understood as 'acts of music made visible', in Wagner's expression inspired by Schopenhauer's metaphysics of music – is a secondary matter: the decisive point is the difference between 'symphonic' form, in which the 'web' of motifs is the basis of the inner cohesion, and 'architectonic' form, consisting of a discernible grouping (using contrast and repetition) of distinct components. (In his four-volume work *Das Geheimnis der Form bei Richard Wagner*, attempting to reduce the musical structures of the music dramas to *Bar* forms, *AAB*, and *Bogen* forms, *ABA*, Alfred Lorenz took the architectural model of musical form as his starting-point, instead of the 'web' principle, as Wagner himself described it metaphorically at the end of his essay 'Zukunftsmusik'. This misapprehension of the basic categories drove Lorenz to acts of interpretative violence when he came to formal details.) The logical consistency with which, from *Das Rheingold* onwards, Wagner developed formal associations, stretching across hundreds and thousands of bars, out of the recurrence and variation or transformation of short motifs or themes is reminiscent of none other than Brahms. As Brahms handled sonata form, development, instead of being restricted to the middle section, extends over the whole movement so that here, too, the formal principle of 'architectonic' grouping of components yields to that of the 'web' of motivic relationships. Thus it emerges that Wagner and Brahms, regarded as antipodes by their contemporaries, shared a central compositional problem: how to develop monumental (whether symphonic or symphonic–dramatic) forms from musical ideas consisting of only a few notes. It need hardly be said that their solutions, as represented by the B major Trio and by *Tristan* (the score of which Brahms studied with admiration), differed in the extreme; but the fact that their problem was to so great an extent the same is symptomatic of the historical situation in German music – by contrast with French and Italian opera – from which Wagner and Brahms alike started out. The spirit of an age, insofar as there is such a thing, is to be found in questions rather than in answers. In terms of stylistic categories, motivic working represents the technical formula for resolving a contradiction that is fundamentally characteristic of the spirit of the 19th century, which Wagner embodied perhaps more perfectly than any other: the contradiction between the taste for the miniature, expressed in the elevation of the lyrical piano piece from a peripheral to a central genre, and the urge towards the monumental, the reflection in the 'anti-world' of music of the economic and technological entrepreneurism of the age. When Nietzsche sarcastically called the composer of the vast *Ring* cycle (in *Der Fall Wagner*) 'our greatest musical miniaturist', he spoke the truth in spite of himself, in that Wagner's monumentality – unlike Handel's, which Wagner despised – proceeds from connections and 'inventions at the level of smallest detail' (Nietzsche).

If then the 'musical logic' resulting from the association between form-building tonality and thematic–motivic processes can be regarded as the technical justification of the assertion of artistic autonomy that Wagner made for musical drama – by analogy with the Beethovenian symphony – the aesthetic attitude expected of the 19th-century audience was dubbed, in a term characteristic of the age, musical 'understanding'. (The 'people' Wagner invoked in the dramatized vision of the finale of *Die Meistersinger* were in historical reality the German educated middle classes.) 'Understanding' involved two things: that the listener on the one hand followed the musical argument, recreating its logic as he heard it, and on the other had an intuitive grasp of the musical expression, which constituted both the substance of the dramatic action and the composer's self-depiction. (The 'orchestral melody' of the music dramas, according to Wagner's Schopenhauerian metaphysics of music, renders audible the 'inmost essence' concealed behind the visible phenomena of the events on the stage; but it is also a commentary in sound giving the composer, as musical narrator, a 'speaking part', so that the 'sound of his voice' is continually heard.) Contrary charges have been levelled against Wagner: that on the one hand leitmotivic technique is too intellectual and requires the listener to cerebrate when he should be enjoying 'direct contemplation'; that on the other, in direct opposition, he weaves musical spells that induce states of intoxication (which Nietzsche felt to be questionable, and Stefan George artistically immoral). Undoubtedly Wagner's music, like all Romantic art, seeks to 'transport' the listener; but being 'beside one's self' (the 'other condition', as Robert Musil calls it) does not exclude by any means the 'circumspection' advocated by Jean Paul and E. T. A. Hoffmann – the ability to recognize widely spaced associations by dint of conceptual effort, and not merely to sense them vaguely. The 'associative magic' of which Thomas Mann speaks is magic, certainly, but one that instead of paralysing the spellbound listener challenges him to use his mind to make the associations; and the Dionysian intoxication described by Nietzsche in *Die Geburt der Tragödie* is not the negation of Apollonian contemplation but leads on to it. The blind frenzy in which enthusiasm for Wagner has sometimes lost itself is as inadequate a response to his work as the pedantry which feels its way through the labyrinth with the aid of Hans von Wolzogen's 'clues', in order to be aware at each and every instant of the 'meaning' of the musical motifs, the relationship of the music to whatever is happening on the stage. There is no need to pay too much attention to Wagner's insistence (in *Oper und Drama*) on the exclusive importance of 'emotional understanding' of music, or his avoidance of technicalities in his theoretical writings (except in some sections of 'Über die Anwendung der Musik auf das Drama'); this is no more than an aesthetic commonplace which goes back to German classicism and even to the Italian Renaissance: art ought to conceal the techniques on which it is based, or as Kant put it, it ought to try to appear as nature.

It has always been recognized that Wagner is aesthetically present in his music dramas, in defiance of the maxim that the dramatist must be invisible behind the events he depicts, but that is no justification for seeking biographical motivations, let alone facts, in the dramatic conceptions. (It is impossible, and it is really unnecessary to try, to tell whether Wagner's love for Mathilde Wesendonck provided the impulse to write *Tristan*, or whether, as Paul Bekker and Ernest Newman thought, the idea of the work, in its demand for realization, conjured up the love.) The aesthetically important thing is that in the music dramas Wagner is an epic writer: he does not allow the *dramatis personae* to become independent, but continually interrupts them with his own comments and asides. First, the mythic action, in which the characters are under inescapable constraints instead of acting freely; secondly the musical predominance of the symphonic 'orchestral melody' (where the 'inner action', the essence of the visible events, takes place) instead of Verdi's *parola scenica*; and finally the prominence of the composer, whose 'institution for expression in the theatre' (Thomas Mann) provides a platform not so much for the characters as – through the characters and above all through the orchestra – for Wagner himself: these are three aspects of the same thing. The choice of subject, the musical technique, and the Romantic principle of expression act together to create, not a thoroughly 'objectivized' action at one remove from the dramatist, but a musical epic, in which the narrator, commenting on the events and reflecting the emotions, is really the principal character.

Ever since the *Sturm und Drang* it was a firmly held belief that the essence of genius was radical originality; meaning, psychologically, that musicians speak of themselves in their music, rather than depict emotions from a detached standpoint, that they 'must be moved themselves, in order to move others' (C. P. E. Bach). In the 19th century, and especially with Wagner, the expressive principle, from being an interpretative aesthetic as it originally was in both opera and keyboard music, became a compositional aesthetic. The audience can sense that it is the composer, not the singers alone, who is moved at Wotan's Farewell or Siegfried's Death, and who communicates his emotion to the listeners through the orchestral melody – the primary musical language of music drama. What the audience experiences has already been experienced by the composer, whose instrumental commentaries combine the roles of unseen puppeteer and ideal spectator. (Wagner's favourite comparison of the 'orchestral melody' with the chorus in Greek tragedy has an unmistakably apologetic function, and conceals the fact that the symphonic reactions and commentaries of the orchestral writing are a consequence of the modern principle of expression, established in art and artistic theory only since the 18th century.)

The postulate of originality, the dominant aesthetic belief of the day, meant not only that music should proceed out of the composer's own emotions, but also that it should be novel in order to rank as authentic and to be accepted in the circles whose opinion counted. The sometimes violent opposition Wagner encountered should not distract attention from the facts that, first, 'epigonal' or 'academic' would in the 19th century have been worse verdicts, and, second, *Tannhäuser* and *Lohengrin*, works displaying no small measure of innovation, were accepted almost unanimously by the 1850s by the educated German middle class – including people like Eduard Hanslick who rejected the later music dramas. It is, moreover, a legend that the musical press failed to rise to the occasion of the Bayreuth Festival of 1876, which was a historical event even before it happened.

It is not hard to recognize in the aesthetic demand for innovation the idea of progress, which informed the self-confidence of the early industrial era. The aesthetic thought of the age was governed by the idea of progress, though not as such, but as bound up in a complicated relationship with the reverence for genius, with the thesis, that is, that the works of genius are outside history and belong in a 'museum of the imagination'. The conversion to the idea of 'classicism' (a concept that did not enter musical aesthetics until about 1800, centuries later than its acceptance in literary theory), together with the growing difficulties of performance, gradually gave rise to a standard repertory. Its backbone in the concert hall consisted of the symphonies of Beethoven and the oratorios of Handel, while in the opera house – aside from the traditionalism of the Paris Opéra, which ensured a relatively long life for individual works from Lully and Rameau to Gluck and finally to Meyerbeer – it was ultimately the works of the musical revolutionary, Wagner himself, that played (along with the Mozart operas) the crucial role in its establishment. Avant-gardism and traditionalism are contradictory but mutually complementary phenomena; and the combination of radical originality with the confident expectation of future classical status is thoroughly characteristic of Wagner. As Stendhal put it: the Romantic of today, however revolutionary his attitudes and behaviour may be, and precisely because they are revolutionary, is sure of being the classic of tomorrow. There is nothing paradoxical about this: it is founded on objective psychological and pragmatic considerations. For although the standardization of the repertory – by contrast with the Italian *stagione* principle – represents on the one hand a contradiction of the principle of novelty, it can on the other hand be a prop for it, as the decriers of the 'musical museum' fail to recognize. A distinction must be made between the qualitative novelty demanded by the 19th century and the purely chronological newness that was taken for granted in the 18th. As long as a musical work was required to make its impact at first hearing (because it was not going to be repeated, as was the rule in earlier times), then it was out of the question that it should be qualitatively new or radical, unless at the cost of predictable failure. Only when there is the chance that a work will be repeated – because of the acknowledgment that something that fails to be understood at first hearing may turn out to be a work of genius, and part of the repertory of the future – is it reasonably possible to attempt something significantly new. The scorn heaped on the 'music of the future' could not disguise the fact that in the 19th century people believed in the future, even if they abhorred it.

Along with his confidence of achieving classical status through his modernity, Wagner made a strict distinction between the authentic version of a work, that in which it should survive as part of the 'museum of the imagination', and unavoidable accommodations to local circumstances in actual productions (such as the Vienna *Tristan*), which he did not actually disown but regarded as incidental. (There was never, by contrast, an 'authentic' version of an Italian opera but only, like variations without a theme, the various realizations that it experienced in different circumstances.) Bayreuth is the institutionalization in musical practice of a principle that the musical scholarship of the same period was documenting in the first historico-critical editions; and Wagner, the scholar among librettists, may well have been conscious of the parallel.

Unlike the Italian and French operas of the 19th century, Wagner's works do not belong to any recognized genre; and the proposition that they constitute a genre in themselves, that of 'music drama', is debatable insofar as it glosses over the fact that they represent an individual recourse, which left composers after Wagner – the opera of the late 19th century is 'post-Wagnerian' in much the same way that the mid-century symphony is 'post-Beethovenian' – hardly any other choice but to be epigons or to sidestep into the fairytale, the musical conversation-piece or naturalism. Wagner should be compared not with Meyerbeer or Verdi but rather with Berlioz, whose works can also be viewed as essays in solving the problem of mediating between symphonic and dramatic music: the problem could not be solved without overstepping the accepted boundaries of the genres, so that each work is *sui generis*.

If, therefore, music drama is not really a genre, there is no sense in Wagnerians like Ludwig Nohl constructing a prehistory for it, as the antithesis of the despised 'opera', tracing it back to Gluck, or even Monteverdi. The dispute over the precedence of words or music, dramatized by Strauss in *Capriccio*, is by no means the cardinal point of operatic history that it is made to appear in such historicizing constructions, which attempt to legitimize Wagner's oeuvre historically by finding precursors for it. The decisive factor was not that Wagner banished 'absolute' melody, bereft of any connection with language and the events on the stage (the melodic writing of Rossini being for him the extreme example), and replaced it by unvarnished declamation, so as not to stifle the drama in the music, but that he developed a vocal style which is both dramatic declamation and yet 'melody' in the full sense of the word. Wagner's solution, a completely individual one, lay in his establishment of a relationship between voice and orchestra that bypassed the conventional pattern of 'melody and accompaniment'; it is, however, wrong to interpret the 'Sprechgesang' as merely the commentary on the symphonic 'orchestral melody'. Rather, the merging of the declamation with the orchestral writing gives the former a melodic character that it could not have assumed on its own. (One reason for putting the orchestra out of sight was to prevent the assumption that, because the orchestra is visible, its contribution is independent of the voices; Wagner 'hid' the orchestra because, not in spite, of the vital importance of its musical role.) Aesthetically, the charge that in Wagner's music dramas the vocal part, which always remains the most important part for the listener–spectator, has only a subordinate role in the musical substance, is wide of the mark; the vocal part takes up into itself what happens musically in the orchestra and makes its aesthetic effect because it calls on more than what is written down for it on the staff. It is the successful mediation between the symphonic and the dramatic that is the essence of Wagnerian music drama: the symphonic is absorbed into the dramatic, rather than colliding with it. Thus the starting-point from which one might evolve a 'poetics' of music drama is not a principle (that of declamation) but a problem – that of permeating declamation with 'melody'. And by contrast with a principle which might institute a musical genre, a problem can admit only of an individual solution.

In view of the fundamental importance that accrued to the symphonic factor in Wagner's music dramas, it is perhaps surprising that his instrumental works, of which only the *Siegfried Idyll* has ever achieved popularity, are mere parerga. The early piano sonatas are apprentice works, representing the concluding phase of his study with Theodor Weinlig; the overtures can be regarded as 'Kapellmeister' music, written before Wagner found his identity; while the *Siegfried Idyll*, with its thematic associations with the third act of *Siegfried*, or the 'Wesendonck' piano sonatas, are private confidences for the ears of initiates rather than concert pieces addressed to a wider public. One explanation for the relative insignificance of 'pure' instrumental music in his output is that the universalism of earlier eras – when, even as late as the Viennese classics, a composer's activities embraced all the musical genres – was replaced in the 19th century by concentration on a few genres, or even only one. This is notably the case with the great composers, as opposed to Kapellmeister who composed on demand. But a more important factor is that the aesthetic postulate of particularity and clarity in musical expression meant that pure instrumental music had no appeal for Wagner, since he regarded it as unclear and unspecific. (The fact that the expressive particularity of Liszt's symphonic poems surprised him shows where, as far as he was concerned, the problem lay; but for him the only solution lay in symphonic drama.) There can be no doubt that Wagner was an instrumental composer of the highest rank, and his influence was as great in the history of the symphony as in the history of musical drama. But it was only in the context of drama that he could operate at that level.

CHAPTER FIVE

Works

I Style

Tracing the history of the reception accorded to the principal categories of Wagnerian style, such as 'music drama', 'Gesamtkunstwerk', 'leitmotif' and 'unending' or 'infinite' melody, it is hard to decide whether the assistance they gave in promoting understanding of the works was greater or less than the harm they did through oversimplification and trivialization. But the attempt to persuade the Wagner exegetes to abandon a vocabulary worn out by misuse would be labour in vain, and the only alternative is to reconstruct the problems concealed behind the façade of these words and so resuscitate the ideas they represent.

The idea of a leitmotif (the term is not Wagner's; it was applied to his works in 1876 by Hans von Wolzogen, who may have found it in Jähns's catalogue of 1871 of Weber's works) as a fixed, recurrent, musical formula, not unlike the 'periodic formulae' in Homer, is simplistic to the point of falsity. Unchanged recurrence is the exception rather than the rule, even in the *Ring*, let alone in *Parsifal* (as long as the musical form and the dramatic significance are always considered conjointly). To counterbalance Debussy's and Stravinsky's malicious references to 'visiting-cards' and 'check-room numbers', amusing though they may be, it should be remembered that the themes and motifs are unceasingly varied, taken apart and merged with or transformed into each other, and that they move gradually closer together or further apart as they are modified. (A 'theme' differs from a 'motif' in its greater extent and complexity: the 'Last Supper theme', as stated at the beginning of *Parsifal*, is a theme; the Spear motif, one element in the Last Supper theme, is a motif.) It is seldom wise to take the earliest form in which a theme or motif appears as necessarily its primary form, from which all subsequent forms derive as secondary variations. Rather, they are all different impressions of the same material, and all principally equal in status; but each impression throws one particular feature of a situation, one trait of a character or one element of an idea into musical relief, without admitting of the motif as 'really' corresponding to one thing and only 'approximately' to another. For example, the Spear motif in the *Ring*, named after its most obvious, most convenient association, does relate to the stage property carried by Wotan. But it also refers to his contract with Fasolt and Fafner, the runes of which are carved on the spear's shaft, and by extension to agreements in general and finally to the connection Wagner sees between all such binding agreements and entanglement in the mythic destiny from which there is no escape. Naming the motifs is not completely arbitrary; but it reduces the intended configuration, which requires quite a lengthy description, to an over-simple object or idea that can be identified by a single word.

If, therefore, the usual distinctions between 'model' and 'variant' or 'exposition' and 'working-out' are irrelevant, or at least doubtful or inadequate, similarly a leitmotif can strictly neither be quoted from one particular place in the score nor be given a name as a dramatic symbol. Hans von Wolzogen's 'clues', identifying the musical structures by particular names (later authors have made changes in detail but have retained the principle) by no means represent the 'original' or 'real' form or meaning; they are simply individual instances taken at random from a very wide range of different musical forms and dramatic functions, which only amount to 'the' motif when viewed as a corpus. Further, it is hardly possible to draw a line, on one side of which a motif is the same one and on the other side of which it is a different one (with a different name) without exercising an arbitrary choice. For example, is the theme of Siegfried as Hero a variant of the Horn Call, or a different motif with a degree of kinship in the material? And what distinguishes the relationship between Horn Call and Hero theme from the connection between the Ring motif and the Valhalla motif, which emerges from the Ring motif by gradual transformation in the interlude between the first two scenes of *Das Rheingold*?

It is possible, on the one hand, with Curt Mey and Walter Engelsmann, to trace very nearly all the motifs in the *Ring* from two basic figurations, and, on the other, to insist on the individual character of each appearance of a motif, in a different musical variant or fulfilling a different dramatic function. Both points of view are justifiable in terms of a network of leitmotifs in which, on the one hand, everything is linked with everything else, and, on the other, each separate instance is unmistakably distinct. The identification and labelling of leitmotifs, like a bridge that one destroys on reaching the other shore, thus fulfils an exclusively heuristic function: the 'clues' utter a first, not a last, word on the musico-dramatic processes and serve merely as a means of entry into the dense system of relationships. The listener whose familiarity with the work enables him constantly to look forwards and backwards is conscious of the musical forms and dramatic functions only as relatives, no longer as absolutes.

The expression 'infinite melody', which Wagner coined in his essay 'Zukunftsmusik' (1860, i.e. around the time of *Tristan*), on the one hand conjures up metaphysical associations of the kind that have gathered around the idea of 'infinity', one of the central categories of the Romantic philosophy of art, and on the other hand admits of a sober, down-to-earth, technical definition: a melody is 'infinite' if it avoids, or bridges, caesuras and cadences. But the word 'infinite' has exerted a fascination that has prevented exegetes from appreciating that what Wagner meant by 'melody' is crucial to the understanding of the term: closer reading of 'Zukunftsmusik' reveals that it is used in a context where Wagner is arguing the distinction between 'melodic' musical passages, which are constantly expressive and significant, and 'un-

melodic' ones, where the music consists of formulae
and 'says' nothing. Thus the implication of 'infinite
melody' is primarily aesthetic and only secondarily
technical: it means that every musical figure must
contain a real 'thought', and that the mere padding
that Wagner condemned in some passages in
Mozart's symphonies should be eschewed. Cadences
are indeed avoided or disguised in 'infinite melody',
but not so much because they are caesuras as because
they are formulae. What Wagner wanted was both
unbroken musical continuity and significance in every
detail, and both postulates are bound into the concept
of 'infinite melody'. A melody is infinite when every
note 'says' something, and it 'says' something when
every moment of the music has dramatic relevance as
well as being inwardly linked to other moments.

Wagner disowned the expression 'music drama' in
'Über die Benennung "Musikdrama"'' (1872), because
it lent itself to being misinterpreted as 'drama serving
a musical purpose'; but it has proved ineradicable
and is always used for the works from *Das Rheingold*
onwards. *Der fliegende Holländer*, *Tannhäuser* and
Lohengrin are 'Romantic operas', but sometimes the
expression is extended to embrace them too. Legi-
timized rather dubiously by reference to various
utterances of Wagner's, they were added to the repertory of the Bayreuth festivals towards the end of the
19th century.

The aesthetic formulae by which Wagner tried to
define the essence of 'music drama' – he failed to
provide any alternative term – appear to be mutually
contradictory: the anticipatory postulate that the

music must be one of the means of expression available to the drama (introduction to *Oper und Drama*) is countered by the retrospective definition that in musical drama the events on the stage are 'the acts of the music made visible' ('Über die Benennung "Musikdrama"'). The discrepancy admits of various explanations, but these seem to complement rather than refute each other. First, it seems that the conception of the *Ring*, of which *Oper und Drama* is the theoretical counterpart, proceeded from a poetico-dramatic scheme which was accompanied to only a very small extent by tangible musical ideas, while the texts of *Tristan* and *Die Meistersinger* were obviously influenced or even determined by clearly defined musical ideas from the start, so that the later theory can be understood as the outcome of experience. Second, the metaphorical definition of 1872 is unmistakably based on Schopenhauer's philosophy, which Wagner first read and assimilated in 1854; in this philosophy music is elevated to the dignity of an 'opus metaphysicum' (Nietzsche) by the assertion that it expresses the innermost basis of the world, the essence behind appearances. The 1851 formula on the other hand is stamped by the philosophy of Feuerbach, with its bias towards corporeal reality (which for Wagner as dramatist meant the stage action) and against abstraction (the 'absolute' music against which Wagner polemicized in *Oper und Drama*). Third, the earlier definition was put forward from the viewpoint of the conception of a musical drama, the later from that of its reception. In *Oper und Drama* he stresses the importance of bringing to life for the audience a poetic intention, by means of music; this is characteristic of a dramatist in the process of planning a work. The contrary idea – that the listener must penetrate through the visible action to the hidden essence revealed in the music – is rather that of an observer who has learnt from Schopenhauer to recognize aesthetic contemplation, immersion in a work of art, while oblivious of self or world, as a vehicle of metaphysics.

The idea of the *Gesamtkunstwerk*, which unleashed a storm of controversy, is either trivial or arrogant. Insofar as it means no more than that the text and the stage presentation of a musical drama are not just the excuse for a 'costumed concert', but are rather functions of the drama, jointly with each other and with the music, then the concept is hardly earth-shaking; but if it represents the thesis that the history of the 'separate' arts in mutual isolation has been a history of decline, and that poetry, music and painting achieve their complete fulfilment and true significance only through being united in musical drama (through a synthesis that claims to restore the idea of Greek tragedy) then it is an assertion of some magnitude. If inclined to mock Wagner's arrogance, one should remember that it was conditioned by the spirit of the 1840s. The Hegelians of the 'Vormärz' period did not allow empirical historical facts to distract them in their grandiose historico-philosophical designs; and when Wagner asserted that both Shakespearean drama and the Beethovenian symphony were elevated or 'redeemed' in musical drama, his intention was to pronounce a historico-philosophical truth which did not exclude the continuing production of 'literary dramas' and symphonies on the lower plane of historical reality. Wagner's thesis should be understood in much the same spirit as Hegel's famous remark about the 'end of art', which does not refer to the existence or non-existence of works of art, but to the presence or absence of the 'world spirit' in art. Wagner's challenging argument was not that symphonic composition was no longer possible but that it was immaterial in the light of historical philosophy; and if, at the end of his life, Wagner thought of writing symphonies, he was not revoking his philosophy of history but contemplating works that would be outside his actual life's work.

That Wagner as harmonist initiated a new era is a commonplace of musical history; some historians are even inclined to regard *Tristan* as the beginning of modern music, just as Baudelaire's *Les fleurs du Mal* (1857) marked the beginning of modern literature. The coincidence of dates is amazing, even if one resists the temptation to indulge in a metaphysical excursus; at all events Baudelaire recognized Wagner's importance. For nearly a century, up to the deaths of Webern and Schoenberg, the style of *Tristan* was the cornerstone of a development whose original impulse was always discernible in its most extreme manifestations. And Wagnerian harmony can be analysed, at least partly, from the viewpoint that the atonal consequences drawn later were already prefigured in its tonality; while, conversely, the fact that the memory of Wagner was still not completely extinct in the 1920s, not only in the music of Schoenberg and Webern but also in that of such 'experimentalists' as Roslavets and Lourié, is no reason for speaking of a 'relapse into Romanticism' in the manner of neo-classical polemics but can rather be interpreted as a sign of the inner unity of a modern music of which *Tristan* was the earliest monument.

Any attempt to describe a harmonic style, some of whose essential characteristics survived the break between tonality and atonality around 1900, leads to almost insuperable terminological difficulties. The expression 'chromatic alteration', one of the basic categories of the style of *Tristan* (according to Ernst Kurth), underlines the fact that a note that impinges on its neighbour as a chromatic passing note or as a suspension began as a variant or chromaticization of a diatonic degree – that is, as an 'alteration'. But it is doubtful whether, or to what extent, harmonic forward movement is determined either by the root progression of the diatonic chord forms or by chromatic semitonal motion; and after 1900, in tonal or atonal derivatives of *Tristan* harmony, it is undeniable that semitonal motion is the real means of connection between chords. Yet if, as is already partly the case in *Tristan*, the essential element in the association of chords is semitonal connection and not root progression (and it can hardly be disputed that it is the function within the association that determines the harmonic significance of a phenomenon), then 'alteration' is strictly an inadequate term, as it seems to imply that chromaticism is secondary and derivative. Rather, chromaticism has achieved a degree of independence from its origins in alteration.

It is part of this independence of chromaticism that the diatonicism of *Die Meistersinger* sounds extraordinarily precarious, in spite of its assured tone of voice; it is like a thin, fragile layer of ice over a groundswell of chromaticism. It is memory rather than corporeal presence, and there is a strand of reflection in its artless nostalgia; but it owes its emotional effect precisely to the listener's sense that it is endangered. By contrast, the chromaticism of *Tristan* relies for its expressive effect on the listener's awareness of deviation from the diatonic background of the chord – that is, on his awareness of the 'alteration': the musical expression is inseparable from the divergence from the norm. To be adequate, a description of Wagnerian harmony would have to clarify its position floating between a tonality that has been attacked by the weakening of the root progressions but not yet completely destroyed, and an atonality anticipated in the increased independence of semitonal motion but not yet reached; and this would have to be defined as clearly as the relationships between the technical features and their expressive role. The emotional and symbolic significance of the 7th chord B–D–F–A and its 'inversions' and enharmonic 'transformations', of which the *Tristan* chord is one, depends on the extent to which either the 'atonal' or the 'tonal' element in the harmony predominates: the resolution of A♯–C♯–E–G♯ on to A–C–E–A in the Tarnhelm motif in *Götterdämmerung* is, poetically, an allegory of alienation, and correlatively, from the compositional viewpoint, a paradigm of semitonal motion independent of any root

progression in the bass. By contrast, the resolution of
the *Tristan* chord F–B–D♯–G♯ on to the altered chord
of the secondary dominant or the subdominant F–B–
D♯–A, which then progresses in turn to the dominant
7th chord of A minor (whose tonic chord is never
directly stated in the *Tristan* prelude but is latent
throughout), symbolizes Tristan's 'sehrende Sehn-
sucht' by its constant postponement of the tonal goal;
this postponement, the 'floating tonality', assumes
that the listener will make his own reference to the
disguised tonal background, the basic root progression from the secondary dominant via the dominant
to the tonic.

The assertion of chromatic independence is closely
associated with the relationship Wagner established
between harmony and counterpoint. In the Tarnhelm
motif the semitonal motion of the individual parts
creates a connection between the chords without the
support of a fundamental bass, so that the progression carries conviction even though it lacks a basis in
the functional theory of tonal harmony; that fact can
be interpreted as a reversal of the traditional relationship between the constituents of composition –
the counterpoint does not rest on the foundations of
a harmonic association but creates its own. It is
myopic to discover the paradigms of Wagnerian
counterpoint only in the explicit motivic combinations such as are encountered at the end of the *Meistersinger* prelude and in the final scene of *Siegfried*.
Wagner's detractors claim that his counterpoint rests
on secondary, literary and dramatic considerations,
and consists of the layering of originally unrelated

121

motifs, which they condemn from a 'purely musical' standpoint (Heinrich Schenker's critique of the *Meistersinger* prelude is typical). But for one thing the practice of forcing disparate motifs to blend above a simple harmonic basis (from which they stand out obtrusively) is at most an extreme example of Wagner's technique of combining motifs; the role of these motifs in less spectacular instances is to provide a contrapuntal function and justification for more complicated chord sequences (in which the polyphony does not stand out so obviously as an unrelated effect, but which are none the less polyphonic for that). Instead of 'polyphonizing' given chords he makes the polyphony create the harmony. Second, the charge of 'literariness' misses the point insofar as it is never possible to separate the musical technique from the poetic intention in any constituent of his composition. It is not just the counterpoint that is 'literary', but the motivic material; and it is aesthetically no disadvantage but an asset, indeed a sign of stylistic unity, if the same characteristics that distinguish the melodic writing also apply to the counterpoint, which is multi-layered melody.

Wagner touched on these issues in a letter to Theodor Uhlig of 31 May 1852: 'I have shown in the third volume of *Oper und Drama* that harmony becomes something real (not just something conceptual) only in polyphonic symphonic music, that is, in the orchestra'. He went on: 'Anyone who separates the harmony from the instrumentation when talking about my music is doing me as great an injustice as someone who separates my music from my text, my song from the words!' In other words, the harmony remains abstract until realized in counterpoint, and the counterpoint remains abstract until realized in orchestration; but for Wagner, as for Weber and E. T. A. Hoffmann, instruments were 'individual personalities with voices'. Thus Wagner's orchestration – recommended as a paradigm by Richard Strauss in his commentary on Berlioz's *Grand traité d'instrumentation* – on the one hand emerges as his art of characterization, his method of making the orchestra speak, and on the other is so intimately fused with his harmony and his counterpoint that the categories blend into each other. 'Sound' (*Klang*), in which 'chord' and 'timbre' meet, is the word that is most exactly applicable to the facts of Wagnerian composition, precisely because the outlines of the conceptual elements are blurred (and 'sound' is the central category of the music of the turn of the century, which lay in Wagner's shadow). It is not enough to analyse Wagner's instrumentation in terms of melodic, polyphonic and harmonic processes: it is not just a 'function' of a 'given' compositional fabric, but is one of the conditions enabling some structures – precisely, the most advanced – to exist in any meaningful way.

Wagner's rhythm has received scant attention, by comparison with his harmony and motivic technique; composers including Stravinsky and Bartók, seeking to emancipate themselves from the Romantic tradition by appealing instead to models from folk music, regarded it as diffuse, fugitive and amorphous, 'bad 19th-century'. Yet it bears witness to a historical change hardly less profound than the more spectacular revolution that took place at the beginning of the 20th century. T. W. Adorno affected to hear in Wagner's rhythms the dictatorial gestures of the Kapellmeister, a certain robustness and inflexibility of beat. But it is undeniable that, at least from *Rheingold* onwards, Wagner was inclined to supplant the regular rhythms or bar-groupings that predominate in Classical and earlier Romantic music with irregular formations, but without intending (as did Beethoven, Schubert and Brahms) that the irregularity be understood as deviation, a variant of a regular foursquare scheme, ever-present behind the exercise of licence: rather, it is self-justifying. 'Foursquare compositional construction', as Wagner disparaged it, is deliberately dissolved into 'musical prose': groups of two and four bars are still frequent, but they are not a norm against which irregularities ought to be judged.

This term 'musical prose' is used in *Oper und Drama* to designate a stage of development that Wagner believed he had moved beyond. He argued that a composer whose music takes into account and reproduces not only the difference between weak and strong syllables, but also the relative degrees of accentuation, is forced to turn verse into prose whenever, for instance, as often happens, the chief accent falls on the third strong syllable in the first line, on the fourth in the second line or on the second in the third line. He was convinced that the dilemma, of either repressing accents or of reducing verse to prose, could be avoided by abandoning accentual verse with end-rhymes in favour of *Stabreim*, verse with free rhythms and alliterative rhymes; but *Stabreim*, which has no rules governing either the number of weak accents in a line or the number of weak syllables between accents, is indistinguishable from prose when set to music. Its rhythmic principle provides no basis for regular groupings, either of beats in a bar, or of bars in a clause or period. And the alliteration has no musical effect.

The inflexibility of beat (which Adorno's ideological pupose led him to exaggerate) and the tendency of the verse to dissolve into 'musical prose' – a tendency that did not reach its extreme until the 20th century, with Schoenberg – appear mutually contradictory, but share one negative characteristic: their common opposition to the 'pulsating' rhythm of Classical and earlier Romantic music. This one negative trait had great historical consequences. The regular movement of strong and weak beats and bars, which Hugo Riemann called 'musical metre', is not entirely done away with in Wagner's rhythm, but it is thrust so far into the background that its continuing presence is felt only feebly. This lack of differentiation between bars and sometimes even between beats is compensated for in Wagner (and in a similar way in Wolf) by the extreme subtlety and complexity of the rhythmic detail; but this complexity runs the risk of being interpreted as diffuseness. The inflexibility of the bars and sometimes of the beats is connected with Wagner's rejection of (along with other worn-out formulae) the simple cadential schemes of Classical and earlier Romantic music, which were the harmonic correlative to the metrical differentiations of accent. The sequence I–IV–V–I, represented by half, one or two bars, is involuntarily heard as weak–strong–weak–strong. The complexity of Wagner's harmony thus causes a loss of 'metrical' differentiation and at the same time, since harmonic complexity gives rise to a corresponding rhythmic complexity, offers compensation for the loss.

The metrical differentiation of bars, yielding a barely vestigial influence in Wagner, was the cornerstone of periodic structure in Classical and earlier Romantic music, and periodic structure in turn was the foundation of those musical forms designated as 'metre on the large scale'. In detail and as a whole, form was based on a balance between parts that could interrelate. By abandoning foursquare compositional construction and pulsating rhythm in the interests of richer, less formula-based harmony and a more exact declamation of the text, with due regard to degrees of accentuation, Wagner renounced an architectonic foundation for musical forms, the principle that was as much the basis of the aria as of the song. He was therefore forced to constitute his forms exclusively according to 'logic', that is to emphasize the principle of thematic–motivic connection and development, which was one of the important form-building elements of Classical and earlier Romantic music. Form as 'architecture' was replaced by form as 'web'. (Lorenz did not appreciate this when he defended Wagner's music against charges of 'formlessness' by trying to reduce it to *Bogen* and *Bar* forms; rather, he should have demonstrated the inapplicability to Wagner's music of the formal concept on which the criticism was based.)

Thus harmony and metre, form and the rhythms of declamation are closely related in Wagner. The harmonic differentiation (advancing to the frontier of atonality) and the complexity of rhythmic detail (running the risk of toppling into diffuseness); the inflexibility of beat and the tendency to dissolve foursquare metre into 'musical prose'; the recoil from worn-out formulae and commonplaces (a sensitivity that produced the idea of 'infinite' melody, meaningful at every moment, as well as the rejection of simple cadential formulae with its destructive consequences for metre); the concern for a declamation that would go beyond the mere distinction between weak and strong syllables, to distinguish the degrees of emphasis; the technique of leitmotif and the establishment of a thematic network or web as the basis of musical form (in place of the architectural principle of the balance between related parts, in detail as well as a whole): all these characteristics of Wagnerian style, taken together, create a systematic association of compositional technique, every element in which can be directly or indirectly derived from every other, without necessitating any differentiation into primary and secondary elements.

II Romantic operas

To speak of Wagner's 'youthful operas' is an overstatement, intended to excuse what Wagner himself, in *Mein Leben*, called the 'wild oats' phase of his taste. After 1833, in the years when he wrote *Die Feen, Das Liebesverbot* and *Rienzi*, Wagner had completed his studies in composition with Theodor Weinlig, and

12. 'Rienzi': engraving from the 'Illustrirte Zeitung' (12 Aug 1843) of the final scene of Act 4 in the first production at Dresden, 1842; the conductor, in contrast to modern practice, is positioned directly in front of the stage with the orchestra behind him

was chorus master and then conductor in Würzburg, Magdeburg and Riga. The composer profited from the conductor's practical experience, but there was nothing out of the ordinary about either career. The only remarkable thing is that Wagner started out in this way. The early operas are an embarrassment to Wagner enthusiasts, not because of technical deficiencies that could be excused on the grounds of his youth, but because they seem as routine as they are derivative: *Das Liebesverbot* and *Rienzi* are 'well-made' operas. It is by no means uncommon for genius to start out as mere talent, but it is surprising for a Romantic – or at least it is contrary to generally held aesthetic expectation. There is little or no sign in the early operas of the revolutionary originality with which Wagner was later to challenge his age. *Die Feen*, after *La donna serpente* by Carlo Gozzi, whose fairytales attracted many German Romantics from E. T. A. Hoffmann onwards, is a Romantic opera in the tradition of Weber and Marschner; motivic recollection fulfils an important function but that is insufficient grounds for speaking of a 'foreshadowing' of Wagnerian music drama, for motivic recall is separated from leitmotif technique by a qualitative leap. *Das Liebesverbot*, derived with dramaturgic virtuosity from Shakespeare's *Measure for Measure*, is an opera after Italian and French models: the work of one who had deserted Weber and Marschner for Donizetti and Auber. And Wagner, who always managed to justify a change in the direction of his own interests as being the will of the world spirit that directed the course of musical history, took the opportunity in an essay on, or against, 'Die deutsche Oper' (1834) to hail the 'cosmopolitan' operatic style, which Schumann had derided as a 'juste milieu', as German opera's salvation from stiffness and academicism. Finally *Rienzi*, based on Bulwer Lytton's novel, was grand opera, aimed at Paris, but modelled less on Meyerbeer than on Spontini, whose *Fernand Cortez* Wagner had heard in Berlin in 1836. A balanced view of the significance and the position of *Rienzi* in Wagner's output requires recognition of the traits of music drama that are anticipated in grand opera and, conversely, the characteristics of grand opera that are retained and preserved in a music drama like *Götterdämmerung*.

The chronological proximity of *Der fliegende Holländer* to *Rienzi* is one of the paradoxes of musical history: that it marks a turning-point in Wagner's development has never been disputed since Wagner himself sketched the outlines of his own historical exegesis in 'Eine Mitteilung an meine Freunde' and *Mein Leben*. Wagner's biographers ascribe a similar importance, as marking a watershed in his development, to *Das Rheingold*, as the work in which the transition from 'Romantic opera' to 'music drama' and from the technique of motivic recall to that of leitmotif was made (those biographers, that is, who are not so set on emphasizing the integration, in terms of a unifying dramaturgical idea, of the entire oeuvre from *Der fliegende Holländer* onwards, as to deny all the leaps in Wagner's development). *Lohengrin* too has been claimed as a 'musical drama' in a positive sense, by comparison with *Tannhäuser*, which is still an 'opera'; while the stylistic upheaval represented by

Tristan is so profound in its repercussions as to necessitate an entirely new concept of music, where the reversal of the relationship between diatonic and chromatic – with the latter becoming the norm, the former the deviation – is merely an external, technical manifestation. But if one is prepared to accept as many as four stylistic stages from *Der fliegende Holländer* onwards, it is only a small step to the standpoint that each of Wagner's musical dramas is *sui generis*, each the outcome of a separate qualitative leap. The divergences between the early operas up to *Rienzi*, which resulted from Wagner's abrupt changes of model, are repeated in the 'Romantic operas' and the 'music dramas' in the form of extreme stylistic differentiation which, as Richard Strauss observed, even extends to the orchestration: each work, even each part of the *Ring*, has a characteristic sound style of its own.

Der fliegende Holländer, with which, according to Wagner, he began his career as a poet and abandoned that of a 'libretto manufacturer', is not put together from numbers but divided into musico-dramatic scenes. The process of drawing separate arias, duets, ensembles and choruses together in complexes, instead of their merely succeeding one another according to the thread of the drama and in an arrangement governed by the desire for variety, was developed in the 18th century and the early 19th, at first in the finales of acts. In *Der fliegende Holländer* it was extended throughout the whole work, though without any question of its being a through-composed music drama. No term exists to distinguish this process as a method in its own aesthetic right from 'number opera' on the one hand and 'music drama' on the other – 'scene opera' would seem odd. (Wagner was aware of the terminological difficulty, but his own attempts to overcome it with such agglomerate expressions as 'song, scene, ballad and chorus' serve to illustrate rather than solve it.) Numbers can be combined in a simple succession, or in an organic interconnection; in either case the form of the separate parts is changed. Since they are no longer required to stand on their own, they can be open in form; there is no need for recurring lines or groups of lines, or for closed forms. The melodic writing is no longer bound by aria schemes but gains the freedom to match word and gesture at any moment in the drama. The decisive aesthetic factor in musical drama is not simply the move towards 'parola scenica' but above all the capacity to effect the move structurally without having the music disintegrate into unconnected fragments.

The development of the kind of expressive, declamatory arioso that predominates in Wagner's works can be described from the viewpoint of stylistic history as a compromise between recitative and aria, but as far as the composer's attempt to solve his problem is concerned the breakthrough was the replacement of the number by the scene. As soon as formal cohesion was assured by the grouping, within a scene, of elements of different character, supporting and complementing each other, the individual parts were relieved of the need to be in closed forms or subjected to the melodic conventions of the aria for the sake of form.

A decade after *Der fliegende Holländer*, Wagner wrote in 'Eine Mitteilung an meine Freunde' (1851) of a leitmotif technique that first emerged from the specific dramaturgical conditions of that particular work, without the composer having previously been aware of it as a methodic principle:

I remember that, before I proceeded to write *Der fliegende Holländer*, I first sketched Senta's ballad in the second act, composing both the text and the melody; in this piece I unwittingly planted the thematic seed of all the music in the opera: it was the poetically condensed image of the whole drama, as it was in my mind's eye; and when I had to find a title for the finished work I was strongly tempted to call it a 'dramatic ballad'. When I came eventually to the composition the thematic image I had already perceived quite involuntarily spread out over the entire drama in a complete, unbroken web; all that was left for me to do was to allow the various thematic germs contained in the ballad to develop to the full, each in its own direction, and all the principal features of the text were arrayed before me in specific thematic shapes of their own making.

It was in fact a great exaggeration to speak of the 'thematic image' of Senta's ballad spreading out 'over the entire drama'. Obviously, when Wagner was looking back at the earlier work, the musical reality became intertwined in his mind with the idea of leit-motif technique, which he had not yet tried in practice. There are only a few passages in the opera – admittedly, those that further the inner action – which are coloured, if not dominated, by the basic motifs of the ballad: the Dutchman's monologue, Erik's narration of his dream, some sections of the Dutchman's and Senta's duet, and the work's close. But if the motivic technique is limited and rudimentary by comparison with the *Ring*, the motifs of recollection, too, for all their dramaturgic prominence, are accessories, not essential to the musical structure; and while in the *Ring* the musical development is based on the leitmotifs, the motifs of recollection in *Der fliegende Holländer* have more the character of interpolations. The regular recurrence of the Dutchman's motif in Erik's narration of his dream, for instance, marks the end of the lines of the text, but does not form the framework or the backbone of the music. And the motifs that symbolically introduce the duet for the Dutchman and Senta (those of the Dutchman and of Redemption) stand out from the musical context like quotations or reminiscences instead of constituting its substance. They have dramaturgic significance, but are not fully integrated in terms of the musical form.

The double title, *Tannhäuser und der Sängerkrieg auf Wartburg*, betrays the fact that in composing the text of his opera Wagner brought together two legends that had no connection in the literary tradition. In the 'Mitteilung an meine Freunde' Wagner wrote:

To the name of my hero Tannhäuser, I added the title of the legend that I combined with the Tannhäuser myth, although originally they had nothing to do with each other. Unfortunately Simrock, whom I so greatly esteemed for his study and resuscitation of the old German legends, later objected to this.

He did not mention that the relationship between

Tannhäuser and Elisabeth, the essential element in
the dramaturgic cohesion of the work, was his own
invention. The legend of Tannhäuser, as transmitted
in *Des Knaben Wunderhorn*, provided the material for
the beginning of the first act, and the conclusion of
the third: Tannhäuser's departure from Venus and
the story of his pilgrimage to Rome. Folksong was
not Wagner's only source: the fact that Heine's poem
Der Tannhäuser is a parody did not prevent him from
adopting some of its features. Heine's Tannhäuser
leaves Venus because he can no longer endure the
ease attending the joys of her *paradis artificiel*: 'Ich
schmachte nach Bitternissen' corresponds to the 'Aus
Freuden sehn' ich mich nach Schmerzen' of Wagner's
hero. And if in Heine Tannhäuser's confession to the
pope is a eulogy of Venus poorly disguised by con-
trition, in Wagner it anticipates Amfortas in speaking
of 'Sehnen, das kein Büssen noch gekühlt'.

In the legend of the Singers' Contest, the art of
Heinrich von Ofterdingen, who plays the part Wagner
gives to Tannhäuser, is demonically inspired. In re-
telling the tale in his *Serapionsbrüder*, E. T. A. Hoffmann even introduced a mention of Venus and her
enchanted mountain, but Wagner was the first to see
that the legend of the Venusberg was cause enough in
itself for the demonic confusion roused by the Heinrich–Tannhäuser song in the contest, without there
being any need for Hoffmann's complicated ghost
story. On the other hand the Wartburg legend seems
to perform no necessary function in the legend of
Tannhäuser: when Tannhäuser cries 'Mein Heil ruht
in Maria' at the end of the first scene, causing the

Venusberg to disappear as if by a magic stroke, it already creates the situation of the end of the second act, when Tannhäuser, oppressed by 'der Sünden Last', joins the pilgrims going to Rome. The purpose of introducing the other legend at all becomes clear only if it is recognized that the contest, filling the second act with histrionic parades and noisy disputes, is merely a façade behind which the tragic relationship between Tannhäuser and Elisabeth works itself out almost without words. His hymn in praise of Venus must be heard as Elisabeth hears it, pierced to the heart by his joyful acclaim of the goddess. Amid the noisy outrage of the knights, as they turn on Tannhäuser with drawn swords, the soundless inner collapse of Elisabeth is the important event. Tannhäuser is another Flying Dutchman, burdened with a curse from which he can be released only by a sacrificial death, that of Elisabeth: 'Nimm hin, o nimm mein Leben: nicht nenn' ich es mehr mein'. The flowering of the pope's staff, the miracle and dramatic climax of the legend of Tannhäuser, is in Wagner's opera merely a metaphor for Tannhäuser's redemption through Elisabeth's death. The essential drama played out in the opera transcends the legendary material that Wagner used.

The music of *Tannhäuser* was composed in Dresden in 1843–5, but in a sense it was never completed. Wagner changed the ending once in Dresden, to make it more striking visually: in the first version the apparition of Venus and the death of Elisabeth were depicted only in the music, not on the stage. For the production in Paris in 1861, a catastrophe in the short term but, as Gounod recognized, a triumph in the long, Wagner rewrote parts of the Venusberg scene and, less drastically, parts of the Singers' Contest. Finally, in 1883, a few weeks before his death, he told Cosima that he still owed the world *Tannhäuser*. The compositional problem, as he seems to have seen it, was not to be solved by mere revision. In the (second) Dresden version the music of the Venusberg scene is impressive in its motivic substance, but it is not sufficiently developed to provide an adequate counterpoise to the scenes dominated by the chorales, songs and marches which were the basis of the work's popularity. On the other hand the revision of 1860–61, which gave the Venusberg music the dramatic weight it needed, resulted in a juxtaposition of old and new sections with obvious stylistic discrepancies. The harmonic writing and orchestration betray only too clearly that Wagner had written *Tristan* in the interim. But it should not be regarded as conclusive that the Paris version, though beyond dispute musically superior in some details, is as a whole inferior to the Dresden version because of its stylistic inconsistency. The demand for stylistic uniformity is both classicist and untheatrical, and measures Wagner, a mannerist and a man of the theatre, by norms that were not his own. The stylistic discrepancies, which constitute inconsistency from the abstract musical point of view, can also be regarded, in a musico-dramatic light, as corresponding to the contrast between the everyday, naturalistic world to which Tannhäuser longs to return and the *paradis artificiel* of Venus, which still holds him inwardly in thrall. They could be said to be a musical weakness that performs a dramatic function.

The principal motif of the tale of the Swan-knight, on which *Lohengrin* is based, the Forbidden Question, reaches back to a magical, pre-Christian era: Lohengrin loses his magic power as soon as he is forced to reveal his name. But this stratum of magic was already overlaid in the medieval epic by the historical action that placed it in the 10th century in the reign of King Henry I and the wars against the Hungarians. There is also no mistaking the autobiographical motivation that drew Wagner to the subject. He wrote in 1851, in the 'Mitteilung an meine Freunde':

Lohengrin sought a woman who would believe in him: who would not ask who he was or whence he came, but would love him as he was and because he was as he appeared to her to be. He sought a woman to whom he would not have to explain or justify himself, but who would love him unconditionally. For this reason he had to conceal his higher nature, for it was precisely the non-discovery, the non-revelation of this higher nature (higher, because it has been raised up) that was his sole guarantee that he was not admired and marvelled at, or humbly – and uncomprehendingly – adored, simply because of that quality. What he longed for was not admiration and adoration but the one thing that could release him from his isolation and satisfy his yearning: love, to be loved, to be understood through love ... But he is unable to shake off the tell-tale aura of his higher nature; he cannot help but appear an object of wonder; the amazement of the commonalty, the venom of envy throw their shadow even into the heart of the loving woman; doubt and jealousy prove to him that he is not understood but only adored, and tear from him the confession of his divinity, with which he returns into his isolation, destroyed.

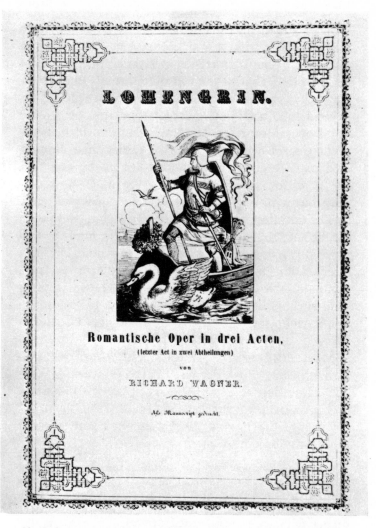

13. 'Lohengrin': title-page of the first edition of the libretto, printed for the first performance on 28 August 1850

139

Wagner's idea that it is Lohengrin's 'higher' nature that summons 'doubt and jealousy' has its origins in an image of himself: he saw in Lohengrin a model of his own fate, that of the 'absolute artist'. But the instinct that guided Wagner as a dramatist reached far beyond the questionable explanation that he offered as his own interpreter. The tragic dialectic at the heart of *Lohengrin*, which is obscured rather than illuminated by Wagner's commentary, lies in the fact that the goal for which Lohengrin yearns is at cross-purposes with the means by which he seeks to reach it. The question he forbids Elsa to ask him, so that he can be sure that she loves, not worships, him, she will inevitably ask sooner or later, even without Ortrud's intervention; an adoration, kept shyly at a distance, might be able to obey him, but a love of a human kind such as he desires cannot comply. In seeking to annul what sets him apart from others, Lohengrin succeeds only in reinforcing it.

Musically *Lohengrin* is traditional, between 'Romantic opera' and 'music drama'. In accordance with Wagner's ambition to establish a symphonic foundation and justification for tragedy and vice versa, the musical unity of a musical drama is analogous to that of a symphonic movement:

Nevertheless the new form of dramatic music must have a musical shape and to do that it must display the unity of a symphonic movement, and it does so if it spreads itself over the whole drama in the closest association with the drama, not merely over isolated, arbitrarily chosen, smaller sections of it.

Just as Senta's Ballad in *Der fliegende Holländer* constituted the starting-point of the composition, as the unifying 'thematic image', so in *Lohengrin*, as Wagner explained in the 'Mitteilung', he attempted to realize a similar unity:

This time I did not already have a complete musical item like the ballad in front of me, but only first shaped the image, in which the thematic radii came together, out of the construction of the scenes, out of their organic growth one from another, and then allowed it to appear everywhere where it was necessary for the comprehension of the principal situations.

The number of motifs or themes that have a structural role in the inner action conveyed by the music (as opposed to the pieces of musical scenery like the king's fanfare or the motif of the Judgment of God) is still very small in *Lohengrin* compared with *Das Rheingold*. Another obvious difference between the motivic technique of *Lohengrin* and the true leitmotif process first developed in the *Ring* is the retention of regular, 'quadratic' periodic structures. The principal motifs are all stated initially as complete periods with antecedent and consequent clauses, which Wagner avoided in his later work. During the work the periods are divided up into smaller structural and motivic components, only to be restored complete at the end: a method reminiscent of, and historically dependent on, the symphonic processes of development and reprise. Antecedent and consequent clauses are separated from each other and the motifs eventually shrink to short quotations which are then always ready to be inserted into the musical text without strain whenever the inner or external action requires it. But these quotations are always perceived as interpolations in the regular periodic structure that provides the framework of the composition, making the impression of additions motivated primarily by textual and dramatic considerations, that is by exterior factors rather than by the substance of the musical text. The idea of leitmotif technique in the stricter sense, replacing quadratic periodic structure as the basis of architectonic musical form as soon as a dense network of motivic combinations ensured coherent musical form, was not realized until the *Ring*.

III Music dramas

The *Ring* took more than a quarter of a century to write, from 1848 to 1874. More amazing than the inconsistencies throughout the work is the degree of unity it displays, a unity less dramatic than epic and symphonic. According to classical tradition, dramatic form had to avoid epic traits. Aristotle laid down in the *Poetics*: 'The poet must take care not to give his tragedy an epic form. By epic I mean consisting of numerous stories, as if, for instance, someone were to try to dramatize the whole content of the *Iliad*'. The Nibelung myth, as Wagner sketched it early in October 1848, contains a large number of stories. Finding the medieval *Nibelungenlied* too diluted, Wagner had turned to the *Edda*, linked the heroic tragedy of the death of Siegfried with the myths of the Germanic gods, and so elevated the events to a drama about the beginning and end of the world. His prose draft of October 1848, *Die Nibelungensage (Mythus)*, later published with the title *Der Nibelungen-Mythus: Als Entwurf zu einem Drama*, includes the whole myth with all its narrative strands, from the theft of the gold and the building of Valhalla to the deaths of Siegfried and Brünnhilde, whereby the curse laid on the gold is lifted. The sketch distinguishes clearly between the prehistory and the action to be presented in the drama. Everything up to the slaying of the dragon and the waking of Brünnhilde is prehistory, and the drama begins only with Hagen's plot and Siegfried's arrival among the Gibichungs. In the first version of his drama, written in prose later in October and in verse in November 1848, with the title *Siegfrieds Tod* (later to be *Götterdämmerung*), this distinction serves to separate the myth of the gods from the heroic tragedy, or what is recalled from what is enacted. The narrative passages expounding the myth are imposed on the action from outside; they are not integrated into it but merely fill in the background. The Norns' scene, Brünnhilde's encounter with the Valkyries (later, in *Götterdämmerung*, with Waltraute alone) and Hagen's dream are all dramaturgic devices. Instead of sustaining the action, the myth remains a pallid memory.

The recognition that *Siegfrieds Tod* was not self-sufficient forced itself on Wagner two years later in Zurich, after his flight from Dresden, when he attempted to set his text and failed. In May and June 1851 he amplified *Siegfrieds Tod* with *Der junge Siegfried* (later *Siegfried*), for partly dramaturgic and partly musical reasons. In November of the same year he told Theodor Uhlig of his plan to enlarge the two-part drama to a four-part one, and the texts of *Die Walküre* and *Das Rheingold* were written in 1852. In the letter to Uhlig he had written:

14. 'Siegfrieds Tod': fragment from the sketches for the Norns' scene, 1850

Music dramas: the Ring

When I came to the complete musical realization and was at last obliged to think about theatrical practicalities, I recognized that what I had in mind was incomplete: the characters owe their immense, striking significance to the wider context, and that context was presented only to the mind, in the epic narratives. To make *Siegfrieds Tod* work, I therefore wrote *Der junge Siegfried*; but the very effect that had, of giving the whole far greater meaning, made it clear to me, as I dwelt on its realization in terms of musical theatre, that it was more than ever necessary to present the whole tale and its background in a directly perceptible form. I see now that to be perfectly understood in the theatre I must have the whole myth performed on the stage.

His argument that only what is actually seen and enacted on the stage will work in the theatre is based on his experience as an operatic composer; it would not apply to non-musical drama, where the epic narrative has a long-standing tradition.

But the dramaturgic difficulty that drove Wagner to expand the tragedy of Siegfried into the four-part *Ring* was closely bound up with a musical and compositional problem. One might well speak of the birth of leitmotif technique out of the dialectic of the epic element in Wagner's drama. To begin with he found it impossible to set *Siegfrieds Tod*. In 1850 he made composition sketches, which survive, for the Norns' scene, in which the myth of the gods is narrated in epic fragments. It was not by chance that these sketches went no further: this first attempt was obviously beset with problems, concerning not the musical declamation in the setting of the text, but the musical drama, the exposition of the central ideas of the mythic tragedy. The sketches lack motivic musical substance. The mythic background which, as Wagner said, gives the characters 'their immense, striking significance' remains musically colourless and thin. There is no question of the myth being brought to life, or presented directly to the senses – which is the function of music in drama according to Wagner's aesthetics. The fragmentary nature of the sketches is closely associated with the dramaturgic weakness of *Siegfrieds Tod*: the rift between the enactment on the stage of the heroic tragedy and the mere narration of the myth.

In Wagner's view, if a musico-dramatic motif was to be fully understood it had to be introduced in association with both words and an event on the stage. In the theatre the visual correlative of what is expressed in the music carries even more weight than the verbal commentary. It is only when a musical motif has been the symbol of something seen on the stage, which establishes its association with the gold, the ring, Valhalla and so on, that it can become a motif of reminiscence or a leitmotif: a means, that is, of linking what is seen and spoken with what is not seen and not spoken. The 1850 sketch of the Norns' scene failed because it needed pregnant, associative, melodic motifs, as the musical means of presenting the narrated myths directly to the senses. Such motifs could not be invented because there were no visual correlatives. In other words, Wagner had not only dramaturgic but also musical reasons for writing first one, and eventually three, dramas to precede *Siegfrieds Tod*, to depict on the stage the events narrated in it: it was essential if he was to create musical motifs capable of portraying the myth of the gods, the background to the heroic tragedy, directly to the senses.

Nevertheless, the relationship of leitmotif technique to the epic element in the *Ring* is complex. It was the narrative character of the Norns' scene that forced Wagner to abandon its composition in 1850. He seems, like Aristotle, to have blamed the epic element in the drama as a whole for his difficulty. In a letter to Liszt of 20 November 1851 he wrote, apropos of expanding the two-part drama to four parts:

the clarity of exposition that this will provide, by allowing everything that at present is narrated at such length either to drop out completely, or at least to be reduced to pithy allusions, will now give me plenty of room to intensify the abundance of associations to the most exciting degree, whereas with the earlier, semi-epic presentation I had laboriously to curtail and weaken everything.

But the presentation of the prehistory of Siegfried's tragedy on the stage, instead of merely in narrative, did not mean that the epic and reflective parts of the drama were reduced: far from shrinking, they grew. In *Götterdämmerung* the Norns' scene is longer than it is in *Siegfrieds Tod*, and a comparison of the Valkyries' scene in *Siegfrieds Tod* with Waltraute's in *Götterdämmerung*, or of the two versions of Hagen's dream, reveals a similar tendency to expand rather than to reduce epic sections. Although this apparently contradicts what Wagner wrote to Liszt, it should cause no surprise. It is in the epic and reflective passages of *Götterdämmerung*, the narratives and the orchestral epic of the Funeral March, that there unfurls that 'associative magic' praised so highly by

147

Thomas Mann. Thus the epic element plays a paradoxical role in the *Ring*: if, as the 1850 sketches show, the epic exposition impeded the motivic technique of composition, on the other hand the epic recapitulation of what has already been shown visually actually creates opportunities for passages particularly rich in motivic development. The epic traits that Wagner the dramatist mistrusted were restored out of musical necessity.

According to the theory that Wagner outlined in *Oper und Drama* in 1851, the 'recurrence of melodic elements', the leitmotif technique, creates the principle behind a 'unified artistic form which stretches not merely over restricted parts of the drama but over the whole drama, linking it all together'. The 'restricted melody' of the traditional kind of aria was to be expanded into the 'infinite melody' that embraces a whole work. The feasibility of extending a motivic association over the whole of a four-part work without monotony depends on the wealth of motifs available. (Exegetes have counted and labelled more than 100 motifs in the *Ring*.) But the compositional need for an abundant and varied supply of motifs is countered by the aesthetic desirability of limiting their number to facilitate immediate comprehension, and two things are essential if the use of leitmotifs is to remain within the bounds of comprehension: first, the number of motifs must be kept small enough for the listener to keep track of them; and second, the musical symbols must have a foundation in the text and, even more important, in an event or object seen on the stage. When the Sword motif is first stated at the end of *Rheingold*, signalling Wotan's 'great thought' that a hero will have to perform the redeeming act that is forbidden to him, the god, it lacks an immediate visual motivation; Wagner conceived, but quickly abandoned, the absurd idea of having a sword on the stage, left behind from the hoard. The problem of resolving this dilemma between conflicting aesthetic and compositional demands may well have been one of the reasons why the composition of the *Ring* took so long. The eventual idea of developing the multitude of motifs he needed out of a small number of initial motifs, the simplicity of which would guarantee the comprehensibility of the motivic system as a whole, released Wagner from the pressure of a paralysing problem, and he recognized it as the decisive innovation introduced by leitmotif technique. In the *Epilogischer Bericht* (1871) he wrote:

In *Das Rheingold* I at once set out along the new path where the first thing I was to find was the plastic nature motifs, which shaped themselves, as they developed in ever more individual ways, into the vehicles for the promptings of the passions motivating the much-ramified action and the characters that expressed themselves in it.

The 'vision' of La Spezia, the inspiration of the prelude to *Rheingold*, was therefore probably not merely an image combining music and stage picture, but also a compositional idea: the possibility of deriving a motivic universe from a single idea (see ex.1). The Nature motif (*a*), a musical image of the elemental, the origin of things, consists of simple sound waves, which go on for no fewer than 136 bars of sublime 'monotony'. Erda's motif (*b*), the musical emblem of the earth goddess, is a minor-key variant of the Nature motif. The rhythmic diminution of Erda's motif, the motif of Wotan's restless wandering (*c*), symbolizes the fear that overcomes Wotan as the result of Erda's prophecy of the gods' doom: the diminution, expressing haste, is the psychological element, and its association with Erda's motif is conceptual. In the *Ring* rising movement means evolution, falling means decline: the

Ex.1
(a)
(b)
(c)
(d)

Nature motif is inverted to produce the motif (*d*) of the gods' downfall ('Götterdämmerung'), the apparent major-mode brightness of which is clouded by the fact that in a tonal context it often represents the flattened supertonic (the Neapolitan degree) of a minor key.

Stabreim, the alliterative verse form, which has been praised and decried in equal measure, character-

izes the text of the *Ring*. In *Oper und Drama* Wagner
made an effort to justify alliteration by a dialectic
interpretation of the history of poetry and of music.
His adoption of the ancient German verse form was
not merely atmospheric, an attempt to assimilate the
diction to the subject of the drama, but, like the myth
he expressed in it, the *Stabreim* was intended as a
means of restoring the 'purely human' in the text.
Wagner sought the human element in what was primeval, and the primeval in the union of music and
poetry, sensed by Rousseau to have existed in an age
before historical factors separated them. In spite of
Wagner's theory, *Stabreim*, as the precondition, has
very little musical importance. But it has a secondary
result which is important, though negative: the verse
entirely lacks metrical regularity. Wagner's lines of
Stabreim differ from old German verse in that the
number of strong accents is irregular: some lines have
two, others three or even four. And the number of
unaccented syllables between the accents is also
undetermined. The consequence of this rhythmic irregularity is that the musical periodic structure breaks
down into prose. And the prose structure of the musical syntax, in which groups of two and four bars are
by no means rare but are no longer the rule and
alternate on equal terms with phrases of three or five
bars, becomes the correlative of leitmotif technique.
From *Rheingold* onwards the basis of Wagner's musical form is no longer primarily syntactic (governed
by correspondences of $2 + 2$, $4 + 4$ or $8 + 8$ bars:
that is, a pattern of antecedent and consequent
clauses) but motivic. The association of motifs that

spreads over the entire *Ring* in a dense network, and the fact that every instant of the music has a motivic raison d'être, compensate for the loss of traditional periodic structure; the constitution of the musical form is 'logical' instead of architectonic, and takes shape as a woven tissue instead of a framework of symmetries.

The argument as to whether leitmotif technique can be traced back to Weber, Grétry or even Monteverdi is as great a waste of time as the controversy as to whether the decisive stage in Wagner's technical evolution is represented by *Der fliegende Holländer*, *Lohengrin* or *Rheingold*. What is important is the recognition that the compositional innovation of the *Ring*, the process of spreading a dense web of leitmotifs over the whole work so that they are almost omnipresent, was a qualitative leap in the history of leitmotif technique (so that it was subsequently possible to distinguish between true leitmotif technique and the technique of motivic recall). In *Lohengrin* the leitmotifs, though sometimes prominent and dramatically significant, are compositionally peripheral: they are interpolations in the periodic structure that provides the musical framework. It was only in the *Ring* that they became essential structural factors.

To a certain extent each of Wagner's musical dramas from *Der fliegende Holländer* onwards can be said to have marked an epoch. If the *Ring* is the first 'music drama', with a primarily symphonic form, based on the interweaving of motifs, *Tristan* can claim to be the source of musical modernity. The *Ring* is Wagner's 'internal' *chef d'oeuvre*, the paradigm of his conception of musical drama, while *Tristan* is his 'external' one, the work of his that had the most profound effect on musical history.

In 1872, in his essay 'Über die Benennung "Musikdrama"', Wagner defined his dramas as 'deeds of music made visible'. The metaphor, encompassing an entire theory, appears to contradict the thesis he had developed 20 years previously, in *Oper und Drama*, namely that music is the means and drama the end. At all events many historians understood it as an acknowledgment of the primacy of music. And anyone seeking biographical justification could attribute the change in Wagner's theory on the one hand to the experience of writing *Tristan*, and on the other to the influence of Schopenhauer, in whose metaphysics of music the visible world of appearances (*Vorstellungen*) is demoted to the mere reflections of the will (*Wille*), which expresses itself musically; it is not words or visual images but only music that penetrates the innermost essence of the world. There is also documentary evidence that appeared to support the thesis that music took precedence in the composition of *Tristan*. In 1854, three years before he wrote the text, Wagner told Liszt: 'I have drafted a *Tristan und Isolde* in my head, the simplest but most full-blooded musical conception': musical, not poetic. In November 1856 he wrote to Princess Marie Wittgenstein that while working on *Siegfried* he had slipped 'unaware into *Tristan*': 'music without words for the present'. And early in 1857 he sent Mathilde Wesendonck something from *Tristan*: music but no words.

Whether the music is subordinate to the text in

15. 'Tristan und Isolde': the first page of the first draft of the libretto, with a sketch for the Sailor's song, 1857

musical drama or the text to the music was not, however, Wagner's primary problem. Those who base the
history of opera on the changing relationship between
words and music are in error when they call him as a
witness. The appearance that Wagner set up, in *Oper
und Drama*, a theory of the precedence of text over
music, which he then put into practice in the *Ring*, is
deceptive and arises from the erroneous equation of
'text' with 'drama'. In Wagner's aesthetic theory
drama is the essence – at once premise and issue – of
the conjunction of text, music and stage action; the
text, exactly like the music, is one of the means, while
the end is the drama. Undoubtedly the later definition
of drama as a 'deed of music made visible' implies a
greater emphasis on music, which had become imbued
with a metaphysical dignity, thanks to Schopenhauer.
But whether the dramatic intention is determined primarily by the text or by the music, the central focus
of Wagner's thought is always the drama. *Tristan*'s
subtitle, 'Handlung' ('action'), is a translation of
'drama'.

The harmony has always been acknowledged as the
most influential innovation of the *Tristan* style, especially since Kurth's *Romantische Harmonik und ihre
Krise in Wagners 'Tristan'* (1920). But what has not
received sufficient recognition is that analysis of harmony is meaningless except in relation to melodic
writing, counterpoint and instrumentation. The
changes in the relationship of the parameters to each
other are even more important historically than the
harmonic changes *per se*; in spite of Berlioz, Wagner
was the first great exponent of the discovery that

'sound' (*Klang*), the central category in the music of around 1900, should be understood in the sense that harmony and instrumentation are inseparable. In ex.2 it is neither the melodic writing (the bass is the *Hauptstimme* or principal part) nor the harmony as such that gives rise to the compelling effect of this motif (of fate, or of the drink of atonement), but the relationship of the elements, a relationship that constitutes a specifically Wagnerian counterpoint. Con-

Ex.2

sidered as an abstract scheme, the sequence of chords in ex.2 is simply incomprehensible and the motif in the bass, if considered on its own merits, and understood as being in E minor, is slight and unappealing. But from the correlation of the harmonic surprise (one can indeed hear a background implication of a diatonic progression B–D$\sharp^7$ = III–V^7 in G$\sharp$ minor), the motivic significance of the bass and the chromatic part-writing in the upper parts, there results a contrapuntal complex as convincing in its effect as it is intriguing in its apparent implications. And the mediation of chromatic and motivic part-writing between chords that are not so much tonally related as juxtaposed to make colouristic effects, which in turn are emphasized by the orchestration, is one of the fundamental stylistic characteristics of the modern music of around 1900, when Wagner's historical influence was at its peak. (To both enthusiastic adherents of this music like Ernst Bloch and opponents like Stefan George, the word 'music' at the beginning of the 20th century was virtually synonymous with 'Wagnerian music', and 'Wagnerian music' with *Tristan*.)

The first scenario of the plot of *Die Meistersinger* dates back to 1845, when Wagner was still Kapellmeister in Dresden. But it was not until the end of the following decade, after he had finished *Tristan*, that Wagner took the project up again, wrote another prose scenario and then, while in Paris in winter 1861–2, the poem. The work's première in Munich signified, against the background of the *succès de scandale* of *Tannhäuser* in Paris, Wagner's assumption of musical hegemony in Germany and in Europe.

The motif of resignation, the love for Eva that Sachs waives, is still missing from the 1845 sketch. While the earliest conception of *Meistersinger* was as a satyr-play to be appended to *Tannhäuser* – a burlesque travesty of the tragic singers' contest – by 1861–2 the proximity to *Tristan* looms large. Sachs renounces Eva so as to avoid sharing the fate of King Mark, and actually refers to the tale. The quotation of the motif of longing from *Tristan* is the outward sign of an inner association between the two works which is of not merely autobiographical but also aesthetic significance. The 'old German' simplicity of *Meistersinger*, represented by diatonicism, is by no means 'naive' but 'sentimental', to use Schiller's categories: not instinctive but reflective and nostalgic. In terms of musical technique this means that modern chromaticism, while reduced and kept in the background, is not expunged from the consciousness: the style of *Tristan* is the latent precondition for the style of *Meistersinger*. The impression that diatonicism has been reinvested with its old, 'classical' rights is completely illusory: what is denied is always present, even though unexpressed. Chromaticism has become the normal language of music, the rule to which diatonicism is now the exception, conspicuous because unusual (this applies to John the Baptist's scenes in *Salome*). The diatonicism of *Die Meistersinger* is somehow dreamlike, not quite real in the 1860s; the style of the work is less a restoration than a reconstruction, it is 'secondary' diatonicism, in the sense of Hegel's 'secondary' nature.

The archaizing tendency of *Meistersinger* also influences the musical forms. The forms of earlier opera were banished from the *Ring* (though they were to return in *Götterdämmerung*, partly because of the requirements of its text, written in 1849, and partly because Wagner ceased to be so dogmatic after *Meistersinger*); but in *Meistersinger* they are much in evidence. There are monologues, songs, ensembles, choruses and dances in plenty, and each act ends like a grand opera, with a massed finale. There is a similar restoration of melody, to which *Meistersinger* owes much of its popularity, though the restoration derives not so much from earlier practice as from leitmotif technique. In the *Ring* and in *Tristan* leitmotifs tend towards the greatest possible brevity (periodic struc-

16. 'Die Meistersinger': beginning of Act 1 scene i in the second
complete draft (orchestral sketch), 1862

159

tures like Siegfried's motif were an exception), but in *Meistersinger* they join together in complex themes or expand into melodies, without it being possible to say whether the motif is a fragment of the melody or the melody a development of the motif. Sometimes it even seems that the differences between the motifs, on which their dramaturgic or allegorical significance is based, are less important than the unity of the tone of voice that joins them together.

An active element in the plot of *Meistersinger* is the conflict between musical conservatism and innovation, represented respectively by Beckmesser who, as a caricature of a critic (more precisely, of Hanslick), is endowed with the attributes of envy, sterility and the inability to understand anything new, and by Walther von Stolzing, the 'natural genius'. This contrast becomes confused in the musical realization. It is true that Beckmesser's creative efforts – the serenade and the mangled Prize Song – are given some of the obvious characteristics of outmoded musical practices: mechanical coloratura, modal melodies and perfunctory accompaniments. On the other hand, Stolzing's songs are anything but 'new' music. They are lyrical, in the form of 'infinite melody', but in the second half of the 19th century 'new' music was not lyrical but 'characteristic', and the supreme example of stylistically advanced, characteristic music in *Meistersinger* is the pantomime for Beckmesser, the traditionalist, in the third act. Wagner as a dramatist may have had the idea of furnishing Stolzing, as the representative of musical progress, with the kind of music that was recognized as progressive in the mid-1860s, but as an experienced man of the theatre he knew better: his triumphant heroic tenor needed music that would have an immediate appeal for the audience, who would identify with the crowd on stage.

The final scene of *Meistersinger*, like the Germanic subject matter of the *Ring*, has been misused for chauvinistic ends. The misuse, though so obvious, had fateful consequences. The final lines, 'Zerging' das Heil'ge Römische Reich in Dunst, uns bliebe doch die heil'ge deutsche Kunst' (this was the first version, but it means exactly the same as the final one) were set by Wagner as early as 1851, 20 years before the German Empire was founded, and they are less an expression of political ambition than a reminiscence of Nietzsche's tenet that art is the only justification of life. Similarly, the gods in the *Ring* are in a decline of which their own guilt is the cause, conceived by Wagner in the spirit of 'demythologization' which he adopted from Feuerbach.

Parsifal, the text of which was finished in 1877 and the music in 1882, is as simple in its formal outline as could be expected of a ritualistic drama that documents Wagner's belief that, since art has become religion, religion may properly become art. He called the piece a 'Bühnenweihfestspiel' ('festival of consecration in a theatre'). The strict symmetry of its external form – the third act repeats the scheme of the first, the second creates a contrast – is architectural, while the inner action is linear, following stepwise a scheme encapsulated in the mysterious prophecy 'Durch Mitleid wissend, der reine Tor'. Parsifal, a

figure of legend, is a passive hero: the decisive action
that is the drama's turning-point is a refusal, his recoil
from the temptations offered by Kundry. He blunders
into the centre of the drama in ignorance of what he
is doing, but the plot is merely the occasion and the
outward aspect of his progress towards recognition.
In the first act, after killing the swan, Parsifal feels a
first intimation of pity. On witnessing Amfortas's
agony, he feels a convulsive pain in his own heart,
but does not yet dare to put the 'redeeming question':
his pity is still dull and inarticulate. In the second act
Parsifal, 'the pure fool', is made 'cosmically clear-
sighted' by Kundry's kiss. He feels in himself the
temptation to which Amfortas succumbed, and per-
ceives ('sees through' in the Schopenhauerian sense)
the world as the unending circle of misery, which
only pity and renunciation can break. The third act
merely carries out what is already foreseeable at the
end of the second, once Parsifal has regained the
spear; uneventful by normal dramatic criteria, it represents a third stage in the inner action – the pity that
is a dull sensation in the first act and recognition in
the second is at last directed outwards in the third as
the 'redeeming act'. And, in spite of the philosophy
of renunciation, Parsifal does not become an anchor-
ite but the Grail king.

The hero's passivity has dramaturgic consequences
which distinguish the 'Bühnenweihfestspiel' from a
drama. Since Parsifal does not act, but only comes to
himself by reacting, the prehistory of the drama had
to be expounded in epic narrations, instead of being
integrated in a sequence of interconnecting actions.

As a result the narrator Gurnemanz, a lay figure dramaturgically, has the biggest part in the work. Yet his narrative, the chief element of exposition, is simultaneously counterpointed with visual actions and images. The motifs associated with the Grail are stated in a scene of prayer, those of Amfortas and Kundry in a scene which has virtually no dramaturgic function – the characters merely make an appearance – but is musically fundamental. All that happens is that the sick Amfortas is carried on to the stage and receives from Kundry a herb which will not relieve his pain. The real purpose of the scene is to provide musical motifs, which would otherwise have only a textual basis in Gurnemanz's narrative, with visual associations. Wagner was not satisfied with a verbal commentary when he introduced a motif; whenever possible he provided a visual equivalent for the musical meaning, which did not have to be a piece of action but could be a tableau.

There seems to be a connection between the epic, ritual character of *Parsifal* and the partial replacement of *Stabreim* by end-rhymes. According to the theory Wagner developed in *Oper und Drama*, *Stabreim* is the verbal expression of emphasis and concentrated feeling, while end-rhyme has a formal, distancing effect.

Generally, the use of musical motifs in *Parsifal* is governed and conditioned by the contrast of chromaticism and diatonicism: the chromaticism that conveys the magic of Klingsor's kingdom also expresses the anguish of Amfortas, while the expressive range of the diatonicism stretches from the naive simplicity of Parsifal's theme to the sublimity of the Grail themes. As categories of musical technique, chromaticism and diatonicism also have an allegorical significance: the insertion of diatonic motifs into the musically opposed sphere of chromaticism, such as the introduction of Grail themes into Amfortas's lamentation in the first act, and Kundry's scene in the second, carries out by musical means a dramaturgic function that cannot escape the listener. And even so apparently insignificant (because too general) a characteristic as two motifs both being chromatic (or diatonic) creates a primary dramatic association: the connection between deception and pain, between Klingsor's garden and Amfortas's complaint, is as unmistakable as, in the diatonic sphere, that between the naivety of the 'pure fool' and the Grail kingship that awaits Parsifal at the end of his path to recognition. In none of Wagner's dramas is the technique of variation, derivation, combination and mixture of motifs so highly developed and differentiated as in *Parsifal*. The fact that the ramifications of the dramatic and motivic dialectic are based on so simple and so obvious a contrast as that between chromaticism and diatonicism, by which the listener can orientate himself, is the proof of Wagner's theatrical genius.

WORKS

Editions: *Richard Wagners Werke*, ed. M. Balling (Leipzig, 1912–29/R1971) [B; inc.]

   Richard Wagner: Sämtliche Werke, ed. C. Dahlhaus, E. Voss and others (Mainz, 1970–) [SW]

Catalogue: J. Deathridge, M. Geck and E. Voss: *Verzeichnis der musikalischen Werke Richard Wagners und ihrer Quellen* (Mainz, 1984) [WWV]

Dates given for MS sources refer to the beginning and end of complete drafts only, including fair copies of librettos and full scores. Dates in square brackets have been deduced from sources other than those mentioned in the same column. Full details of all autograph MSS (including single musical sketches prior to first complete drafts), copies in other hands as well as first and subsequent major prints are to be found in WWV. For a discussion of terminology see WWV (foreword) and J. Deathridge: 'The Nomenclature of Wagner's Sketches', *PRMA*, ci (1974–5), 75. All texts are by Wagner unless otherwise stated.

NA – Nationalarchiv der Richard-Wagner-Stiftung, Bayreuth   RWG – Richard-Wagner-Gedenkstätte der Stadt Bayreuth

Text
MSS (autograph) $\left\{\begin{array}{l}\text{ps – prose sketch (outline)}\\\text{pd – prose draft (detailed)}\\\text{vd – verse draft}\end{array}\right.$

Music
MSS (autograph) $\left\{\begin{array}{l}\text{fcd – first complete draft (outline)}\\\text{scd – second complete draft (detailed)}\\\text{ffs – first full score (draft)}\\\text{sfs – second full score (fair copy)}\\\text{(for those works where only a single}\\\text{complete draft and/or full score}\\\text{exists: cd, fs)}\\\text{pm – performance material}\end{array}\right.$

Prints $\left\{\begin{array}{l}\text{vs – vocal score}\\\text{fs – full score}\\\text{ps – piano score}\end{array}\right.$

Writings: *Gesammelte Schriften und Dichtungen*, i–x (Leipzig, 1871–3, 1883/R1976) [GS]

   Sämtliche Schriften und Dichtungen, i–xvi (Leipzig, n.d. [1911–16]) [SS]

   Richard Wagner's Prose Works, ed. and trans. W. A. Ellis, i–viii (London 1892–99/R1972) [PW]

   Das Braune Buch: Tagebuchaufzeichnungen 1865–82, ed. J. Bergfeld (Zurich and Freiburg, 1975; Eng. trans., London, 1981) [BB]

Numbers in the right-hand column denote references in the text.

165

STAGE WORKS (COMPLETE)

WWV	Title (genre, libretto)	Composition, sources	1st perf.; cond.	Publication	Dedication, remarks	
32	Die Feen (Grosse romantische Oper in 3 Akten, after C. Gozzi: La donna serpente)	text: pd, vd (both lost), [Jan–Feb 1833, Leipzig]; rev. dialogue, GB-Lbm, NA, vd¹, vd², [sum. 1834, Leipzig]; vd³, [Würzburg]; music: cd, NA, fs (lost), Feb 1833–Jan 1834, Würzburg ov. (end): cd, 27 Dec 1833; fs, 6 Jan 1834 Act 1: 20 Feb–24 May 1833; fs (end), 6 Aug 1833 Act 2 (end): cd, 27 Sept 1833; fs, 1 Dec 1833 Act 3 (end): cd, 7 Dec 1833; fs, 1 Jan 1834 Act 2 scene v (scena and aria, Ada), rev.: cd, NA, [spr. 1834], Leipzig	Munich, Königliches Hof- und National-theater, 29 June 1888; F. Fischer ov.: Magdeburg, 10 Jan 1835; Wagner	lib: Mannheim, 1888; SW 22 vs: Mannheim, 1888 fs: c1890 (orchestration rev. H. Levi); B xiii; SW 1	pm (not autograph), D-Mbs, from lost fs or copy	11, 12, 48, 82, 127, 129
38	Das Liebesverbot oder Die Novize von Palermo (grosse komische Oper in 2 Akten, after Shakespeare: Measure for Measure)	text: pd (lost), vd, GB-Lbm, [mid June–Dec 1834, Rudolstadt and Magdeburg]; Fr. trans.: vd, Lbm, [aut. 1839, Paris] music: cd, NA, fs (lost), Jan 1835–[March 1836], Magdeburg Act 1 (begin): cd, 23 Jan 1835 Act 2 (end): cd, 30 Dec 1835 arrs. from nos. 2, 9, 11 (in Fr.): pm, NA, [Feb–March 1840, Paris]	Magdeburg, Stadt-theater, 29 March 1836; Wagner 2 duets from Act 1: Magdeburg, Stadttheater, 6 April 1835; Wagner	lib: Leipzig, 1911/ R1981; SW 22 vs: Leipzig, 1922/R1982 fs: B xiv; SW 2 Karnevalslied, from no.11, vs (in Ger.): Stuttgart, 1837 Gesang der Isabella, from no.6, vs (in Ger.): Munich, 1896	copy of lost fs in Wittelsbacher Ausgleichsfonds, Munich	14, 15, 21, 24, 48, 82, 127, 129
49	Rienzi, der Letzte der Tribunen (grosse tragische Oper in 5 Akten, after E. Bulwer Lytton: Rienzi: the Last of the Roman Tribunes)	text: ps, US-PHci, pd, vd, NA, [June/July 1837, Blasewitz and Dresden; June]– Aug 1838, Mitau and Riga; Fr. trans.: vd, NA, [sum. 1839–wint. 1839/40] music: cd, NA, fs (lost), Aug 1838–Nov 1840, Riga and Paris ov.: 1st draft (begin), 20 Sept 1840; cd (end), 23 Oct 1840; fs (end), [19 Nov 1840]	Dresden, Königlich Sächsisches Hoftheater, 20 Oct 1842; C. Reissiger	lib: Dresden, 1842; Hamburg, 1844; Berlin, 1847; SW 23 vs: Dresden, 1844 fs: Dresden, 1844 (shortened version); SW 3	Friedrich August II, King of Saxony; pm (inc., not autograph), D-Dlb, from lost fs or copy; for Wagner's revs. see SW 3/v and WWV 49 Erläuterungen	17, 18, 19, 22, 24, 25, 37, 48, 82, 127, 128, 129, 130, 131

No.	Title	Composition	Première	Publication	Remarks	References
		Act 1: cd, 7 Aug–6 Dec 1838; fs, [8 Sept 1838]–6 Feb 1839 Act 2: cd, 6 Feb–9 April 1839; fs (end), 12 Sept 1839 Act 3: cd, 15 Feb–7 July 1840; fs, 6 June–11 Aug 1840 Act 4: cd, 10 July–29 Aug 1840; fs (begin), 14 Aug 1840 Act 5: cd, 5 Sept–19 Sept 1840 Prelude to Act 3 for perf. on 2 evenings [Jan 1843]: cd, private collection, fs, NA, S-Smf				21, 22, 24, 25, 27, 37, 43, 44, 48, 63, 72, 84, 85, 114, 130, 131–4, 140, 152
63	Der fliegende Holländer (romantische Oper in 3 Aufzügen, after H. Heine: Aus den Memoiren des Herrn von Schnabelewopski)	text: pd (in Fr.), F-Pn, [2–6 May 1840]; pd (in Ger.), RWG, [early 1841]; vd (in Ger.), RWG, 18–28 May 1841, Meudon Senta's Ballad, Song of Scottish Sailors, Song of the Dutchman's Crew: vd (in Fr.), GB-Lbm, May–June 1840 music: cd (lost), fs, NA, July–Nov 1841, Meudon and Paris ov. (end): cd, 5 Nov 1841; fs, [19 Nov 1841] Act 1 (begin): cd, 23 July 1841 Act 2 (end of Senta's Ballad): cd, 31 July 1841 Act 2 (begin no.5): cd, 4 Aug [1841] Act 2 (end): cd, 13 Aug [1841] Act 3 (end): cd, 22 Aug 1841; fs, 21 Oct 1841 Senta's Ballad, Song of Scottish Sailors, Song of the Dutchman's Crew: cd, fs (both partly lost), NA, RWG, US-NYp, [May–July 1840] end of ov., 1860: ffs, NA, 19 Jan 1860, sfs, GB-Lbm, [shortly before 16 March 1860]	Dresden, Königlich Sächsisches Hoftheater, 2 Jan 1843; Wagner	lib: Dresden, 1843; Zurich, 1852; Munich, 1864; SW 24 vs: Dresden, 1844; Berlin, 1909 (Weingartner version) fs: Dresden, 1844; Berlin, 1896 (Weingartner version); SW 4 (orig. version with later alterations in separate vol.) ov. with rev. ending of 1860, fs: 1861	Ida von Lüttichau (née von Knobelsdorf); orig. version in 1 act; orchestration rev. 1846, 1852; ending modified, 1860	

WWV	Title (genre, libretto)	Composition, sources	1st perf.; cond.	Publication	Dedication, remarks	
70	Tannhäuser und der Sängerkrieg auf Wartburg (grosse romantische Oper in 3 Akten (1859–60: Handlung in 3 Aufzügen))	text: stage 1: June 1842–April 1843, Aussig, Teplitz and Dresden; pd¹, NA (with orig. title 'Der Venusberg'), 28 June–6 July 1842; pd², NA, 8 July 1842 (end); vd¹ (lost); vd², NA, [shortly before 7 April 1843 with later alterations] stage 2: [early 1847, Dresden]; pd, vd (lost) stage 3: [Sept 1859–Feb/March 1861, Paris]; vd¹, vd² (in Ger.), NA, private collection stage 4: [Aug/Sept 1861, Vienna–early 1865, Munich]; vd¹, vd² (both partly lost), Geheimarchiv, Munich music: stage 1: [July 1843]–April 1845, Teplitz and Dresden; preliminary sketches, private collections, *D-LEu*, *Mbs*, RWG, *S-Smf*; cd, private collection, NA; fs (destroyed during lithographing in 1845) ov. (end): cd, 11 Jan 1845 Act 1: cd, Nov 1843–27 Jan 1844 Act 2: cd, 7 Sept–15 Oct 1844 Act 3: cd, 19 Dec–29 Dec 1844, fs (end), 13 April 1845 stage 2: [Oct 1845]–May 1847, Dresden; cd, NA, 30 April 1847 (end); fs, NA, 7 May 1847 (end) stage 3: [Aug/Sept 1860–March 1861, Paris] Act 1 scene i: cd, NA, fs, NA, 28 Jan 1861 (end); Act 1 scene ii: fcd, NA, scd, NA, 18 Oct 1860 (end), fs, NA; further MSS in *A-Wn*, *D-Mbs*, NA, RWG, Wagnermuseum, Eisenach, *F-Pn*, *Po* stage 4: [probably aut. 1861, Vienna–sum. 1867, Munich]; fs (partly not autograph), private collection, pm (not autograph), *D-Mbs*	stage 1: Dresden, Königlich Sächsisches Hoftheater, 19 Oct 1845; Wagner stage 2: Dresden, Königlich Sächsisches Hoftheater, 1 Aug 1847; Wagner stage 3: Paris, Opéra, 13 March 1861; L. Dietsch stage 4: Munich, Königliches Hof- und Nationaltheater, 1 Aug 1867; H. von Bülow	stage 1 lib: Dresden, 1845; SW 25 vs: Dresden, 1846; SW 20/i fs: Dresden, 1845; B iii; SW 5 stage 2 lib: Dresden, 1847; SW 25 vs: Dresden, 1852 fs: Dresden, 1860; B iii; SW 5 stage 3 lib: Paris, 1861; SW 25 vs: Paris, 1861 fs: B iii; SW 6 stage 4 lib: Munich, 1867; SW 25 vs: Berlin and Dresden, 1876 fs: Berlin, *c*1888; B iii; SW 6	Camille Erard (stage 2, 1860); see WWV 70 *Erläuterungen*	22, 24, 25, 28, 29, 37, 43, 44, 84, 104, 114, 130, 134–8, 157

	Title	Sources	First performance	Publications	Remarks	Pages
75	Lohengrin (romantische Oper in 3 Akten)	text: pd, NA, 3 Aug 1845, Marienbad (end); vd, private collection, 27 Nov 1845 [Dresden] (end) music: fcd (partly lost), private collections, D-Mbs, NA, US-NYp, STu; scd, NA; fs, NA; [May 1846]–April 1848, Dresden Prelude: scd (end), 29 Aug [1847], fs (begin), 1 Jan 1848 Act 1: scd, 12 May–8 June 1847 Act 2: scd, 18 June–2 Aug 1847 Act 3: fcd (end), 30 July 1846; scd, 9 Sept 1846–5 March 1847; fs (end), 28 April 1848 arrs. for concerts in Zurich, May 1853, (mostly lost), NA arrs. for concerts in St Petersburg and Budapest, 1863, NA, H-Bo, private collection	Weimar, Grossherzogliches Hof-Theater, 28 Aug 1850; Liszt Act 1 finale (in concert): Dresden, Königlich Sächsisches Hoftheater, 22 Sept 1848; Wagner	lib: Weimar, 1850; SW 26 vs: Leipzig, 1851 fs: Leipzig, 1852; B iv; SW 7	Liszt; Prelude composed last but orchd first; orig. version of lib in SW 26	31, 34, 37, 40, 44, 45, 46, 64, 84, 104, 114, 130, 138–42, 152
86	Der Ring des Nibelungen (ein Bühnenfestspiel für drei Tage und einen Vorabend)		as a cycle: Bayreuth, Festspielhaus, 13, 14, 16, 17 Aug 1876; H. Richter		'Im Vertrauen auf den deutschen Geist entworfen und zum Ruhme seines erhabenen Wohlthäters des Königs Ludwig II von Bayern vollendet' copy by Friedrich Wölfel of lost fs, NA; pm for 1st perf. (not autograph) D-Mbs	33, 36, 37, 42, 47, 50, 54, 55, 57, 60, 65, 70, 72, 73, 78, 83, 84, 88, 95, 96, 100, 111, 112, 113, 116, 131, 134, 141, 142–52, 155, 158, 161
86a	Vorabend: Das Rheingold	text: ps, pd, vd, NA, [Oct/Nov 1851]–Nov 1852, Albisbrunn and Zurich pd, 23–31 March 1852; vd, 15 Sept–3 Nov 1852 music: cd, NA, ffs (partly lost), NA, US-NYp, PRu; sfs (lost), Nov 1853–Sept 1854, Zurich; cd, 1 Nov 1853–14 Jan 1854; ffs, 1 Feb–28 May 1854; sfs, 15 Feb–26 Sept 1854 arrs. for concerts in Vienna, 1862–3, private collections, A-Wgm	Munich, Königliches Hof- und Nationaltheater, 22 Sept 1869; F. Wüllner excerpts from scenes i, ii, iv (in concert): Vienna, Theater an der Wien, 26 Dec 1862; Wagner	lib: Zurich, 1853; SW 29/ii vs: Mainz, 1861 fs: Mainz, 1873; SW 10		36, 38, 39, 40, 47, 48, 55, 99, 113, 114, 124, 130, 141, 143, 149, 151, 152

WWV	Title (genre, libretto)	Composition, sources	1st perf.; cond.	Publication	Dedication, remarks	
86b	Erster Tag: Die Walküre (in 3 Aufzügen)	text: ps, pd, vd, NA, [Nov/Dec 1851]–July 1852, Albisbrunn and Zurich Act 1: pd (begin), 17 May 1852; vd, 1–11 June [1852] Act 2: vd, 12–23 June [1852] Act 3 (end): pd, 26 May 1852; vd, 1 July 1852 music: cd, ffs, NA, sfs (lost), June 1854–March 1856, Zurich, London, Seelisberg and Zurich Act 1: cd, 28 June–1 Sept 1854; ffs (end), 3 April 1855; sfs (begin), 14 July 1855 Act 2: cd, 4 Sept–18 Nov 1854; ffs, 7 April–20 Sept 1855 Act 3: cd, 20 Nov–27 Dec 1854; ffs, 8 Oct 1855–20 March 1856; sfs (end), 23 March 1856 arrs. for concerts in Vienna, 1862–3, private collection, A-Wgm, NA, RWG, US-NYpm, Wc	Munich, Königliches Hof- und Nationaltheater, 26 June 1870; Wüllner excerpts from Acts 1, 3 (in concert): Vienna, Theater an der Wien, 26 Dec 1862; Wagner	lib: Zurich, 1853; SW 29/ii vs: Mainz, 1865 fs: Mainz, 1874; SW 11 'Walkürenritt': Mainz, 1876	copy by Alois Niest of lost sfs, D-Mbs; 'Walkürenritt', 'Wintersturme wichen dem Wonnemond', arr. pf by C. Tausig (1863, 1866) approved by Wagner but not identical with his arrs.	36, 40, 48, 55, 73, 143
86c	Zweiter Tag: Siegfried (in 3 Aufzügen)	text: ps, pd, NA, vd¹, private collection, vd², NA, May 1851–[Nov/Dec 1852]; pd, 24 May–1 June 1851; vd¹, 3 June–24 June 1851 [1st rev., Nov/Dec 1852, 2nd rev., 1856] music: fcd, scd, ffs, sfs (only Acts 1–2), NA, [Sept 1856]–Aug 1857, Zurich (end scd Act 2); Dec 1864–Dec 1865, Munich (ffs Act 2); March 1869–Feb 1871, Tribschen (Act 3) Act 1: fcd (end), 20 Jan 1857; scd, 22 Sept 1856–5 Feb 1857; ffs, 11 Oct 1856–31 March 1857; sfs (begin), 12 May 1857 Act 2: fcd, 22 May–30 July 1857; scd, 18 June–9 Aug 1857; ffs, 22 Dec 1864–2 Dec 1865; sfs (end), 23 Feb 1869 Act 3: fcd, 1 March–14 June 1869; scd, 25 June–5 Aug 1869; ffs, 25 Aug 1869–5 Feb 1871 arrs. of 'Schmiedelieder' for concert in Vienna, 1863, NA, RWG, H-Bo	Bayreuth, Festspielhaus, 16 Aug 1876; Richter 2 Schmiedelieder from Act 1 (in concert): Vienna, Theater an der Wien, 1 Jan 1863; Wagner	lib: Zurich, 1853; SW 29/ii vs: Mainz, 1871 fs: Mainz, 1875; SW 12		36, 41, 50, 54, 55, 71, 109, 121, 143, 153

86d	Dritter Tag: Götterdämmerung (Vorspiel und 3 Aufzügen)	text: pd, NA, vd¹, private collection, vd², CH-W, vd³, NA, Oct 1848–Dec 1852, Dresden and Zurich; pd (end), 20 Oct 1848 [prol late Oct 1848]; vd¹, 12–28 Nov 1848; vd², [late 1848/early 1849]; vd³ (end), 15 Dec 1852 [1st rev.: 1848/9; 2nd rev.: Nov/Dec 1852] music: fcd, scd, fs, NA, Oct 1869–Nov 1874, Tribschen and Bayreuth Prol (begin): fcd, 2 Oct 1869; scd, 11 Jan 1870; fs, 3 May 1873 Act 1: fcd, 7 Feb–5 June 1870; scd (end), 2 July 1870; fs (end), 24 Dec 1873 Act 2: fcd, 24 June–25 Oct 1871; scd, 5 July–19 Nov 1871; fs (end), 26 June 1874 Act 3: fcd, 4 Jan–10 April 1872; scd, 9 Feb–22 July 1872; fs, 10 June–21 Nov 1874	Bayreuth, Festspielhaus, 17 Aug 1876; Richter excerpts from prol, Acts 1, 3 (in concert): Vienna, Musikvereinssaal, 25 March, 6 May 1875; Wagner	lib: Zurich, 1853; SW 29/ii vs: Mainz, 1875 fs: Mainz, 1876; SW 13	musical sketches and 2 inc. drafts of prol (1 dated 12 Aug 1850), US-Wc, private collection	33, 41, 57, 60, 120, 130, 143, 147, 158
90	Tristan und Isolde (Handlung in 3 Aufzügen)	text: ps, pd, vd, NA, [aut. 1854]–Sept 1857, Zurich pd (begin), 20 Aug 1857; vd (end), 18 Sept 1857 music: fcd, scd, fs, NA, Oct 1857–Aug 1859, Zurich, Venice and Lucerne Act 1 (with Prelude): fcd, 1 Oct–31 Dec 1857; scd, 5 Nov 1857–13 Jan 1858 Act 2: fcd, 4 May–1 July 1858; scd, 5 July–9 March 1859; fs (end), 18 March 1859 Act 3: fcd, 9 April–16 July 1859; scd, 1 May–19 July 1859; fs (end), 6 Aug 1859 concert ending to Prelude: Dec 1859, Paris	Munich, Königliches Hof und Nationaltheater, 10 June 1865; Bülow Prelude (with Bülow's concert ending): Prague, 12 March 1859; Bülow Prelude (with Wagner's concert ending): Paris, Théâtre-Italien, 25 Jan 1860; Wagner	lib: Leipzig, 1859; SW 27 vs: Leipzig, 1860; fs: Leipzig, 1860; B v; SW 8 Prelude with Wagner's concert ending: Leipzig, 1860	earliest dated sketches: 19 Dec 1856; practice of ending Prelude with conclusion of Act 3 introduced by Wagner, 26 Feb 1863, St Petersburg	40, 41, 42, 43, 44, 45, 49, 50, 70, 71, 73, 99, 102, 106, 114, 116, 118, 119, 120, 121, 131, 137, 152–7, 158

WWV	Title (genre, libretto)	Composition, sources	1st perf.; cond.	Publication	Dedication, remarks	
96	Die Meistersinger von Nürnberg (in 3 Aufzügen)	text: pd¹ (end), 16 July 1845, Marienbad; pd², pd³, vd, NA, Schott, Mainz, Nov 1861–Jan 1862, Vienna and Paris Act 1 (end): vd, 5 Jan 1862 Act 2 (end): vd, 16 Jan 1862 Act 3 (end): pd³, 18 Nov 1861; vd, 25 Jan 1862 music: fcd, scd, NA, fs, D-Ngm, April–Dec 1862, Biebrich and Vienna; Feb 1866–Oct 1867, Geneva and Tribschen Prelude: scd, 13–20 April 1862; fs (begin), [3 June 1862] Act 1 (end): fcd, [Feb 1866]; scd, 21 Feb 1866; fs, 23 March 1866 Act 2: fcd, 15 May–6 Sept 1866; scd, 8 June–23 Sept 1866. fs, 22 March–22 June 1867 Act 3: fcd, 2 Oct 1866–7 Feb 1867; scd, 8 Oct 1866–5 March 1867: fs, 26 June–24 Oct 1867 concert ending to Walther's Trial Song from Act 1: 12 July 1865, Munich	Munich, Königliches Hof- und Nationaltheater, 21 June 1868: Bülow Prelude: Leipzig, Gewandhaus, 1 Nov 1862: Wagner 'Versammlung der Meistersingerzunft' and Walther's Trial Song from Act 1: Vienna, Theater an der Wien, 26 Dec 1862; Wagner conclusion of Act 3 (from Sachs's 'Verachtet mir die Meister nicht'): Linz, 4 April 1868: Bruckner	lib: Mainz, 1862; SW 28 vs: Mainz, 1868 fs: Mainz, 1868; SW 9 Prelude, fs: Mainz, 1866	King Ludwig II of Bavaria; earliest dated sketch ('Wach auf' chorus): Jan 1862; entitled 'Komische Oper' in pd¹, 'Grosse komische Oper' in pd² and pd³, 'Oper' in poster for 1st perf.	31, 45, 46, 47, 48, 51, 52, 53, 70, 96, 100, 116, 120, 121, 122, 157–61
111	Parsifal (ein Bühnenweihfestspiel in 3 Aufzügen)	text: ps (lost), pd¹, RWG, pd², vd, NA, April 1857, Zurich; Aug 1865, Munich; [Jan]–April 1877, Bayreuth; ps, end of April (not Good Friday, see SW 30); pd³, 27–30 Aug [1865]; pd² (end), 23 Feb 1877; vd (end), 19 April 1877	Bayreuth, Festspielhaus, 26 July 1882; Levi Prelude: Bayreuth, 25 Dec 1878; Wagner	lib: Mainz, 1877; SW 30 vs: Mainz, 1882 fs: Mainz, 1883; SW 14		41, 51, 53, 54, 62-4, 65, 84, 96, 111, 112, 161-4

music: fcd, scd, fs, NA, [Sept 1877]–Dec 1881, Bayreuth and Palermo
Act 1: fcd (end), 29 Jan 1878; scd, 25 Sept 1877–31 Jan 1878; fs, 23 Aug 1879–25 April 1881
Act 2: fcd (end), 30 Sept [1878]; scd, 13 March–11 Oct 1878; fs, 6 June–20 Oct 1881
Act 3: fcd, 30 Oct 1878–16 April [1879]; scd, 14 Nov 1878–26 April 1879; fs, 8 Nov–25 Dec 1881

STAGE WORKS (INCOMPLETE OR PROJECTED)

WWV	Title (genre, libretto)	Composition, sources	Publication	Remarks	
1	Leubald (Trauerspiel in 5 Aufzügen)	[1826-1828, Dresden and Leipzig], vd, NA	extracts from Act 5: Leipzig, 1908; SS 16 complete: SW 31	no music survives; ? none written	6
6	Schäferoper (after Goethe: Die Laune des Verliebten), inc., lost	early 1830, Leipzig		entitled 'Schäferoper' in Red Pocket-Book, 'Schäferspiel' in *Mein Leben*	10
31	Die Hochzeit (Oper, adapted from J. Büsching: Ritterzeit und Ritterwesen), inc.	text: pd, vd, [Oct/Nov 1832, Pravonin and Prague] music (Introduction, Chorus, Septet): cd (lost), fs NA, Dec 1832–March 1833, Leipzig and Würzburg cd (begin): 5 Dec 1832; fs (end): 1 March 1833	B xii; SW 15	frag. 1st perf. Rostock, Stadttheater, 13 Feb 1933	10, 11
40	Die hohe Braut (grosse Oper in 5 Akten, after H. Koenig: Die hohe Braut)	text: pd^1, pd^2, private collection, pd^3 (in Fr.), *GB-Lbm*, [probably July 1836, Königsberg; Paris, 1840] vd (lost), [25 July–6 Sept 1842, Dresden] music: not set; no sketches survive	Prague, 1848 (lib to setting by J. B. Kittl); SS 11; SW 31	Wagner offered lib to C. G. Reissiger, 1842; Kittl's setting (Bianca und Giuseppe oder Die Franzosen vor Nizza) 1st perf. Prague, 19 Feb 1848	15

WWV	Title (genre, libretto)	Composition, sources	Publication	Remarks	
48	Männerlist grösser als Frauenlist oder Die glückliche Bärenfamilie (komische Oper in 2 Akten, after 1001 Nights)	text: vd (lost), copy (not autograph), NA, presumably sum. 1838, Riga music: lost	vd copy: SS 11; SW 31	according to *Autobiographische Skizze*, 1842–3, composition discontinued after 2 nos.	17
66	Die Sarazenin (Oper in 5 Akten), scenario	text: ps, private collection, pd (lost), copy (not autograph) of pd (now lost), [1841, Paris; early 1843, Dresden] music: not set; no sketches survive	ps: SW 31 pd: Bayreuth, 1889; SS 11; PW 8; SW 31		25
67	Die Bergwerke zu Falun (Oper in 3 Akten), scenario	text: pd¹, *D-Dla*, pd² (lost), [Feb]–March 1842, Paris; pd¹ (end), 5 March 1842 music: not set; no sketches survive	pd¹, copy (not autograph) of pd²: Bayreuth, 1905; SS 11; *19th Century Music*, v (1981–2), 201; SW 31	written for J. Dessauer; later offered to A. Röckel who did not set it	25
76	Friedrich I ([? Oper] in 5 Akten), frag. scenario	text: ps, pd¹, pd² frags., NA, Oct 1846 [wint. 1848–9, Dresden]; ps (end), 31 Oct 1846 music: not set; no sketches survive	SS 11; SW 31	orig. planned as an opera, not a play without music, as Wagner later claimed; see WWV 76 *Erläuterungen*	33
80	Jesus von Nazareth ([? Oper] in 5 Akten), scenario	text: pd, NA, early 1849, Dresden, [? 30 March–16 April 1849, see WWV 80 *Erläuterungen*] music: not set; one sketch survives, *S-Smf*	pd: Leipzig, 1887; PW 8; SS 11; SW 31	entitled 'Tragödie' and 'Drama' in *Mein Leben*	33
81	Achilleus ([? Oper] in 3 Akten), projected	early 1849, Dresden; Feb–July 1850, Paris and Zurich	notes on 'Achilleus' (Leipzig, 1885; misleadingly described in SS 12 as 'Bruchstücke eines Dramas "Achilleus"') probably relate to Wagner's theoretical writings 1849–50, not the projected opera	in correspondence (Feb, July 1850), orig. planned as an opera; called a 'purely dramatic poem' in a letter to Ludwig II, 1865	33
82	Wieland der Schmied (Heldenoper in 3 Akten), scenario	text: pd¹, pd², pd³, private collection, [Dec 1849, Zurich]–March 1850, Paris; pd², pd³ (end), 11 March 1850 music: not set; no sketches survive	pd²: GS 3; PW 1; SS 3 pd¹⁻³: SW 31	offered to Berlioz (via Liszt), A. Röckel, W. Weissheimer, but none set it; Wagner changed 'Heldenoper' to 'als Drama entworfen' in GS, cf WWV 76, 80, 81	33, 34

WWV	Title	Composition, sources	1st perf.; cond.	Publication	Remarks
89	Die Sieger ([? Oper in 3 Akten]), projected	text: ps, NA, May 1856, Zurich; ps (end), 16 May 1856	music: not set; no sketches survive	ps: Leipzig, 1885; PW 8; SS 11; SW 31	hopes of its composition mentioned in Cosima's diaries (11 Jan 1878)
99	Luther ([? Oper]), projected	text: ps, RWG, Aug 1868, Tribschen; ps (middle, end), 19 Aug, 22 Aug 1868	music: not set; no sketches survive	ps: Bayreuth, 1937; BB; SW 31	
100	Lustspiel in 1 Akt, scenario	text: pd, RWG, Aug/Sept 1868, Tribschen; pd (end), 1 Sept [1868]	music: not set; no sketches survive	pd: BB; SW 31	
102	Eine Kapitulation (Lustspiel in antiker Manier)	text: pd, RWG, vd, NA, [Nov 1870]		pd: BB; SW 31 vd: GS 9; PW 5; SS 9; SW 31	alternative title in vd: Nicht kapitulirt: Antikes Lustspiel in 1 Akt frei nach Aristophanes: von E. Schlossenbach: Musik von Hans Richter; according to Cosima's diaries (16 Dec 1870) Richter sketched some music

INCIDENTAL MUSIC

WWV	Title	Composition, sources	1st perf.; cond.	Publication	Remarks
12	Overture to Schiller: Die Braut von Messina, lost	sum./aut. 1830, Leipzig			possibly identical with WWV 13, see ORCHESTRAL
24	Overture, e, and stage music to E. Raupach: König Enzio	ov.: cd, GB-Lbm, fs, NA, wint. 1831–2, Leipzig; fs (end), 3 Feb 1832 stage music: lost	Leipzig, Königlich Sächsisches Hoftheater, 17 Feb 1832; H. Dorn	fs: Leipzig and London, 1907; SW 18/i; ps: Leipzig and London, 1908; SW 18/i	for 2 frags., gui, ? from stage music, see WWV 24 Erläuterungen
25	Entreactes tragiques no.1, D no.2, c	[probably early 1832] no.1: cd, D-Bds, fs frag., GB-Lbm no.2: cd, D-Bds			possibly part of stage music for WWV 24; not discussed by Wagner and probably never completed
36	[Overture and 4 numbers] to W. Schmale: Beim Antritt des neuen Jahres	cd, GB-Lbm, RWG, fs, NA, [end Dec 1834, Magdeburg]	Magdeburg, Stadttheater, 1 Jan 1835; Wagner with text by Cornelius; Bayreuth, Markgräfliches Opernhaus, 22 May 1873; A. Ritter	s: B xvi; SW 16	with new text written by P. Cornelius for Wagner's 60th birthday entitled 'Künstlerweihe'

WWV	Title	Composition, sources	1st perf.; cond.	Publication	Remarks	
37	Overture, E♭, and stage music to T. Apel: Columbus	ov.: cd, fs (lost), copy of fs (not autograph), D-B, pm, F-Pn, GB-Cfm, [Dec 1834–Jan 1835, Magdeburg] stage music: lost	Magdeburg, Stadttheater, c25 Feb 1835; Wagner	ov., fs: Leipzig and London, 1907; SW 18/ii ps: Leipzig and London, 1907 sketches: SW 15	for discussion of date of 1st perf. and lost stage music see WWV 37 Erläuterungen	15, 18, 24
41	[Music] to J. Singer: Die letzte Heiden-verschwörung in Preussen oder Der Deutsche Ritterorden in Königsberg	sketches, GB-Lbm, fs (lost), [probably Feb 1837, Königsberg]	? Königsberg, Stadttheater, 17 Feb 1837			17

ORCHESTRAL

WWV	Title, key	Composition, sources	1st perf.; cond.	Publication	Dedication, remarks	
10	Overture, B♭, 'Drumbeat Overture' ('Paukenschlag-Ouvertüre'), lost	sum. 1830, Leipzig	Leipzig, Königlich Sächsisches Hoftheater, 25 Dec 1830; Dorn		according to Dorn (1838), ov. in 6/8 with recurring drum beat	
11	Political Overture, frag., lost	probably Sept 1830, Leipzig			not identical with Ov., E♭, WWV 17	
13	[Orchestral piece], e, frag.	fs, private collection, [probably 1830, Leipzig]		SW 18/i	? identical with WWV 12, see INCIDENTAL MUSIC	
14	Overture, C, lost	late 1830, Leipzig			according to Cosima's diaries (15 Dec 1878), in 6/8	
17	Overture, E♭, probably frag., lost	spr. 1831, Leipzig			not identical with WWV 11	
20	Overture, d (Concert Overture no.1)	Sept–Nov 1831, Leipzig fs (both versions), NA version 1: fs (end), 26 Sept 1831 version 2: fs (end), 4 Nov 1831	version 2: Leipzig, Königlich Sächsisches Hoftheater, 25 Dec 1831; probably Dorn	B xx (version 2); SW 18/i (both versions)	called Concert Overture for 1st perf.	8

No.	Title	Composition / sources	Première	Editions	Notes	Pages
27	Concert Overture no.2, C	March 1832, Leipzig sketches, GB-Lbm, cd, NA, private collection, fs, NA fs (end), 17 March 1832	Leipzig, Musikverein Euterpe, c end March 1832; Wagner	B xx; SW 18/i		10
29	Symphony, C	[probably April–June 1832, Leipzig] cd, US-Wc, fs (lost), pm (not autograph), D-B, fs (not autograph), NA	Prague, Ständisches Konservatorium, Nov 1832; D. Weber	Leipzig, 1911; B xx; SW 18/i	according to Cosima's diaries (14 March 1878), Wagner composed a 'Trio zum Scherzo' in 1878 which has not survived; rev. for private perf. Venice, La Fenice, 25 Dec 1882	11
35	Symphony, E, frag.	Aug 1834, Lauchstädt and Rudolstadt cd (lost), 4–29 Aug 1834			mentioned in Mein Leben; cd sold by Ludwig Rosenthal, Munich (catalogue 153, c1913): 1st movt, Allegro con spirito; 2nd movt, Adagio cantabile (29 bars)	14
39	Overture 'Polonia', C	[May–July 1836, Berlin] cd, private collections, fs, NA, pm, NA, F-Pn, GB-Lbm	? Königsberg, Stadttheater, wint. 1836–7; Wagner;? London, Queen's Hall, 2 Jan 1905; H. Wood (see WWV 39 Erläuterungen)	fs: Leipzig and London, 1907; SW 18/ii ps: Leipzig and London, 1908		15
42	Overture 'Rule Britannia', D	March 1837, Königsberg cd, NA, fs, GB-Lbm fs (end), 15 March 1837	probably Riga, Schwarzhäupter-Saal, 19 March 1838; Wagner	fs: Leipzig and London, 1907; SW 18/ii ps: London. 1905		17, 18
59	Eine Faust-Ouvertüre, d (orig. 1st movt of projected Faust Symphony)	version 1: Dec 1839–Jan 1840, Paris sketches, NA, US-PHci, private collection, fcd, NA, US-NH, scd (frag.), Wagnermuseum, Eisenach, fs, NA fcd (end), 13 Dec 1839 fs (end), 12 Jan 1840 version 2: Jan 1855, Zurich fs, NA, 17 Jan 1855 (end)	version 1: Dresden, Palais des königlichen grossen Gartens, 22 July 1844 (as 'Overture'); Wagner version 2: Zurich, Casino, 23 Jan 1855; Wagner	version 1: SW 18/iii version 2: Leipzig, 1855; B xviii; SW 18/iii	rev., Paris, 1840–41 and Dresden before 1st perf.	20–21, 38

WWV	Title, key	Composition, sources	1st perf.; cond.	Publication	Dedication, remarks	
73	Trauermusik (on motifs from Weber's Euryanthe), wind insts	1st half of Nov 1844, Dresden cd, RWG, fs, *D-Bds* fs (end), 15 Nov 1844	Dresden, during transfer of Weber's remains to Catholic Cemetery, Friedrichstadt, 14 Dec 1844	fs: B xx; SW 18/ii ps: Dresden, 1860	title 'Trauersinfonie' in fs (B xx) and ps not authentic	30
97	Huldigungsmarsch, Eb, for Ludwig II of Bavaria, military band	Aug 1864, Starnberg cd, ffs, NA, sfs, Wittelsbacher Ausgleichsfonds, Munich	Munich, 5 Oct 1864; J. Siebenkäs	fs: Mainz, 1890; B xviii; SW 18/iii ps: Mainz, 1865	'Zum neunzehnten Geburtstage Seines Majestät des Königs Ludwig II' (sfs); version for large orch by J. J. Raff (Mainz, 1871)	48
98	Romeo und Julie, sketches	April-May 1868, Tribschen 1st sketch, NA, 21 April 1868, 2nd sketch, RWG, May [1868]		Karlsruhe, 1943; Zurich, 1956; BB		
103	Siegfried Idyll, E, small orch	[Oct]-Dec 1870, Tribschen cd, NA, ffs, Wagner Museum, Tribschen, sfs, NA	Tribschen, 25 Dec 1870; Wagner	fs: Mainz, 1878; B xviii; SW 18/iii, ps: Mainz, 1878	'Tribschener Idyll ... als Symphonischer Geburtstagsgruss Seiner Cosima dargestellt von ihrem Richard' (sfs); orig. entitled 'Symphonie'	49, 67, 109
104	Kaisermarsch, Bb, with concluding chorus	[Jan]-March 1871, Tribschen cd, NA, (end), 25 Feb 1871 fs, NA, (end), 15 March 1871	Berlin, 14 April 1871 (1st public perf.: Leipzig, Stadttheater, 23 April 1871; G. Schmidt)	fs: Leipzig, 1871; B xviii; SW 18/iii ps: Leipzig, 1871		
110	Grosser Festmarsch, G	[Jan-March 1876, Bayreuth] fcd, NA, (end), 15 Feb [1876] scd, *I-Bc*, (end), 20 Feb 1876 ffs, NA, sfs, *US-Cn*	Philadelphia, 10 May 1876; T. Thomas	fs: Mainz, 1876; B xviii; SW 18/iii ps: Mainz, 1876; Cincinnati, 1876	'Composed and Dedicated to the Women's Centennial Committee by Richard Wagner' (ps: Cincinnati, 1876); (for centenary of the declaration of independence of USA)	61

During 1846-7 and the second half of the 1870s Wagner considered writing a number of orchestral works – mainly symphonies and overtures – for which he made several sketches that cannot be assigned to specific works or projects. For a discussion and transcription of some of the sketches, see WWV 78 Sinfonien (Skizzen) and WWV 107 Pläne zu Ouvertüren und Sinfonien.

WWV	Title, key	Composition, sources	1st perf.	Publication	Remarks
4	String Quartet, D, lost	aut. 1829, Leipzig			mentioned in Red Pocket-Book and autobiographical writings
91b	Träume, solo vn, 13 insts	Dec 1857, Zurich; fs, NA, 18 Dec 1857 (end)	Zurich, 23 Dec 1857	Mainz, 1878; B xx; SW 18/iii	see also WWV 91a ii (SONGS AND ARIAS)

PIANO

(for two hands unless otherwise stated)

WWV	Title, key	Composition, sources	Publication	Dedication, remarks
2	Sonata, d, lost	sum. 1829, Leipzig		Wagner's 'first sonata' (*Mein Leben*)
5	Sonata, f, lost	aut. 1829, Leipzig		mentioned in Red Pocket-Book
16	Sonata, B♭, 4 hands, lost	early 1831, Leipzig		also orchd according to *Mein Leben* and Red Pocket-Book
21	Sonata, B♭, op.1	aut. 1831, Leipzig MS, private collection	Leipzig, 1832, 2/1862; SW 19	C. T. Weinlig; 'op.1' orig. in Wagner's letter to his sister Ottilie, 3 March 1832; not in MS or 1st print
22	Fantasie (Fantasia), f♯	aut. 1831, Leipzig; fcd, NA, 27 Nov 1831 (end); scd, RWG	Leipzig, 1905; SW 19	
23a	Polonaise, D	[late 1831/early 1832, Leipzig] MS, private collection	MT, cxiv (1973), 26; SW 21	
23b	Polonaise, D, op.2, 4 hands	[end 1831/early 1832], Leipzig; no sources survive	Leipzig, 1832; SW 19	'op.2' not in 1st printing but advertised thus by Breitkopf & Härtel
26	Grosse Sonate, A, op.4	[early 1832, Leipzig] MS, NA	Cologne, 1960; SW 19	'op.4' on title-page of autograph MS
64	[Piano piece], E, 'Albumblatt für E. B. Kietz "Lied ohne Worte"'	Dec 1840, Paris fcd, RWG, scd, NA, 31 Dec 1840 (end)	Vienna, 1911; SW 19	no title on fcd and scd (traditional title in dedicatory poem to Kietz); no clear evidence that poem is related to pf piece
84	[Polka], G	29 May 1853, Zurich MS, NA	SW 19	no title on MS; for title 'Polka' see WWV 84 *Erläuterungen*

< unused>
</>

WWV	Title, key	Composition, sources	Publication	Dedication, remarks	
85	Sonate, A♭	[first half of June 1853, Zurich] MS, NA	Leipzig, 1878 (as Eine Sonate für das Album von Frau M[athilde] W[iesendonck]); SW 19	'Sonate für Mathilde Wesendonck' (autograph MS); pubn title deliberately gives the (probably misleading) impression that it was to be an 'occasional work' only (cf Cosima Wagner's letter to Schott, 17 Dec 1877)	109
88	Züricher Vielliebchen-Walzer, E♭	May 1854, Zurich MS, NA, 31 May 1854 (end)	Die Musik, i/20–21 (1901–2), suppl.; SW 19	Marie Luckemeyer (sister of Mathilde Wesendonck)	109
93	[Theme], A♭ (wrongly known as 'Porazzi' theme)	1858, Venice; 1881, Palermo	SW 21: facs. in E. Newman: *R. Wagner*, iv, opposite 405 (New York edn.)	for 'Porazzi' theme, see MISCELLANEOUS	
94	In das Album der Fürstin M[etternich], C	June 1861, Paris fcd, NA, 18 June 1861 (end) scd, private collection	Leipzig, 1871; SW 19		
95	Ankunft bei den schwarzen Schwänen, Albumblatt, A♭	July 1861, Paris sketch, NA, cd, private collection, 29 July 1861 (end)	Leipzig, 1891; SW 19	'Seiner edlen Wirthin Frau Gräfin von Pourtalès zur Erinnerung' (cd)	
108	Albumblatt, E♭	Jan 1875, Bayreuth sketch, NA, fcd, Wagner Museum, Tribschen, scd, NA, 1 Feb 1875 (end)	Mainz, 1876; SW 19	Frau Betty Schott	

CHORAL

WWV	Title, forces (text)	Composition, sources	1st perf.; cond.	Publication	Dedication, remarks	
19a	Fugue 'Dein ist das Reich'	[aut. 1831–wint. 1831–2, Leipzig] MS, NA		SW 21		
44	Volks-Hymne, 'Nicolay', solo vv, chorus, orch (H. von Brackel)	[aut. 1837, Riga] cd, fs, NA	Riga, Stadttheater, 21 Nov 1837; probably Wagner	B xvi; SW 16		18
51	Gesang am Grabe (H. von Brackel), lost	29 Dec 1838–4 Jan 1839	Riga, Jakobi-Kirchhof, 4 Jan 1839		? identical with musical sketch, NA, to 'Wir senken Dich in's finstre Grab . . .', see WWV	

No.	Title	Composition	Performance	Publication	Remarks	
68	Festgesang 'Der Tag erscheint', male vv / male vv, brass insts (C. C. Hohlfeld)	[May 1843, Dresden] fs, private collection, NA	a cappella: Dresden, 7 June 1843, Wagner; with insts: probably Dresden, 25 May 1911		title 'Weihegruss' in 1st printing not authentic	
69	Das Liebesmahl der Apostel: eine biblische Szene, male vv, orch	April–June 1843, Dresden text: ps, pd, *D-Bds*, vd (lost) pd (end), 21 April 1843 music: fcd (lost), scd (partly lost), NA, RWG, *US-Wc*, fs, private collection; fcd (begin), 14 May [1843]; scd (end), 24 June [1843]; fs (end), 29 June 1843	Dresden, Frauenkirche, 6 July 1843; Wagner	fs: Leipzig, 1845; B xvi; SW 16 vs: Leipzig, 1845	Charlotte Emilie Weinlig; orch pts. rev. for 1st printing	30
71a	Gruss seiner Treuen an Friedrich August den Geliebten bei seiner Zurückkunft aus England den 9. August 1844, Im treuen Sachsenland', male vv, wind band	[Aug 1844, Dresden] cd, *D-Bds*, fs (lost)	Pillnitz, nr. Dresden, 12 Aug 1844; Reissiger	fs: SW 16; vv only: Dresden, 1844; B xvi	also for 1v, pf, see SONGS AND ARIAS	
72	An Webers Grabe, male vv	early Nov 1844, Dresden text: vd, NA, 10 Nov 1844 (end) music: fs, private collection	Dresden-Friedrichstadt, Catholic Cemetery, 15 Dec 1844; Wagner	Leipzig, 1872; B xvi; SW 16	written for the transfer of Weber's remains from London to Dresden, see Trauermusik (ORCHESTRAL)	30
101	Wahlspruch für die deutsche Feuerwehr 'Treue sei unsre Zier', male vv	Nov 1869, Lucerne MS, private collection, 8 Nov 1869 (end)		Speyer, 1870; SW 21		
106	Kinder-Katechismus zu Kosels Geburtstag 'Sagt mir Kinder, was blüht am Maitag?', solo v, children's vv, pf/orch	pf version: Dec 1873, Bayreuth; cd, fs, NA orch version: Dec 1874, Bayreuth; fs, NA, 14 Dec 1874 (end)	pf version: Bayreuth, 25 Dec 1873 orch version: Bayreuth, 25 Dec 1874	Mainz, 1937; SW 21		
113	'Ihr Kinder, geschwinde, geschwinde' ('antiker Chorgesang'), children's vv	[Dec 1880, Bayreuth] MS, NA	Bayreuth, 25 Dec 1880	SW 21		

SONGS AND ARIAS

(for 1v, pf unless otherwise stated)

WWV	Title, forces (text)	Composition, sources	Publication	Dedication, remarks
3	Arie, lost	1829, Leipzig		existence and circumstances of 1st perf. in 'Kintschy's Schweizerhütte' (*Mein Leben*) are doubtful
7	[Songs] (unidentified), frag.	[1828–30, Leipzig] MS, NA	SW 21	
8	Arie, lost	spr. 1830, Leipzig		? part of Schäferoper, see STAGE WORKS (INCOMPLETE OR PROJECTED)
15	Sieben Kompositionen zu Goethes Faust: 1, Lied der Soldaten, male vv; 2, Bauer unter der Linde, S, T, mixed vv; 3, Branders Lied, B; 4, Lied des Mephistopheles, i: 'Es war einmal ein König', B, male vv; 5, Lied des Mephistopheles, ii: 'Was machst du mir vor Liebchens Tür', B; 6, Gretchen am Spinnrade, S; 7, Melodram (Gretchen, spoken text)	[early 1831, Leipzig] MS no.6 only, NA; complete MS (not autograph except for title-page), NA	B xv; Weimar, 1916; SW 17	MS copy (not autograph), NA, dated 1832; 'op.5' on title-page in another hand; copy could be rev. form of an earlier composition
28	Szene und Arie, S, orch, lost	early 1832, Leipzig		1st perf.: Leipzig, Königlich Sächsisches Hoftheater, 22 April 1832, cond. Wagner
30	Glockentöne (T. Apel), lost	12 Oct 1832, Pravonin, nr. Prague		entitled 'Abendglocken' in letter to Apel (12 Oct 1832), 'Glockentöne' in *Mein Leben*; text probably identical with Apel's poem Der Entfernten
50	Der Tannenbaum (G. Scheurlin)	[aut. 1838, Riga] cd frag, private collection, autograph copy of cd, 1868, US-NYpm	*Europa*, 1839, no.4; Berlin, 1871; B xv; Munich, 1921; SW 17	composed Riga, 1838, not earlier in Königsberg as in *Mein Leben*; US-NYpm copy made for Cosima's 31st birthday (also WWV 53, 55, 57)
53	Dors mon enfant (author unknown)	[aut. 1839, Paris] cd (lost); autograph copies: 1840, RWG, ?1845, private collection, 1868, US-NYpm	*Europa*, 1841, no.3; Paris, 1870; B xv; Munich, 1921; SW 17	dedication to 'Madame la Baronne de Cater' in 1870 print (also WWV 55, 57 below) made without Wagner's permission; US-NYpm copy made for Cosima's 31st birthday (also WWV 50, 55, 57); for chronology of WWV 53–8, see WWV

54	Extase (V. Hugo), frag.	[aut. 1839, Paris] MS, GB-Lbm	SW 17	for chronology of WWV 53–8, see WWV	
55	Attente (V. Hugo)	[aut. 1839, Paris] cd, private collection; copies: ?1845, private collection, 1868, US-NYpm	Europa, 1842, no.1; Paris, 1870; B xv; Munich, 1921; SW 17	dedication to 'Madame la Baronne de Cater' in 1870 print (also WWV 53, 57) made without Wagner's permission; US-NYpm copy made for Cosima's 31st birthday (also WWV 50, 53, 57); for chronology of WWV 53–8, see WWV	
56	La tombe dit à la rose (V. Hugo), frag.	[aut. 1839, Paris] MS, GB-Lbm	SW 17	for chronology of WWV 53–8, see WWV	
57	Mignonne (P. de Ronsard)	[aut. 1839, Paris] cd, A-Wn; copies: ?1845, private collection, 1868, US-NYpm	Europa, 1843, no.2; Paris, 1870; B xv; Munich, 1921; SW 17	dedication to 'Madame la Baronne de Cater' in 1870 print (also WWV 53, 55) made without Wagner's permission; US-NYpm copy made for Cosima's 31st birthday (also WWV 50, 53, 55); for chronology of WWV 53–8, see WWV	19
58	Tout n'est qu'images fugitives (Soupir) (J. Reboul)	[aut. 1839, Paris] cd, NA	B xv; SW 17	for chronology of WWV 53–8, see WWV	
60	Les deux grenadiers, Bar (H. Heine, trans. F. A. Loeve-Veimar)	[Dec 1839–early 1840, Paris] cd (partly lost), NA	Paris, 1840; Mainz, 1843 (Fr. and Ger.); B xv; Munich, 1921 (Fr. and Ger.); SW 17	H. Heine; composed not before 17 Dec 1839 (see WWV 60 Erläuterungen)	
61	Adieux de Marie Stuart, S (P. J. de Béranger)	March 1840, Paris fcd (partly lost), GB-Lbm, NA, scd, NA, (end) 26 March 1840, copy of scd, US-STu	Revue Musicale S.I.M., 1913, no.5; B xv; SW 17		
71b	Gruss seiner Treuen an Friedrich August den Geliebten bei seiner Zurückkunft aus England den 9. August 1844, 'Im treuen Sachsenland'	Aug 1844, Dresden	Dresden, 1844; B xv; SW 17		

WWV	Title, forces (text)	Composition, sources	Publication	Dedication, remarks	
91a	Fünf Gedichte für eine Frauenstimme (M. Wesendonck):	Nov 1857–Oct 1858, Zurich and Venice	Mainz, 1862; B xv; Leipzig, 1954 (Ger. and Eng.); SW 17 (all versions)	1st printing: 1, Der Engel (version 2); 2, Stehe still! (version 2); 3, Im Treibhaus (version 3); 4, Schmerzen (version 3); 5, Träume (version 3); songs 1st perf. in this form, Laubenheim, nr. Mainz, 30 July 1862; composed in different sequence (see below)	42
	1, Der Engel	version 1 [late Nov 1857]: cd, NA; version 2 [Oct 1858]: cd, Schott, Mainz			
	2, Träume	version 1: cd, NA, 4 Dec 1857 (end); version 2: cd, NA, 5 Dec 1857 (end); version 3: cd, Schott, Mainz, [Oct 1858]		also version for solo vn, chamber orch (see CHAMBER MUSIC); Wagner added 'Studie zu Tristan und Isolde' to cd, version 3	42
	3, Schmerzen	version 1: cd, NA, 17 Dec 1857 (end); version 2: cd, CS-Pnm, [Oct 1858]; version 3: cd, Schott, Mainz, [Oct 1858]			
	4, Stehe still!	version 1: cd, NA, 22 Feb 1858 (end); version 2: cd, Schott, Mainz, [Oct 1858]		version 1 without title	
	5, Im Treibhaus	version 1: cd, NA, 1 May 1858 (end); version 2: cd, private collection, [Oct 1858]; version 3: cd, Schott, Mainz, [Oct 1858]		Wagner added 'Studie zu Tristan und Isolde' to cd, version 3	
92	Es ist bestimmt in Gottes Rat, draft	[Jan 1858, Paris] MS, NA	SW 21		
105	Der Worte viele sind gemacht (Song for Louis Kraft)	22 April 1871, Leipzig MSS, D-LEs - NA	Allgemeines Reichs-Commersbuch für deutsche Studenten, ed. M. von der Werra, Leipzig, 1875; MMR, xiii (1883), 90; SW 21		

WWV	Works, forces (text)	Composition, sources	1st perf.; cond.	Publication, remarks	
19b	Four-part double fugue	[aut.–wint. 1831, ? spr. 1832] MS, *US-Wc*		*Die Musik*, xi/34–40 (1911–12); SW 21	12
33	new ending (Allegro) to Aria no.15 (Aubry) from H. Marschner: Der Vampyr	Sept 1833, Würzburg fs, NA, 23 Sept 1833 (end)	Würzburg, Stadttheater, 29 Sept 1833; Aubry: Albert Wagner	B xv; SW 15; addl text also by Wagner	
43	'Sanfte Wehmut will sich regen', B solo (K. von Holtei) aria for K. Blum: Mary, Max und Michel	Aug 1837, Riga cd, NA, 19 Aug [1837] (end) fs, NA	Riga, Stadttheater, 1 Sept 1837; Wagner; Max: K. W. Günther	B xv; SW 15; no evidence for title 'Romanze' in Glasenapp's biography and B xv	18
45	Aria for J. Weigl: Die Schweizerfamilie, B solo (author unknown), lost	probably Dec 1837, Riga	probably Riga, Stadttheater, 22 Dec 1837; B solo: F. W. Scheibler	mentioned in Red Pocket-Book and *Mein Leben*	18
52	'Norma il predise', B solo, male vv (author unknown), aria (Orovist) for Bellini: Norma	[late Sept/early Oct 1839, Paris] fs, NA	not perf. in Wagner's lifetime	B xv; SW 15; written for L. Lablache who, according to Wagner's letter to G. E. Anders (13 Oct 1839), refused to sing it	19
65	'Descendons gaiment la courtille' (? by M. Dumersan), chorus for Dumersan and Dupeuty: La descente de la courtille	[probably Jan 1841, Paris] cd, *GB-Lbm*, fs, NA	possibly Paris, Théâtre des Variétés, 20 Jan 1841	B xvi; SW 15; no evidence that chorus was perf.; date given is 1st perf. of vaudeville for which it was written	19
112	Weihnachten 1877, 'Willkommen in Wahnfried', presumably children's vv, frag.	Dec 1877, Bayreuth MS, NA		SW 21; title in MS in Cosima's hand	

Various musical greetings, frags.: leaf with title 'Parzifal' to Mathilde Wesendonck (SW 30, p.13); 'Canto anticcho italiano', 1861, for P. Cornelius (see Cornelius's letter to his sister, 17 Nov 1861); souvenir, 1864, for J. Rebel (*Die Musik*, i (1901–2), after p.1940); 'Quasi-Graziöses Thema', 1872, for J. S. Svendsen, NA; 'Porazzi' theme ('Adagio', Palermo, 2 and 4 March 1882), transcr. with incorrect designation in C. von Westernhagen: *R. Wagner: sein Werk, sein Wesen, seine Welt* (Zurich, 1956), 453 (see also WWV 93, 107)

ARRANGEMENTS, ORCHESTRATIONS

WWV	Arrangement, orchestration	Date, sources	1st perf.; cond.	Publication, remarks	
9	Beethoven: Symphony no.9, pf 2 hands	[sum. 1830–Easter 1831, Leipzig] MS, NA		SW 20/ii	7
18	Haydn: Symphony no.103, pf 2 hands, lost	sum. 1831, Leipzig		mentioned in undated letter to Breitkopf & Härtel (letter received 14 Aug 1831)	10
34	Bellini: Cavatina from Il pirata, orchestration, lost	Nov–Dec 1833, Würzburg		mentioned and wrongly dated in Mein Leben (see WWV)	12
46a	Bellini: Norma, additions and changes to orchestration	[probably Dec 1837, Riga] MS, CH-Zz	probably Riga, Stadttheater, 11 Dec 1837; Wagner	SW 20/iii	18
46b	Meyerbeer: Cavatina, 'Robert, toi que j'aime' from Robert le diable, transcr. of harp pt.	[probably Nov 1838, Riga] MS, US-STu	probably Riga, Stadttheater, 30 Nov 1838; Wagner	SW 20/iii	18
46c	Weber: Hunting Chorus from Euryanthe, arr. vv, 12 hn	[probably Jan 1839, Riga] MS, US-STu	Riga, Schwarz-häupter-Saal, 17 Jan 1839; Wagner	SW 20/iii	18
47	Rossini: duet 'Die Seemänner' ('Li marinari') from Les soirées musicales, orchestration	[probably spr. 1838, Riga] fs, pm, RWG	probably Riga, Schwarzhäupter-Saal, 19 March 1838; Wagner	SW 20/iii	18
62	Paris arrs.:	[aut. 1840, Paris–July 1842, Teplitz and Dresden]		SW 20/iii; both Richard and Paul Wagner made arrs., Paris, early 1840s; pubd arrs. from Donizetti's Les Martyrs (June 1840) designated 'par Wagner' are therefore not incl.	20
62a	Suites for Cornets à pistons (potpourris), lost	[probably aut. 1840, Paris]			
62b	Donizetti: La favorite, arrs.	[Dec 1840–April 1841, Paris] MSS frags., F-Pn		vs, arr. for str qt, arr. for 2 vn: Paris and Berlin, 1841 (Schlesinger)	20

No.	Title	Sources / dates	Premiere	Publication	Ref
62c	H. Herz: Grande fantaisie sur La romanesca, arrs., pf. 4 hands	[early 1841, Paris]		Paris, 1841 (Troupenas)	20
62d	Halévy: Le guitarrero, arrs.	[Feb–April 1841, Paris] MSS frags, *F-Pn*, *GB-Lbm*, private collection		ps of ov., arr. for 2 vn: Paris, 1841 (Schlesinger); arr. for str qt: Paris and Berlin, 1841 (Schlesinger)	20
62e	Halévy: La reine de Chypre, arrs.	[Dec 1841–April 1842, Paris; June–July 1842, Teplitz]		vs, arr. for str qt, arr. for 2 vn: Paris, 1842 (Schlesinger)	20
62f	Auber: Zanetta, ou Jouer avec le feu, arrs., str qt	[July 1842, Teplitz and Dresden]		Paris, 1842–3 (Troupenas)	20
74	Spontini: La vestale, inst addns, lost	[probably Nov 1844]	Dresden, Königlich Sächsisches Hof-theater, 29 Nov 1844; Spontini	mentioned in *Mein Leben*; see WWV 74 *Erläuterungen*	
77	Gluck: Iphigénie en Aulide, arr.	[Dec 1846–Jan 1847, Dresden] text: vd, NA music: vs, fs, NA	Dresden, Königlich Sächsisches Hoftheater, 24 Feb 1847; Wagner	lib: Dresden, 1847; Leipzig, 1859; SW 20/iv / vs: Leipzig, 1858 / fs: ov. only with Zurich ending (WWV 87, see below): Leipzig, 1888; SW 20/iv	26
79	Palestrina: Stabat mater, arr.	Feb–early March 1848, Dresden	Dresden, Königlich Sächsisches Hoftheater, 8 March 1848; Wagner	Leipzig, 1878; SW 20/iii	
83	Mozart: Don Giovanni, arr., lost	[early Nov 1850, Zurich] only a single leaf in *D-LEu* has survived	Zurich, Stadt-Theater, 8 Nov 1850; Wagner	for more detailed account of arr., see WWV 83 *Erläuterungen*	38
87	Gluck: Ov. to Iphigénie en Aulide, concert ending	[early March 1854, Zurich] cd, NA, fs [lost], pm (not autograph), *CH-Zz*	Zurich, 7 March 1854; Wagner	fs: *NZM*, Jg.91 (1854); with the rest of ov. in Wagner's 1847 reinstrumentation: Leipzig, 1888; SW 20/iv	38
109	J. Strauss: Waltz op.333 (Wein, Weib und Gesang), instructions for orchestration	[May 1875] MS, *D-Bds*	?Bayreuth, 22 May 1875		

WORKS OF DOUBTFUL AUTHENTICITY

Incidental music for J. A. Gleich: Der Berggeist, Magdeburg, 1834–5, lost
'Fischerlied', vv, gui. for Peppino, Naples, 1880
Adagio, cl, str qt: wrongly attrib. Wagner in B xx; slow movt of op.23 by H. J. Baermann (1821); see *NZM*, Jg.115 (1964), 166

AUTOGRAPH FACSIMILES

Der Ring des Nibelungen (Berlin, 1919) [from private print of poem, 1853]
Die Meistersinger von Nürnberg (Munich, 1922) [fs]
Tristan und Isolde (Munich, 1923) [fs]
Siegfried-Idyll (Munich, 1923) [fs]
Parsifal (Munich, 1925) [fs]
5 Gedichte für eine Frauenstimme (Wesendonck-Lieder) (Leipzig, 1962)
Lohengrin, preludes to Acts 1 and 3 (Leipzig, 1975) [fs]
Kinder-Katechismus zu Kosel's Geburtstag (Mainz, 1983)
Die Meistersinger von Nürnberg (lib, 1862) with essay by E. Voss (Mainz, 1983)

WRITINGS, SPEECHES

This list includes most of Wagner's writings, reviews, speeches, open letters and letters on specific subjects published (not always with complete justification) in SS; occasional poems and dedications as well as prose drafts and texts of the stage works in GS and SS are excluded. (It should be noted that the texts of the stage works in the Collected Writings often differ from the finished works.)
The list does not claim to be complete. Wagner wrote a great deal that was published in obscure newspapers and periodicals that are often difficult to obtain today. He also published many essays, reviews and speeches either anonymously or under a pseudonym. A detailed catalogue must await further research.
Numbers to the right of each column denote references in the text.

Title, date	GS, SS	PW	
Die deutsche Oper, 1834	xii	viii	13, 130
Pasticcio, 1834	xii	viii	14
Eine Kritik aus Magdeburg, 1835	xvi	—	
Aus Magdeburg, 1836	xii	—	14
Das Liebesverbot: Bericht über eine erste Opernaufführung, 1836	i	vii	
Bellinis *Norma*, 1837 [review of perf. in Magdeburg first pubd in F. Lippmann: 'Ein neu entdecktes Autograph Richard Wagners', *Musicae scientiae collectanea: Festschrift Karl Gustav Fellerer* (Cologne, 1973)]	—	—	

Title, date	GS, SS	PW	
Zwei Zeitungs-Anzeigen aus Riga [i, Theateranzeige; ii, Konzertanzeige], 1837, 1839	xvi	—	
Der dramatische Gesang, 1837 [?]	xii	—	
Bellini. Ein Wort zu seiner Zeit, 1837	xii	viii	
Über Meyerbeers *Hugenotten*, ?1840	xii	—	
Eine Pilgerfahrt zu Beethoven, novella, 1840	i	vii	70
Über deutsche Musik, 1840	i	vii	
Der Virtuos und der Künstler, 1840	i	vii	
Stabat mater de Pergolese par Lvoff, 1840	xii	vii	
Über die Ouvertüre, 1840–41	i	vii	24

Title, date	GS, SS	PW
Ein Theater in Zürich, 1851	v	iii
Über die 'Goethestiftung': Brief an Franz Liszt, 1851	v	iii
Eine Mitteilung an meine Freunde, 1851	iv	i	36, 37, 72, 89, 130, 133, 134, 138, 141
Erinnerungen an Spontini, 1851	v	iii
Über die musikalische Berichterstattung in der Eidgenössischen Zeitung, 1851	xvi	—
Zur Empfehlung Gottfried Sempers, 1851	xvi	—
Über musikalische Kritik: Brief an den Herausgeber der Neuen Zeitschrift für Musik, 1852	v	iii
Über die Aufführung des Tannhäuser: eine Mitteilung an die Dirigenten und Darsteller dieser Oper, 1852	v	iii
Bemerkungen zur Aufführung der Oper Der fliegende Holländer, 1852	v	iii
Beethoven's Heroische Symphonie, 1852 [explanatory programme]	v	iii
Ouvertüre zu Koriolan, 1852 [explanatory programme]	v	iii
Ouvertüre zu Tannhäuser, 1852 [explanatory programme]	v	iii
Vieuxtemps, 1852	xvi	—
Wilhelm Baumgartners Lieder, 1852	xii	—
Zum musikalischen Vortrag der Tannhäuser–Ouvertüre [letter to G. Schmidt], 1852	xvi	—
Zum Vortrag Beethovens [letter to Uhlig], 1852	xvi	—
Tannhäuser, i: Einzug der Gäste auf Wartburg; ii: Tannhäusers Romfahrt, 1853 [explanatory programme]	xvi	—
Vorspiel zu Lohengrin, 1853 [explanatory programme]	v	iii
Lohengrin, i: Männerszene und Brautzug; ii: Hochzeitmusik und Brautlied, 1853 [explanatory programme]	xvi	—
Ouvertüre zum Fliegenden Holländer, 1853, [explanatory programme]	v	iii
Über die programmatischen Erklärungen zu den Konzerten im Mai 1853 [prefatory remarks], 1853	xvi	—
Vorlesung der Dichtung des Ring des Nibelungen [invitation], 1853	xvi	—
Vorwort zum ersten Druck des Ring des Nibelungen, 1853	xii	—
Beethoven's Cis moll-Quartett, 1854 [explanatory programme]	xii	—
Gluck's Ouvertüre zu Iphigénie in Aulis, 1854	v	iii
Empfehlung einer Streichquartett-Vereinigung, 1854	xvi	—
Dante – Schopenhauer [letter to Liszt], 1855	xvi	—
Über die Leitung einer Mozart-Feier, 1856	xvi	—
Über Franz Liszts symphonische Dichtungen: Brief an M[arie zu Sayn] W[ittgenstein], 1857	v	iii	82
Entwurf eines Amnestiegesuches an den Sächsischen Justizminister Behr, 1858	xvi	—
Metaphysik der Geschlechtsliebe, 1858	xii	—
Tristan und Isolde: Vorspiel, 1859 [explanatory programme]	xii	—
Nachruf an L. Spohr und Chordirektor W. Fischer: brieflich an einen älteren Freund in Dresden, 1860	v	iii
Ein Brief an Hector Berlioz, 1860	vii	iii
'Zukunftsmusik': an einen französischen Freund (F. Villot) als Vorwort zu einer Prosa-Übersetzung meiner Operndichtungen, 1860	vii	iii	43, 74, 98, 114
Bericht über die Aufführung des Tannhäuser in Paris, 1861	vii	iii
Vom Wiener Hofoperntheater, 1861	xii	—
Gräfin Egmont ballet by Rota [review pubd under pseud. in Oesterreichische Zeitung, 8 Oct 1861 and in E. Kastner: Wagner-Catalog, 1878], 1861	—	—
Vorwort zur Herausgabe der Dichtung des Bühnenfestspieles Der Ring des Nibelungen, 1862	vi	iii	95
Drei Schreiben an die Direktion der Philharmonischen Gesellschaft in St Petersburg, 1862–6	xvi	—
Das Wiener Hofoperntheater, 1863	vii	iii
Tristan und Isolde: Vorspiel und Schluss, 1863 [explanatory programme]	xii	—

Title, date	GS, SS	PW
Aufforderung zur Erwerbung von Patronatscheinen, 1871	xvi	—
Eine Mitteilung an die deutschen Wagner-Vereine, 1871	xvi	—
Über die Wagner-Vereine [letter to the Weimar Intendant von Loën], 1871	xvi	—
Vorwort zu GS 3/4, 1871	iii	vii
Censuren: Vorbericht, 1872	viii	iv
An Friedrich Nietzsche, 1872	ix	v
Über Schauspieler und Sänger, 1872	ix	v
Schreiben an den Bürgermeister von Bologna, 1872	ix	v
Brief über das Schauspielerwesen an einen Schauspieler, 1872	ix	v
Ein Einblick in das heutige deutsche Opernwesen, 1872	ix	v
Über die Benennung 'Musikdrama', 1872	ix	v	77, 115, 116, 153
Ankündigung der Aufführung der 9. Symphonie für den 22. Mai 1872	xvi	
Ankündigung für den 22. Mai 1872 [laying of foundation-stone in Bayreuth]	xvi	
Dank an die Bürger von Bayreuth, 1872	xvi	iii
Vorwort zu GS 5/6, 1872	v	
Zirkular an die Patrone über ihre Anwesenheit bei der Grundsteinlegung, 1872	xvi	
Zwei Erklärungen in der Augsburger Allgemeine Zeitung über die Oper Theodor Körner von Wendelin Weissheimer, 1872	xvi	
Zwei Berichtigungen im Musikalischen Wochenblatt [i, 2. Report of the Academic Wagner Society, Berlin; ii, Brockhaus Konversationslexikon], 1872–3	xvi	
Einleitung zu einer Vorlesung der Götterdämmerung vor einem auserwählten Zuhörerkreise in Berlin, 1873	ix	v
Zum Vortrag der neunten Symphonie Beethovens, 1873	ix	v
Schlussbericht über die Umstände und Schicksale, welche die Ausführung des Bühnenfestspieles Der Ring des Nibelungen bis zur Gründung von Wagner-Vereinen begleiteten, 1873	ix	v
Das Bühnenfestspielhaus zu Bayreuth: nebst einem Bericht über die Grundsteinlegung desselben, 1873	ix	v
An die Patrone der Bühnenfestspiele in Bayreuth, 1873	xii	—

Title, date	GS, SS	PW	
Mein Leben, i–iii, 1865–75 (pubd privately, 1870–75); iv, 1879–80 (pubd privately, 1881); i–iv, abridged (Munich, 1911) [suppressed passages 1st pubd in Die Musik, xxiii (1929–30), 725; Eng. trans. in E. Newman: Fact and Fiction about Wagner (London, 1931), 199]; rev. ed. M. Gregor-Dellin (Munich, 1963, 1976, 1983)	xiii–xv	—	2, 5, 7, 8, 11, 12, 14, 15, 16, 17, 19, 20, 21, 22, 26, 28, 30, 36, 39, 41, 45, 49, 51, 53, 66, 90, 91, 127, 130
Über eine Opernaufführung in Leipzig: Brief an den Herausgeber des Musikalischen Wochenblattes, 1874	x	vi	
Zwei Erklärungen (i. Notgedrungene Erklärung; ii. Die 'Presse' zu den 'Proben'), 1874, 1875	xvi	—	
Götterdämmerung, i: Vorspiel; ii: Hagens Wacht; iii: Siegfrieds Tod; iv: Schluss des letzten Aktes, 1875 [explanatory programmes]			
Einladungsschreiben an die Sänger für Proben und Aufführungen des Bühnenfestspiels Der Ring des Nibelungen, 1875	xvi		
An die geehrten Patrone der Bühnenfestspiele von 1876, 1876	xii	—	
Abschiedswort an die Künstler (zum ersten Festspiel), 1876	xvi	—	
An die Künstler (zum ersten Festspiel), 1876	xvi	—	
An die Orchestermitglieder (zum ersten Festspiel), 1876	xvi	—	
Ankündigung der Festspiele für 1876	xvi	—	
Ansprache nach Schluss der Götterdämmerung, 1876	xvi	—	
Letzte Bitte an meine lieben Genossen. Letzter Wunsch (zum ersten Festspiel), 1876			
Über Bewerbungen zu den Festspielen, 1876	xvi	—	
Über den Gebrauch des Textbuches, 1876	xvi	—	
Über den Hervorruf (zum ersten Festspiel), 1876	xvi	—	
An die geehrten Vorstände der Richard Wagnervereine, 1877	x	vi	
Entwurf, veröffentlicht mit den Statuten des Patronatvereines, 1877	x	vi	
Ansprache an die Abgesandten des Bayreuther Patronats, 1877	xii	vi	
Ankündigung der Aufführung des Parsifal, 1877	xii	vi	

Zur Einführung [for 1st issue of *Bayreuther Blätter*], 1878	x	vi	
Modern, 1878	x	vi	
Publikum und Popularität, 1878	x	vi	
Ein Rückblick auf die Bühnenfestspiele des Jahres 1876, 1878	x	vi	
Ein Wort zur Einführung der Arbeit Hans von Wolzogens *Über Verrottung und Errettung der deutschen Sprache*, 1879	x	vi	
Erklärung an die Mitglieder des Patronatvereines, 1879	x	vi	
Zur Einführung in das Jahr 1880, 1879	x	vi	
Wollen wir hoffen?, 1879	x	vi	
Über das Opern-Dichten und Komponieren, 1879	x	vi	71
Über das Dichten und Komponieren im Besonderen, 1879	x	vi	71
Über die Anwendung der Musik auf das Drama, 1879	x	vi	71, 82, 102
Offenes Schreiben an Herrn Ernst von Weber, Verfasser der Schrift *Die Folterkammern der Wissenschaft*, 1879	x	vi	
Religion und Kunst, 1880	x	vi	71, 85
'Was nützt diese Erkenntnis?': ein Nachtrag zu *Religion und Kunst*, 1880	x	vi	
Zur Mitteilung an die geehrten Patrone der Bühnenfestspiele in Bayreuth, 1880	x	vi	
An König Ludwig II. über die Aufführung des *Parsifal*, 1880	xvi		71
Zur Einführung der Arbeit des Grafen Gobineau *Ein Urteil über die jetzige Weltlage*, 1881	x	vi	
Ausführungen zu *Religion und Kunst*: 'Erkenne dich selbst'; Heldentum und Christentum, 1881	x	vi	71
Brief an H. v. Wolzogen, 1882	x	vi	
Offenes Schreiben an Herrn Friedrich Schön in Worms, 1882	x	vi	
Das Bühnenweihfestspiel in Bayreuth 1882, 1882	x	vi	
Bericht über die Wiederaufführung eines Jugendwerkes: an den Herausgeber des *Musikalischen Wochenblattes*, 1882	x	vi	
Parsifal: Vorspiel, 1882 [explanatory programme]	xii		
Danksagung an die Bayreuther Bürgerschaft, 1882	xvi		
An die geehrten Vorstände der noch bestehenden lokalen Wagner-Vereine, 1882	xvi		66
Brief an H. v. Stein, 1883	x	vi	
Über das Weibliche im Menschlichen, 1883, inc.	xii		
Metaphysik, Kunst und religion, Moral, Christentum [aphorisms]	xii		

ANTHOLOGIES, OTHER EDITIONS

E. L. Burlingame, ed. and trans.: *Art, Life and Theories of Richard Wagner Selected from his Writings* (New York, 1875, 2/1909)

C. G. Glasenapp and H. von Stein: *Wagner-Lexikon: Hauptbegriffe der Kunst- und Weltanschauung Richard Wagners in wörtlichen Anführungen aus seinen Schriften* (Stuttgart, 1883)

C. F. Glasenapp: *Wagner-Encyclopädie: Hauptperscheinungen der Kunst- und Kulturgeschichte im Lichte der Anschauung Richard Wagners* (Leipzig, 1891)

W. Golther, ed.: *Richard Wagner: Gesammelte Schriften und Dichtungen in 10 Bänden* (Berlin, 1913) [incl. prefatory life and works, suppl. vol. of notes and commentary]

E. Bücken, ed.: *Richard Wagner: Die Hauptschriften* (Leipzig, 1937, rev., abridged 2/1956 by E. Rappl)

A. Lorenz, ed.: *Richard Wagner: Ausgewählte Schriften und Briefe* (Berlin, 1938)

M. Gregor-Dellin, ed.: *Richard Wagner: Mein Leben* (Munich, 1963, 1976, 1983) [1st authentic edn.]

A. Goldman and E. Sprinchorn, eds.: *Wagner on Music and Drama: a Compendium of Richard Wagner's Prose Works* (New York, 1964/R1977) [trans. W. A. Ellis]

R. Jacobs and G. Skelton, eds. and trans.: *Wagner Writes from Paris: Stories, Essays and Articles by the Young Composer* (London, 1973)

Bibliography

CATALOGUES, BIBLIOGRAPHIES, RELATED STUDIES

E. Kastner: *Wagner-Catalog: chronologisches Verzeichniss der von und über Richard Wagner erschienenen Schriften, Musikwerke* (Offenbach, 1878/R1966)

N. Oesterlein: *Katalog einer Richard Wagner-Bibliothek: nach den vorliegenden Originalien zu einem authentischen Nachschlagebuch durch die gesammte insbesondere deutsche Wagner-Literatur bearbeitet und veröffentlicht* (Leipzig, 1882–95/R1970)

H. Silège: *Bibliographie wagnérienne française* (Paris, 1902)

O. Strobel: *Genie am Werk: Richard Wagners Schaffen und Wirken im Spiegel eigenhandschriftlicher Urkunden: Führer durch die einmalige Ausstellung einer umfassenden Auswahl von Schätzen aus dem Archiv des Hauses Wahnfried* (Bayreuth, 1933, rev. 2/1934)

E. M. Terry: *A Richard Wagner Dictionary* (New York, 1939/R1971)

O. Strobel: 'Richard-Wagner-Forschungsstätte und Archiv des Hauses Wahnfried', *Das Bayerland*, lii (1942), 457; repr. in *Bayreuth: die Stadt Richard Wagners*, ed. O. Strobel and L. Deubner (Munich, 2/1943), 39

H. Barth, ed.: *Internationale Wagner-Bibliographie: 1945–55* (Bayreuth, 1956); *1956–60* (1961); *1961–6* (1968)

A. Ziino, ed.: *Antologia della critica wagneriana in Italia* (Messina, 1970)

H.-M. Plesske: *Richard Wagner in der Dichtung: Bibliographie deutschsprachiger Veröffentlichungen* (Bayreuth, 1971)

H. Kirchmeyer: *Das zeitgenössische Wagner-Bild*, i: *Wagner in Dresden* (Regensburg, 1972); ii: *Dokumente 1842–45* (1967); iii: *Dokumente 1846–50* (1968)

H. F. G. Klein: *Erst- und Frühdrucke der Textbücher von Richard Wagner: Bibliographie* (Tutzing, 1979)

J. Deathridge, M. Geck and E. Voss: *Verzeichnis der musikalischen Werke Richard Wagners und ihrer Quellen* (Mainz, 1984)

ICONOGRAPHICAL STUDIES

E. Fuchs and E. Kreowski: *Richard Wagner in der Karikatur* (Berlin, 1907)

E. W. Engel: *Richard Wagners Leben und Werke im Bilde* (Leipzig, 1913/R1922)

194

Bibliography

R. Bory: *La vie et l'oeuvre de Richard Wagner par l'image* (Lausanne, 1938; Ger. trans., 1938)

W. Schuh: *Renoir und Wagner* (Stuttgart, 1959)

M. Geck: *Die Bildnisse Richard Wagners* (Munich, 1970)

H. Barth, D. Mack and E. Voss: *Wagner: sein Leben, sein Werk und seine Welt in zeitgenössischen Bildern und Texten* (Vienna, 1975/*R*1982; Eng. trans., 1975)

D. Mack and E. Voss, eds.: *Richard Wagner: Leben und Werk in Daten und Bildern* (Frankfurt am Main, 1978)

O. Bauer: *Richard Wagner: die Bühnenwerke von der Uraufführung bis heute* (Berlin, 1982)

M. Gregor-Dellin: *Richard Wagner: eine Biographie in Bildern* (Munich, 1982)

C. Osborne: *The World Theatre of Wagner* (Oxford, 1982)

CORRESPONDENCE
(*catalogues, anthologies, collected editions*)

Ernst v. Weber: bisher ungedruckte Briefe (Dresden, 1883) [several Wagner letters 1879–81]

L. Herbeck: *Johann Herbeck: ein Lebensbild* (Vienna, 1885) [letters between Wagner and Johann Herbeck]

O. Kitzler: *Musikalische Erinnerungen mit Briefen von Wagner . . .* (Brno, 1904)

W. Altmann: *Richard Wagners Briefe nach Zeitfolge und Inhalt: ein Beitrag zur Lebensgeschichte des Meisters* (Lepizig, 1905/*R*1971)

Helbing, auction catalogue, 11 May 1909, Munich [25 autograph letters from collection of Hofrat Edgar Hanfstaengl]

J. Joachim and A. Moser, eds.: *Briefe von und an Joachim*, i (Berlin, 1911)

M. Huch, ed.: 'Drei unbekannte Schreiben Richard Wagners an Gustav Hölzel', *Die Musik*, xii (1912–13), 171

'Lettres inédites de Wagner à Léon Leroy et Gaspérini', *ReM*, iv/11 (1923), 139

W. Altmann, ed.: 'Briefe Wagners an Editha von Rhaden', *Die Musik*, xvi (1923–4), 712

K. Obser, ed.: 'Unveröffentlichte Briefe Richard Wagners', *Wissen und Leben: neue Schweizer Rundschau* [Zurich], xvii (20 Jan 1924)

R. Sternfeld: 'Richard Wagner in seinen Briefen an "Das Kind" ', *Die Musik*, xix (1926–7), 1

G. F. Winternitz, ed.: 'Drei unbekannte Wagner-Briefe', *Die Musik*, xxv (1932–3), 357

195

H. Ziegler: 'Wagners Briefwechsel mit seinem Verleger Fritzsch', *Die Musik*, xxvi (1933–4), 5

G. Kinsky, ed.: 'Fünf ungedruckte Briefe Wagners an Meyerbeer', *SMz*, lxxiv (1934), 705

A. Hedley: 'An Unpublished Wagner Letter', *ML*, xix (1938), 18

M. Becker, ed.: 'Neue Briefe Richard Wagners von seinem zweiten Pariser Aufenthalt, *Die Musik*, xxxv (1942–3), 137

P. P. Kies: 'Four New Wagner Letters', *Research Studies* (State College of Washington), xvii (1949), 209

H. A. Fiechtner: 'Neugefundene Wagnerbriefe', *Das Musikleben*, iii (1950), 129

J. N. Burk, ed.: *Letters of Richard Wagner: the Burrell Collection* (London, 1951; Ger. text and trans., 1953)

A. Zinsstag, ed.: *Zur Erinnerung an Malwida von Meysenbug* (Basle, 1956) [containing 9 unpubd Wagner letters]

G. Marbach: 'Seien Sie ganz mein Freund – Richard Wagner an Otto Bach', *NZM*, Jg.119 (1958), 207

D. Härtwig: 'Ein unbekannter Wagner-Brief in Schwerin', *Musik und Gesellschaft*, x (1960), 653

'Richard Wagner und die arme Wiener Hofoper: ein unbekannter Briefwechsel aus dem Archiv des ehemaligen Wiener Obersthofmeisteramtes', *Musik und Gesellschaft*, xiii (1963), 283

W. Grupe: 'Wagner-Briefe im Deutschen Zentralarchiv, Abteilung Merseburg', *Musik und Gesellschaft*, xiv (1964), 682

M. Ullrichowa, ed.: 'Fünf neu aufgefundene Briefe von Richard Wagner', *BMw* (1964), suppl.

G. Strobel and W. Wolf, eds.: *Richard Wagner: Sämtliche Briefe* (Leipzig, 1967–)

'Douze lettres inédites de Richard Wagner à Édouard Schuré', *RdM*, liv (1968), 206

H. Oesterheld: 'Dokumente zur Musikgeschichte Meiningens', *Neue Beiträge zur Regerforschung und Musikgeschichte Meiningens*, Südthüringer Forschung, vi, 1970 [5 letters to Duke Georg II of Saxe-Meiningen and his wife]

P. Slezak: 'Richard Wagner an Angelo Tessarini: ein bisher unbekannter Brief Richard Wagners', *ÖMz*, xxix (1974), 31

R. P. Locke: *Fenway Court: annual report of the Isabella Stewart Gardner Museum* (Boston, 1975) [letters from Bayreuth]

J. Heyne: 'Ein unbekannter Brief Richard Wagners', *Musik und Gesellschaft*, xxviii (1978), 164 [to King Friedrich August II of Saxony]

Bibliography

Musikantiquariat Hans Schneider: catalogues 215 [Richard Wagner, ii: Documents, 1850–64], 222 ['Gruss an die Schweiz', Zurich antiquarian fair], 223 [Richard Wagner, iii: Documents, 1865–83] (Tutzing, 1978)

E. Voss: 'Wagners "Sämtliche Briefe"?', *Melos/NZM*, iv (1978), 219

J. Deathridge: 'Wagner und Spontini: mit einem unveröffentlichten Brief Richard Wagners', *Jb der Bayerischen Staatsoper* (1979), 68

——: 'Wagner und sein erster Lehrmeister: mit einem unveröffentlichten Brief Richard Wagners', *Bayerische Staatsoper: Programmheft zur Neuinszenierung Die Meistersinger von Nürnberg* (Munich, 1979), 71

M. Eger: 'Der Briefwechsel Richard und Cosima Wagner: Geschichte und Relikte einer vernichteten Korrespondenz', *Bayreuther Festspiele: Programmheft IV. Das Rheingold* (Bayreuth, 1979), 1

J. Deathridge: ' "Diesen Messias glaubte und wusste ich in Ihrer Person gefunden zu haben": ein unveröffentlichter Briefentwurf Richard Wagners an den Münchener Intendanten Theodor von Küstner', *Jb der Bayerischen Staatsoper* (Munich, 1980), 75

(*individual publications*)

F. Hueffer, ed.: *Briefwechsel zwischen Wagner und Liszt* (Leipzig, 1887, 2/1900, rev. and enlarged 3/1910 by E. Kloss; Eng. trans., 1888/*R*1973)

E. Wille: *15 Briefe des Meisters, nebst Erinnerungen und Erläuterungen* (Leipzig, 1887, 2/1908 by W. Golther, rev. 3/1935 by C. F. Meyer)

H. von Wolzogen, ed.: *Richard Wagner's Briefe an Theodor Uhlig, Wilhelm Fischer, Ferdinand Heine* (Leipzig, 1888; Eng. trans., 1890) [see also O. Strobel: 'Unbekannte Lebensdokumente Richard Wagners: 2 unveröffentlichte Briefe Wagners an Theodor Uhlig', *Die Sonne*, x (1933), 69, and J. N. Burk, ed.: *Letters of Richard Wagner: the Burrell Collection* (London, 1951), 607–41]

H. S. Chamberlain, ed.: *Richard Wagners echte Briefe an Ferdinand Praeger* (Bayreuth, 1894, rev. 2/1908)

La Mara [pseud. of M. Lipsius], ed.: *Richard Wagners Brief an August Röckel* (Leipzig, 1894, 2/1912; Eng. trans., 1897)

J. Hoffmann, ed.: *Richard und Cosima Wagner an Maler Josef Hoffmann* (Bayreuth, 1896) [letters in facs.]

Wagner

E. Kastner, ed.: *Briefe von Richard Wagner an seine Zeitgenossen* (Berlin, 1897)

A. Heintz, ed.: *Briefe Richard Wagner's an Otto Wesendonk* (Charlottenburg, 1898, enlarged 2/1905 by W. Golther; Eng. trans., 1911/*R*1972)

K. Heckel, ed.: *Briefe Richard Wagners an Emil Heckel: zur Entstehungsgeschichte der Bühnenfestspiele in Bayreuth* (Berlin, 1899, 3/1911; Eng. trans., 1899)

W. Golther, ed.: *Richard Wagner an Mathilde Wesendonk: Tagebuchblätter und Briefe 1853–1871* (Leipzig, 1904, rev. 30/1906; Eng. trans., 1905) [see also J. Kapp: 'Unterdrückte Dokumente aus den Briefen Richard Wagners an Mathilde Wesendonk', *Die Musik*, xxiii (1930–31), 877, and O. Strobel: 'Ueber einen unbekannten Brief Richard Wagners an Mathilde Wesendonk und seine Geschichte', *Bayreuther Festspielführer 1937*, 152]

D. Spitzer, ed.: *Briefe Richard Wagners an eine Putzmacherin* (Vienna, 1906, enlarged edn., 1967 by L. Kusche; Eng. trans., 1941)

C. F. Glasenapp, ed.: *Familienbriefe von Richard Wagner 1832–1874* (Berlin, 1907; Eng. trans., 1911/*R*1972)

——: *Bayreuther Briefe von Richard Wagner (1871–1883)* (Berlin, 1907, 2/1912; Eng. trans., 1912/*R*1972)

E. Kloss, ed.: *Richard Wagner an seine Künstler* (Berlin, 1908)

H. von Wolzogen, ed.: *Richard Wagner an Minna Wagner* (Berlin, 1908; Eng. trans., 1909/*R*1972)

E. Kloss, ed.: *Richard Wagner an Freunde und Zeitgenossen* (Berlin, 1909)

T. Apel, ed.: *Richard Wagner an Theodor Apel* (Leipzig, 1910)

W. Altmann, ed.: *Richard Wagners Briefwechsel mit seinen Verlegern: Briefwechsel mit Breitkopf & Härtel* (Leipzig, 1911); *Briefwechsel mit B. Schott's Söhne* (Mainz, 1911)

F. von Hornstein, ed.: *Zwei unveröffentlichte Briefe Richard Wagners an Robert von Hornstein* (Munich, 1911)

E. Förster-Nietzsche: *Wagner und Nietzsche zur Zeit ihrer Freundschaft: Erinnerungsgabe zu Friedrich Nietzsches 70. Geburtstag den 15. Oktober 1914* (Munich, 1915; Eng. trans., 1922 as *The Nietzsche–Wagner Correspondence*)

J. G. Prod'homme: 'Wagner and the Paris Opéra: Unpublished Letters (February–March, 1861)', *MQ*, i (1915), 216

D. Thode, ed.: *Richard Wagners Briefe an Hans von Bülow* (Jena, 1916)

S. von Hausegger, ed.: *Richard Wagners Briefe an Frau Julie Ritter* (Munich, 1920)

Bibliography

W. Altmann, ed.; *Richard Wagner und Albert Niemann: ein Gedenkbuch mit bisher unveröffentlichten Briefen* (Berlin, 1924)

L. Karpath, ed.: *Richard Wagner: Briefe an Hans Richter* (Berlin, 1924)

H. Scholz, ed.: *Richard Wagner an Mathilde Maier (1862–1878)* (Leipzig, 1930)

H. J. Moser: 'Zwanzig Richard-Wagner-Dokumente', *Deutsche Rundschau*, lvii (1931), 42, 133

E. Lenrow, ed. and trans.: *The Letters of Richard Wagner to Anton Pusinelli* (New York, 1932/R1972)

J. Tiersot, ed.: *Lettres françaises de Richard Wagner* (Paris, 1935)

W. Schuh, ed. and trans.: *Die Briefe Richard Wagners an Judith Gautier* (Zurich, 1936, enlarged, with Fr. orig., 1964 as *Richard et Cosima Wagner: Lettres à Judith Gautier*, ed. L. Guichard)

O. Strobel: 'Liszt an Wagner: zwei unveröffentlichte Briefe', *Bayreuther Festspielführer 1936*, 128

O. Strobel, ed.: *König Ludwig II. und Richard Wagner: Briefwechsel*, v: *Neue Urkunden zur Lebensgeschichte Richard Wagners, 1864–1882* (Karlsruhe, 1936–9)

C. H. N. Garrigues: *Ein ideales Sängerpaar: Ludwig Schnorr von Carolsfeld und Malwina Schnorr von Carolsfeld, geb. Garrigues* (Copenhagen, 1937) [see also O. Strobel: 'Richard Wagner und Malwina Schnorr von Carolsfeld', *König Ludwig II. und Richard Wagner*, v: *Neue Urkunden zur Lebensgeschichte Richard Wagners, 1864–1882* (Karlsruhe, 1936–9), xvii–1]

O. Strobel: 'Anton Bruckner huldigt Richard Wagner: ein unveröffentlichter Brief', *Bayreuther Festspielführer 1938*, 35

W. Jerger, ed.: *Wagner-Nietzsches Briefwechsel während des Tribschener Idylls* (Berne, 1951)

L. Strecker: *Richard Wagner als Verlagsgefährte: eine Darstellung mit Briefen und Dokumenten* (Mainz, 1951)

W. Keller, ed.: *Richard Wagner: Briefe an Wilhelm Baumgartner 1850–1861* (Zurich, 1976)

PERIODICALS

Bayreuther Blätter, i–lxi (1878–1938)

Revue wagnérienne, i–iii (1885–8/R1971)

Richard Wagner-Jb, i (1886)

The Meister: the Quarterly Journal of the London Branch of the Wagner Society, i–viii (1885–95)

Richard Wagner-Jb, i–v (1906–8, 1912–13)

Tribschener Blätter: Mitteilungen der Gesellschaft Richard-Wagner-Museum Tribschen (Lucerne, 1956–)

199

*Feuilles Wagnériennes: bulletin d'information de l'association
Wagnérienne de Belgique* (Brussels, 1960–)
Wagner (new ser.), ed. S. Spencer (London, 1980–)

CONTEMPORARY ESSAYS

F. Liszt: *Lohengrin et Tannhaeuser de Richard Wagner* (Leipzig,
1851; Ger. trans., 1852)

J. Raff: *Die Wagnerfrage: kritisch beleuchtet*, i: *Wagners letzte
künstlerische Kundgebung im 'Lohengrin'* (Brunswick, 1854) [no
more pubd]

F. Liszt: 'Richard Wagners Rheingold', *NZM*, xliii (1855), 1

H. von Bülow: *Über Richard Wagner's Faust-Ouvertüre: eine
erläuternde Mittheilung an die Dirigenten, Spieler und Hörer
dieses Werkes* (Leipzig, 1860)

Champfleury [pseud. of H. Husson]: *Richard Wagner* (Paris,
1860)

C. Baudelaire: *Richard Wagner et Tannhaeuser à Paris* (Paris,
1861; Eng. trans., 1964) [orig. pubd in *Revue européenne* (Paris,
1 April 1861); monograph incl. new section]

F. Nietzsche: *Die Geburt der Tragödie aus dem Geiste der Musik*
(Leipzig, 1872, 2/1878, enlarged 3/1886; Eng. trans., 1967)

H. Porges: *Die Aufführung von Beethovens 9. Symphonie unter
Richard Wagner in Bayreuth* (Leipzig, 1872)

E. Dannreuther: *Richard Wagner: his Tendencies and Theories*
(London, 1873)

E. Hanslick: *Die Moderne Oper* (Berlin, 1875)

E. Schuré: *Le drame musical*, ii: *Richard Wagner: son oeuvre et
son idée* (Paris, 1875, rev. 4/1895; Eng. trans., 1910)

C. F. Glasenapp: *Richard Wagner's Leben und Wirken* (Kassel,
1876–7 [see 'Principal biographies']

W. Mohr: *Richard Wagner und das Kunstwerk der Zukunft im
Lichte der Bayreuther Aufführung betrachtet* (Cologne, 1876)

M. Plüddemann: *Die Bühnenfestspiele in Bayreuth: ihre Gegenwart
und ihre Zukunft* (Leipzig, 1877)

H. Porges: *Die Bühnenproben zu den Bayreuther Festspielen des
Jahres 1876* (Leipzig, 1877, repr. 1896; Eng. trans., 1983)

F. von Hausegger: *Richard Wagner und Schopenhauer* (Leipzig,
1878, 2/1892)

J. Gautier: *Wagner et son oeuvre poétique depuis Rienzi jusqu'à
Parsifal* (Paris, 1882)

R. Pohl: *Gesammelte Schriften über Musik und Musiker*, i: *Richard
Wagner* (Leipzig, 1883/*R*1973)

Bibliography

PERSONAL ACCOUNTS, REMINISCENCES

M. von Meysenbug: *Memoiren einer Idealistin* (Berlin, ?1868–76)

H. Dorn: *Aus meinem Leben* (Berlin, 1870)

F. Nietzsche: *Unzeitgemässe Betrachtungen*, iv: *Richard Wagner in Bayreuth* (Chemnitz, 1876; Eng. trans., 1910)

H. Dorn: *Ergebnisse aus Erlebnissen* (Berlin, 1877)

R. Pohl: 'Richard Wagner', *Sammlung musikalischer Vorträge*, v/53–4, ed. P. Waldersee (1883), 123–98

H. von Wolzogen: *Erinnerungen an Richard Wagner* (Vienna, 1883, enlarged 2/1891; Eng. trans., 1894)

C. Mendès: *Richard Wagner* (Paris, 1886)

K. Heckel: *Die Bühnenfestspiele in Bayreuth* (Leipzig, 1891)

F. Weingartner: *Bayreuth (1876–1896)* (Leipzig, 1896, rev. 2/1904)

A. Lavignac: *Le voyage artistique à Bayreuth* (Paris, 1897; Eng. trans., 1898)

W. Weissheimer: *Erlebnisse mit Richard Wagner, Franz Liszt und vielen anderen Zeitgenossen nebst deren Briefen* (Stuttgart, 1898)

E. Schuré: *Souvenirs sur Richard Wagner* (Paris, 1900)

L. Schemann: *Meine Erinnerungen an Richard Wagner* (Stuttgart, 1902)

M. Kietz: *Richard Wagner in den Jahren 1842–1849 und 1873–1875: Erinnerungen von Gustav Adolph Kietz* (Dresden, 1905)

H. Zumpe: *Persönliche Erinnerungen nebst Mitteilungen aus seinen Tagebuchblättern und Briefen* (Munich, 1905)

E. Michotte: *La visite de Richard Wagner à Rossini (Paris 1860)* (Paris, 1906; Eng. trans., 1968)

E. Humperdinck: 'Parsifal-Skizzen: persönliche Erinnerungen an die erste Aufführung des Bühnenweihfestspieles am 25. Juli 1882', *Die Zeit* (Vienna, 1907); repr. in *Bayreuther Festspielführer 1927*, 215

A. Neumann: *Erinnerungen an Richard Wagner* (Leipzig, 1907; Eng. trans., 1908/*R*1976)

J. Gautier: *Le collier des jours: le troisième rang du collier* (Juven, 1909, rev. edn. in *Mercure de France*, 1943; Eng. trans., 1910)

J. Hey: *Richard Wagner als Vortragsmeister: Erinnerungen*, ed. H. Hey (Leipzig, 1911)

L. Frankenstein, ed.: *Theodor Uhlig: Musikalische Schriften* (Regensburg, 1913)

E. von Possart: *Erstrebtes und Erlebtes: Erinnerungen aus meiner Bühnentätigkeit* (Berlin, 1916)

201

M. Fehr: *Unter Wagners Taktstock: 30 Winterthurer- und Zür-cherbriefe aus der Zeit der Wagnerkonzerte in Zürich 1852* (Winterthur, 1922)

S. Wagner: *Erinnerungen* (Stuttgart, 1923, enlarged 2/1935)

F. Klose: *Bayreuth: Eindrücke und Erlebnisse* (Regensburg, 1929)

E. Thierbach, ed.: *Die Briefe Cosima Wagners an Friedrich Nietzsche* (Weimar, 1938–40)

W. Krienitz: 'Felix Mottls Tagebuchaufzeichnungen aus den Jahren 1873–1876', *Neue Wagner-Forschungen*, i, ed. O. Strobel (Bayreuth, 1943), 167–234

M. Gregor-Dellin and D. Mack, eds.: *Cosima Wagner: die Tage-bücher 1869–1883* (Munich and Zurich, 1976–7; Eng. trans., 1978–9)

PRINCIPAL BIOGRAPHIES

C. F. Glasenapp: *Richard Wagners Leben und Wirken* (Kassel, 1876–7, rev., enlarged 2/1882, rev., enlarged 3/1894–1911 as *Das Leben Richard Wagners*, rev. 5/1910–23; Eng. trans. of 3rd edition rev., enlarged 1900–08/*R*1977 by W. A. Ellis as *Life of Richard Wagner* [vols. iv–vi by Ellis alone])

M. Burrell: *Richard Wagner: his Life and Works from 1813–1834* (London, 1898)

M. Koch: *Richard Wagner* (Berlin, 1907–18)

E. Newman: *The Life of Richard Wagner* (London, 1933–47/ *R*1976)

M. Fehr: *Richard Wagners Schweitzer Zeit*, i [1849–55] (Aarau and Leipzig, 1934); ii [1855–72, 1883] (Aarau and Frankfurt am Main, 1954)

C. von Westernhagen: *Richard Wagner: sein Werk, sein Wesen, seine Welt* (Zurich, 1956)

R. W. Gutman: *Richard Wagner: the Man, his Mind, and his Music* (New York and London, 1968)

C. von Westernhagen: *Wagner* (Zurich, 1968; Eng. trans., 1979)

M. Gregor-Dellin: *Richard Wagner: sein Leben, sein Werk, sein Jahrhundert* (Munich, 1980/*R*1983)

OTHER BIOGRAPHICAL AND RELATED STUDIES

F. Hueffer: *Richard Wagner* (London, 1872, 3/1912)

A. Jullien: *Richard Wagner: sa vie et ses oeuvres* (Paris, 1886; Eng. trans., 1892, repr. 1910/*R*1974)

H. S. Chamberlain: *Richard Wagner* (Munich, 1896, 3/1911; Eng. trans., 1897/*R*1974)

E. Newman: *A Study of Wagner* (London, 1899/*R*1974)

Bibliography

W. Kienzl: *Die Gesamtkunst des XIX. Jahrhunderts: Richard Wagner* (Munich, 1903, rev. 2/1908)

M. Semper: *Das Münchener Festspielhaus: Gottfried Semper und Richard Wagner* (Hamburg, 1906)

J. Hey: *Richard Wagner als Vortragsmeister: Erinnerungen*, ed. H. Hey (Leipzig, 1911)

C. von Ehrenfels: *Richard Wagner und seine Apostaten* (Vienna, 1913)

E. Newman: *Wagner as Man and Artist* (London, 1914, rev. 2/1924/R1963)

J. Kniese: *Der Kampf zweier Welten um das Bayreuther Erbe: Julius Knieses Tagebuchblätter aus dem Jahre 1883* (Leipzig, 1931)

E. Newman: *Fact and Fiction about Wagner* (London, 1931)

G. de Pourtalès: *Wagner: histoire d'un artiste* (Paris, 1932, enlarged 2/1942; Eng. trans., 1932/R1972)

E. Stemplinger: *Richard Wagner in München (1864–1870): Legende und Wirklichkeit* (Munich, 1933)

E. Bücken: *Richard Wagner* (Wildpark-Potsdam, 1934, 2/1943)

W. Reihlen: 'Die Stammtafel Richard Wagners (Leipziger Abschnitt)', *Familiengeschichtliche Blätter*, xxxviii (1940), 170

——: 'Die Eltern Richard Wagners', *Familiengeschichtliche Blätter*, xli (1943), 41

O. Strobel: *Neue Wagnerforschungen* (Karlsruhe, 1943)

W. Rauschenberger: 'Die Abstammung Richard Wagners', *Familiengeschichtliche Blätter*, xlii (1944), 9

L. Strecker: *Richard Wagner als Verlagsgefährte: eine Darstellung mit Briefen und Dokumenten* (Mainz, 1951)

O. Strobel: *Richard Wagner: Leben und Schaffen: eine Zeittafel* (Bayreuth, 1952)

H. Mayer: *Richard Wagners geistige Entwicklung* (Düsseldorf and Hamburg, 1954)

H. Engel: 'Wagner und Spontini', *AMw*, xii (1955), 167

W. Vordtriede: 'Richard Wagners "Tod in Venedig" ', *Euphorion*, lii (1958–9), 378

H. Mayer: *Richard Wagner in Selbstzeugnissen und Bilddokumenten* (Reinbek bei Hamburg, 1959; Eng. trans., 1972)

O. Daube: *Richard Wagner: 'Ich schreibe keine Symphonien mehr': Richard Wagners Lehrjahre nach den erhaltenen Dokumenten* (Cologne, 1960)

C. von Westernhagen: *Richard Wagners Dresdener Bibliothek 1842–1849: neue Dokumente zur Geschichte seines Schaffens* (Wiesbaden, 1966)

203

R. Hollinrake: 'The Title-Page of Wagner's "Mein Leben" ', *ML*, li (1970), 415

M. Gregor-Dellin: *Wagner Chronik: Daten zu Leben und Werk* (Munich, 1972)

J. Bergfeld, ed.: *Richard Wagner: Tagebuchaufzeichnungen 1865–1882: 'Das braune Buch'* (Zurich, 1975; Eng. trans., 1981)

G. Skelton: *Richard and Cosima Wagner: Biography of a Marriage* (London, 1982)

BAYREUTH: POLITICS AND INFLUENCE

W. Schuler: *Der Bayreuther Kreis von seiner Entstehung bis zum Ausgang der wilhelminischen Ära: Wagnerkult und Kulturreform im Geiste völkischer Weltanschauung* (Münster, 1971)

M. Karbaum: *Studien zur Geschichte der Bayreuther Festspiele* (Regensburg, 1976)

E. Voss: *Die Dirigenten der Bayreuther Festspiele* (Regensburg, 1976)

H. Zelinsky: *Richard Wagner – ein deutsches Thema* (Frankfurt am Main, 1976)

J. Deathridge: 'Bayreuth's National Front', *Times Literary Supplement* (5 Aug 1977)

S. Grossmann-Vendrey: *Bayreuth in der deutschen Presse* (Regensburg, 1977)

R. Hartford: *Bayreuth: the Early Years* (London, 1980)

B. W. Wessling, ed.: *Bayreuth im Dritten Reich* (Weinheim and Basle, 1983)

PRODUCTION STUDIES

A. Appia: *La mise en scène du drame wagnérien* (Paris, 1895); ed. E. Stadler in *Theaterjb der Schweizerischen Gesellschaft für Theaterkultur*, xxviii–xxix (Berne, 1963)

——: *Die Musik und die Inszenierung* (Munich, 1899; Fr. orig., 1963; Eng. trans., 1962)

F. A. Geissler: 'Wagner und die Opernregie', *Richard Wagner-Jb*, i (1906), 251

A. Heuss: 'Musik und Szene bei Wagner: ein Beispiel aus "Tristan und Isolde" und zugleich ein kleiner Beitrag zur Charakteristik Gustav Mahlers als Regisseur', *Die Musik*, xii (1912–13), 207

H. de Curzon: *L'oeuvre de Richard Wagner à Paris et ses interprètes, 1850–1914* (Paris, 1920)

D. M. Oenslager: 'A Project for the *Ring*', *Theatre Arts Monthly*, xi (1927), 35

F. Rühlmann: *Richard Wagners theatralische Sendung: ein Beitrag*

Bibliography

zur Geschichte und zur Systematik der Opernregie (Brunswick, 1935)

A. Bahr-Mildenburg: *Darstellung der Werke Richard Wagners aus dem Geiste der Dichtung und Musik: Tristan und Isolde: vollständige Regiebearbeitung sämtlicher Partien mit Notenbeispielen* (Leipzig, 1936)

E. Preetorius: *Vom Bühnenbild bei Richard Wagner* (Haarlem, 1938)

K. F. Richter: *Die Antinomien der szenischen Dramaturgie im Werk Richard Wagners* (diss., U. of Munich, 1956)

K. H. Ruppel, ed.: *Wieland Wagner inszeniert Richard Wagner* (Konstanz, 1960)

K. Neupert: 'Die Besetzung der Bayreuther Festspiele 1876–1960', *Internationale Wagner-Bibliographie: 1956–60*, ed. H. Barth (Bayreuth, 1961), 47–119

W. Wagner, ed.: *Richard Wagner und das neue Bayreuth* (Munich, 1962)

K. Hommel: *Die Separatvorstellungen vor König Ludwig II. von Bayern* (Munich, 1963)

D. Steinbeck: *Inszenierungsformen des 'Tannhäuser'* (*1845–1904*): *Untersuchungen zur Systematik der Opernregie* (Regensburg, 1964)

G. Skelton: *Wagner at Bayreuth: Experiment and Tradition* (London, 1965, rev., enlarged 2/1976)

D. Steinbeck, ed.: *Richard Wagners Tannhäuser-Szenarium: das Vorbild der Erstaufführungen mit der Kostümbeschreibung und den Dekorationsplänen* (Berlin, 1968)

P. Turing: *New Bayreuth* (London, 1969, rev. 2/1971)

M. and D. Petzet: *Die Richard-Wagner-Bühne König Ludwigs II.* (Munich, 1970)

W. E. Schäfer: *Wieland Wagner: Persönlichkeit und Leistung* (Tübingen, 1970)

D. Steinbeck: 'Richard Wagners "Lohengrin"-Szenarium', *Kleine Schriften der Gesellschaft für Theatergeschichte*, xxv (Berlin, 1972), 3–44

H. Barth, ed.: *Der Festspielhügel: 100 Jahre Bayreuther Festspiele in einer repräsentativen Dokumentation* (Bayreuth, 1973, 2/1976)

C.-F. Baumann: *Bühnentechnik im Bayreuther Festspielhaus* (Munich, 1973)

L. Lucas: *Die Festspiel-Idee Richard Wagners* (Regensburg, 1973)

G. Zeh: *Das Bayreuther Bühnenkostüm* (Munich, 1973)

D. Mack: *Der Bayreuther Inszenierungsstil* (Regensburg, 1975)

D. Mack, ed.: *Theaterarbeit an Wagners Ring* (Munich, 1979)

LITERARY AND PHILOSOPHICAL STUDIES

F. Nietzsche: *Der Fall Wagner* (Leipzig, 1888; Eng. trans., 1967)

H. Dinger: *Richard Wagners geistige Entwicklung: Versuch einer Darstellung der Weltanschauung Richard Wagners*, i: *Die Weltanschauung Richard Wagners in den Grundzügen ihrer Entwicklung* (Leipzig, 1892) [no more pubd]

H. Lichtenberger: *Richard Wagner: poète et penseur* (Paris, 1898, 5/1911; Ger. trans., 2/1904)

W. Golther: *Richard Wagner als Dichter* (Berlin, 1904; Eng. trans., 1905)

R. Sternfeld: *Schiller und Wagner* (Berlin, 1905)

P. Moos: *Richard Wagner als Ästhetiker: Versuch einer kritischen Darstellung* (Berlin, 1906)

E. Dujardin: '*La revue wagnérienne*', *ReM*, iv/11 (1923), 237; pubd separately (New York, 1977)

K. Hildebrandt: *Wagner und Nietzsche: ihr Kampf gegen das 19. Jahrhundert* (Breslau, 1924)

A. Drews: *Der Ideengehalt von Richard Wagners dramatischen Dichtungen im Zusammenhange mit seinem Leben und seiner Weltanschauung, nebst einem Anhang: Nietzsche und Wagner* (Leipzig, 1931)

G. Woolley: *Richard Wagner et le symbolisme français* (Paris, 1931)

K. Jäckel: *Richard Wagner in der französischen Literatur* (Breslau, 1931–2)

G. Abraham: 'Nietzsche's Attitude to Wagner: a Fresh View', *ML*, xiii (1932), 64; repr. in *Slavonic and Romantic Music: Essays and Studies* (London, 1968), 313

P. Claudel: 'Richard Wagner: rêverie d'un poëte français', *Revue de Paris* (15 July 1934); ed. M. Malicet (Paris, 1970)

E. Ruprecht: *Der Mythos bei Wagner und Nietzsche* (Berlin, 1938)

H. Schneider: *Richard Wagner und das germanische Altertum* (Tübingen, 1939)

A. Schmitz: 'Der Mythos der Kunst in den Schriften Richard Wagners', *Beiträge zur christlichen Philosophie*, iii (Mainz, 1948)

P. A. Loos: *Richard Wagner: Vollendung und Tragik der deutschen Romantik* (Berne and Munich, 1952)

W. Vetter: 'Richard Wagner und die Griechen', *Mf*, vi (1953), 111

A. Carlsson: 'Das mythische Wahnbild Richard Wagners', *Deutsche Vierteljahrsschrift für Literaturwissenschaft und Geistesgeschichte*, xxix (1955), 237

M. Gregor-Dellin: *Wagner und kein Ende: Richard Wagner im*

Bibliography

Spiegel von Thomas Manns Prosawerk: eine Studie (Bayreuth, 1958)

E. Bloch: 'Paradoxa und Pastorale in Wagners Musik', *Merkur*, xiii (1959), 405–35; repr. in *Verfremdungen*, i (Frankfurt am Main, 1962), and *Literarische Aufsätze* (Frankfurt am Main, 1965)

E. Mann, ed.: *T. Mann: Wagner und unsere Zeit: Aufsätze, Betrachtungen, Briefe* (Frankfurt am Main, 1963); Eng. trans. of 2 essays in *T. Mann: Essays of Three Decades* (New York and London, 1947)

F. Egermann: 'Aischyleische Motive in Richard Wagners Dichtung von "Tristan und Isolde" ', *DJbM*, ix (1965), 40

L. Siegel: 'Wagner and the Romanticism of E. T. A. Hoffmann', *MQ*, li (1965), 597

B. Magee: *Aspects of Wagner* (London, 1968, rev. 2/1972)

D. Bancroft: 'Claudel on Wagner', *ML*, 1 (1969), 439

M. Gregor-Dellin: *Richard Wagner: die Revolution als Oper* (Munich, 1973)

E. Koppen: *Dekadenter Wagnerismus: Studien zur europäischen Literatur des Fin de siècle* (Berlin and New York, 1973)

C. Dahlhaus: 'Wagners Berlioz-Kritik und die Ästhetik des Hässlichen', *Festschrift für Arno Volk* (Copenhagen, 1974), 107

K. G. Just: 'Richard Wagner – ein Dichter? Marginalien zum Opernlibretto des 19. Jahrhunderts', *Richard Wagner: von der Oper zum Musikdrama*, ed. S. Kunze (Berne and Munich, 1978), 79

R. Furness: *Wagner and Literature* (Manchester, 1982)

R. Hollinrake: *Nietzsche, Wagner and the Philosophy of Pessimism* (London, 1982)

D. Ingenschay-Goch: *Richard Wagners neu erfundener Mythos: zur Rezeption und Reproduktion des germanischen Mythos in seinen Operntexten* (Bonn, 1982)

ANALYSIS AND CRITICISM: GENERAL STUDIES

L. Nohl: *Das moderne Musikdrama* (Vienna, 1884)

H. Bulthaupt: 'Richard Wagner', *Dramaturgie der Oper*, ii (Leipzig, 1887, rev. 2/1902)

W. A. Ellis: *Richard Wagner as Poet, Musician and Mystic* (London, 1887)

H. von Wolzogen: *Wagneriana: gesammelte Aufsätze über Richard Wagners Werke vom Ring bis zum Gral* (Bayreuth, 1888)

L. Torchi: *Riccardo Wagner: studio critico* (Bologna, 1890)

H. E. Krehbiel: *Studies in the Wagnerian Drama* (New York, 1891/R1975)

H. S. Chamberlain: *Das Drama Richard Wagners: eine Anregung* (Leipzig, 1892, 3/1908/*R*1973; Eng. trans., 1915)

A. Prüfer: *Die Bühnenfestspiele in Bayreuth* (Leipzig, 1899, rev., enlarged, 1909 as *Das Werk von Bayreuth*)

W. J. Henderson: *Richard Wagner: his Life and his Dramas* (New York, 1901, 2/1923, rev. 2/1971/*R*1971)

A. Seidl: *Wagneriana* (Berlin, 1901–2)

G. Adler: *Richard Wagner: Vorlesungen gehalten an der Universität zu Wien* (Munich, 1904, 2/1923)

H. von Wolzogen: *Musikalisch-dramatische Parallelen: Beiträge zur Erkenntnis von der Musik als Ausdruck* (Leipzig, 1906)

A. Seidl: *Neue Wagneriana: gesammelte Aufsätze und Studien* (Regensburg, 1914)

A. Halm: *Von Grenzen und Ländern der Musik* (Munich, 1916)

P. Bekker: *Richard Wagner: das Leben im Werke* (Stuttgart, 1924; Eng. trans., 1931/*R*1970)

A. Lorenz: *Das Geheimnis der Form bei Richard Wagner*, i: *Der musikalische Aufbau des Bühnenfestspieles Der Ring des Nibelungen* (Berlin, 1924/*R*1966); ii: *Der musikalische Aufbau von Richard Wagners 'Tristan und Isolde'* (Berlin, 1926/*R*1966); iii: *Der musikalische Aufbau von Richard Wagners 'Die Meistersinger von Nürnberg'* (Berlin, 1930/*R*1966); iv: *Der musikalische Aufbau von Richard Wagners 'Parsifal'* (Berlin, 1933/*R*1966)

O. Strobel: *Richard Wagner über sein Schaffen: ein Beitrag zur 'Künstlerästhetik'* (Munich, 1924)

——: 'Richard Wagners Originalpartituren', *AMz*, lv (1928), 307

H. Pfitzner: *Werk und Wiedergabe*, Gesammelte Schriften, iii (Augsburg, 1929)

V. d'Indy: *Richard Wagner et son influence sur l'art musical français* (Paris, 1930)

W. Engelsmann: *Wagners klingendes Universum* (Potsdam, 1933)

T. Mann: 'Leiden und Grösse Richard Wagners', *Neue Rundschau*, xliv (1933), 450–501; repr. in *Gesammelte Werke*, ix (Berlin and Frankfurt, 1960), 363–426; Eng. trans., in *T. Mann: Past Masters and other Papers* (London, 1933), 15–96

L. Gilman: *Wagner's Operas* (New York, 1937)

E. Newman: *Wagner Nights* (London, 1949/*R*1961 and 1977); as *The Wagner Operas* (New York, 1949/*R*1963)

O. Strobel: 'Eingebung und bewusste Arbeit im musikalischen Schaffen Richard Wagners', *Bayreuther Festspielbuch 1951*, 88

T. W. Adorno: *Versuch über Wagner* (Berlin and Frankfurt am Main, 1952/*R*1964; repr. in Gesammelte Schriften, xi (1971); Eng. trans., 1981)

Bibliography

P. A. Loos: *Richard Wagner: Vollendung und Tragik der deutschen Romantik* (Berne and Munich, 1952)

H. Blümer: *Über den Tonarten-Charakter bei Richard Wagner* (diss., U. of Munich, 1958)

E. A. Lippman: 'The Aesthetic Theories of Richard Wagner', *MQ*, xliv (1958), 209

W. Serauky: 'Richard Wagner in Vergangenheit und Gegenwart', *DJbM*, iii (1958), 7

J. M. Stein: *Richard Wagner and the Synthesis of the Arts* (Detroit, 1960/*R*1973)

H. von Stein: *Dichtung und Musik im Werk Richard Wagners* (Berlin, 1962)

C. von Westernhagen: *Von Holländer zum Parsifal: neue Wagner Studien* (Freiburg, 1962)

H. Gál: *Richard Wagner: Versuch einer Würdigung* (Frankfurt am Main, 1963; Eng. trans., 1976)

G. Knepler: 'Richard Wagners musikalische Gestaltungs-prinzipien', *BMw*, v (1963), 33

J. Mainka: 'Sonatenform, Leitmotiv und Charakterbegleitung', *BMw*, v (1963), 11

E. Arro: 'Richard Wagners Rigaer Wanderjahre: über einige baltische Züge im Schaffen Wagners', *Musik des Ostens*, iii (1965), 123–68

C. Dahlhaus: 'Wagners Begriff der "dichterisch-musikalischen Periode"', *Beiträge zur Geschichte der Musikanschauungen im 19. Jahrhundert*, i. ed. W. Salmen (Regensburg, 1965), 179

H. Mayer: *Anmerkungen zu Wagner* (Frankfurt am Main, 1966)

H. F. Redlich: 'Wagnerian Elements in pre-Wagnerian Operas', *Essays Presented to Egon Wellesz* (Oxford, 1966)

C. Dahlhaus: 'Eduard Hanslick und der musikalische Formbe-griff', *Mf*, xx (1967), 145

K. Overhoff: *Die Musikdramen Richard Wagners: eine thematisch-musikalische Interpretation* (Salzburg, 1968)

M. Geck: 'Richard Wagner und die ältere Musik', *Die Ausbreitung des Historismus über die Musik*, ed. W. Wiora (Regensburg, 1969), 123

R. Raphael: *Richard Wagner* (New York, 1969)

Colloquium Verdi–Wagner: Rome 1969 [AnMc, no.11 (1972)]

C. Dahlhaus: *Die Bedeutung des Gestischen in Wagners Musik-dramen* (Munich, 1970)

——: 'Wagner and Program Music', *Studies in Romanticism*, ix (1970), 3; Ger. orig. in *Jb des Staatlichen Institut für Musik-forschung Preussischer Kulturbesitz* (Berlin, 1973)

——: 'Soziologische Dechiffrierung von Musik: zu Theodor W. Adornos Wagnerkritik', *International Review of Music Aesthetics and Sociology*, i (1970), 137

C. Dahlhaus, ed.: *Das Drama Richard Wagners als musikalisches Kunstwerk* (Regensburg, 1970)

S. Kunze: 'Naturszenen in Wagners Musikdrama', *Gf MKB, Bonn 1970*, 199

E. Voss: *Studien zur Instrumentation Richard Wagners* (Regensburg, 1970)

C. Dahlhaus: *Die Musikdramen Richard Wagners* (Velber, 1971; Eng. trans., 1979)

——: *Wagners Konzeption des musikalischen Dramas* (Regensburg, 1971)

——: 'Zur Geschichte der Leitmotivtechnik bei Wagner', *Richard Wagner: Werk und Wirkung* (Regensburg, 1971), 17

A. Sommer: *Die Komplikationen des musikalischen Rhythmus in den Bühnenwerken Richard Wagners* (Giebing, 1971)

R. Bailey: 'The Evolution of Wagner's Compositional Procedure after Lohengrin', *IMSCR, xi Copenhagen 1972*, 240

E. Lichtenhahn: 'Die "Popularitätsfrage" in Richard Wagners Pariser Schriften', *Schweizer Beiträge zur Musikwissenschaft*, i (1972), 143

U. Jung: *Die Rezeption der Kunst Richard Wagners in Italien* (Regensburg, 1974)

J. Deathridge: 'The Nomenclature of Wagner's Sketches', *PRMA*, ci (1974–5), 75

K. Kropfinger: *Wagner und Beethoven: Untersuchungen zur Beethoven-Rezeption Richard Wagners* (Regensburg, 1975)

P. Petersen: 'Die dichterisch-musikalische Periode: ein verkannter Begriff Richard Wagners', *Hamburger Jb für Musikwissenschaft*, II (1977), 105

S. Kunze: 'Über den Kunstcharakter des Wagnerschen Musikdramas', *Richard Wagner: von der Oper zum Musikdrama*, ed. S. Kunze (Berne and Munich, 1978), 9

H. K. Metzger and R. Riehn, eds.: *Richard Wagner: wie antisemitisch darf ein Künstler sein?*, Musik-Konzepte, no.5 (Munich, 1978)

P. Wapnewski: *Der traurige Gott: Richard Wagner in seinen Helden* (Munich, 1978)

P. Boulez: 'Anmerkung zur musikalischen Struktur', *Theaterarbeit an Wagners Ring*, ed. D. Mack (Munich, 1979), 243

P. Burbidge and R. Sutton, eds.: *The Wagner Companion* (London, 1979)

R. Holloway: *Debussy and Wagner* (London, 1979)

Bibliography

N. Josephson: 'Tonale Strukturen im musikdramatischen Schaffen Richard Wagners', *Mf*, xxxii (1979), 141

H. E. Renk: 'Anmerkungen zur Beziehung zwischen Musiktheater und Semiotik', *Theaterarbeit an Wagners Ring*, ed. D. Mack (Munich, 1979), 275

A. D. Sessa: *Richard Wagner and the English* (Rutherford, Madison, Teaneck and London, 1979)

E. Voss: 'Noch einmal: das Geheimnis der Form bei Richard Wagner', *Theaterarbeit an Wagners Ring*, ed. D. Mack (Munich, 1979), 251

A. Newcomb: 'The Birth of Music out of the Spirit of Drama', *19th Century Music*, v (1981–2), 38

D. Borchmeyer: *Das Theater Richard Wagners* (Munich, 1982)

R. Brinkmann: 'Richard Wagner der Erzähler', *ÖMz*, xxxvii (1982), 297

M. Ewans: *Wagner and Aeschylus: the 'Ring' and the 'Oresteia'* (London, 1982)

C. Dahlhaus: 'Wagner's "A Communication to my Friends": Reminiscence and Adaptation', *MT*, cxxiv (1983), 89

J. Deathridge: 'Cataloguing Wagner', *MT*, cxxiv (1983), 92

ANALYSIS AND CRITICISM: INDIVIDUAL STUDIES
(early operas: Die Hochzeit to Lohengrin)

A. Smolian: *The Themes of 'Tannhäuser'* (London, 1891)

W. Golther: 'Rienzi: ein musikalisches Drama', *Die Musik*, i (1901–2), 1833

F. Muncker: 'Richard Wagners Operntext "Die Hochzeit" ', *Die Musik*, i (1901–2), 1824

W. Tappert: 'Die drei verschiedenen Schlüsse des Tannhäuser vor der jetzigen, endgültigen Fassung', *Die Musik*, i (1901–2), 1844

W. Altmann: 'Richard Wagner und die Berliner General-Intendantur: Verhandlungen über den "Fliegenden Holländer" und "Tannhäuser" ', *Die Musik*, ii (1902–3), no.2, p.331, no.3, pp.92, 304

W. Golther: 'Die französische und die deutsche Tannhäuser-Dichtung', *Die Musik*, ii (1902–3), 271

F. Panzer: 'Richard Wagners Tannhäuser: sein Aufbau und seine Quellen', *Die Musik*, vii (1907–8), 11

H. Dinger: 'Zu Richard Wagners "Rienzi" ', *Richard Wagner-Jb*, iii (1908), 88–132

E. Istel: 'Richard Wagners Oper "Das Liebesverbot" auf Grund der handschriftlichen Originalpartitur dargestellt', *Die Musik*, viii (1908–9), 3–47

E. Kloss: 'Richard Wagner über "Lohengrin": Aussprüche des

Meisters über sein Werk', *Richard Wagner-Jb*, iii (1908), 132–88

E. Istel: 'Wagners erste Oper "Die Hochzeit" auf Grund der autographen Paritur dargestellt', *Die Musik*, ix (1909–10), 331

H. Porges: 'Ueber Richard Wagner's "Lohengrin" ', *Bayreuther Blätter*, xxxii (1909), 173

A. Heuss: 'Zum Thema, Musik und Szene bei Wagner: im Anschluss an Wagners Aufsatz, Bemerkungen zur Aufführung der Oper "Der fliegende Holländer" ', *Die Musik*, x (1910–11), 3, 81

W. Krienitz: *Richard Wagners 'Feen'* (Munich, 1910)

M. Graf: 'Richard Wagner im "Fliegenden Holländer" ', *Schriften zur angewandten Seelenkunde*, ed. S. Freud, ix (Leipzig and Vienna, 1911/R1970)

J. Kapp: 'Die Urschrift von Richard Wagners "Lohengrin"-Dichtung', *Die Musik*, xi (1911–12), 88

M. Koch: 'Die Quellen der "Hochzeit" ', *Richard Wagner-Jb*, iv (1912), 105

E. Istel: 'Autographe Regiebemerkungen Wagners zum "Fliegenden Holländer" ', *Die Musik*, xii (1912–13), 214

E. Mehler: 'Beiträge zur Wagner-Forschung: unveröffentlichte Stücke aus "Rienzi", "Holländer" und "Tannhäuser" ', *Die Musik*, xii (1912–13), 195

E. Lindner: *Richard Wagner über 'Tannhäuser': Aussprüche des Meisters über sein Werk* (Leipzig, 1914)

H. von Wolzogen: *Richard Wagner über den 'Fliegenden Holländer': die Entstehung, Gestaltung und Darstellung des Werkes aus den Schriften und Briefen des Meisters zusammengestellt* (Leipzig, 1914)

J. G. Robertson: 'The Genesis of Wagner's Drama "Tannhäuser" ', *Modern Language Review*, xviii (1923), 458

O. Strobel: 'Wagners Prosaentwurf zum "Fliegenden Holländer" ', *Bayreuther Blätter*, lvi (1933), 157

H. Nathan: *Das Rezitativ der Frühopern Richard Wagners: ein Beitrag zur Stilistik des Opernrezitativs in der ersten Hälfte des 19. Jahrhunderts* (diss., U. of Berlin, 1934)

A. Lorenz: 'Der musikalische Aufbau von Wagners "Lohengrin" ', *Bayreuther Festspielführer 1936*, 189

O. Strobel: 'Die Urgestalt des "Lohengrin": Wagners erster dichterischer Entwurf', *Bayreuther Festspielführer 1936*, 141–71

G. Abraham: ' "The Flying Dutchman": Original Version', *ML*, xx (1939), 412

H. Engel: 'Über Richard Wagners Oper "Das Liebesverbot" ', *Festschrift Friedrich Blume* (Kassel, 1963), 80

Bibliography

D. Steinbeck: 'Zur Textkritik der Venus-Szenen im "Tannhäuser" ', *Mf*, xix (1966), 412

G. Abraham: 'A Lost Wagner Aria', *MT*, cx (1969), 927

M. Geck: 'Rienzi-Philologie', *Das Drama Richard Wagners als musikalisches Kunstwerk*, ed. C. Dahlhaus (Regensburg, 1970), 183

C. Hopkinson: *Tannhäuser: an Examination of 36 Editions* (Tutzing, 1973)

P. S. Machlin: 'Wagner, Durand and "The Flying Dutchman": the 1852 Revisions of the Overture', *ML*, lv (1974), 410

——: *The Flying Dutchman: Sketches, Revisions and Analysis* (diss., U. of California, Berkeley, 1976)

R. Strohm, ed.: *Dokumente und Texte zu 'Rienzi, der Letzte der Tribunen'*, R. Wagner: Sämtliche Werke, xxiii (Mainz, 1976)

J. Deathridge: *Wagner's Rienzi: a Reappraisal based on a Study of the Sketches and Drafts* (Oxford, 1977)

R. Strohm: 'Dramatic Time and Operatic Form in Wagner's "Tannhäuser" ', *PRMA*, civ (1977–8), 1

J. Deathridge: 'Eine verschollene Wagner-Arie?', *Melos/NZM*, iv (1978), 208

I. Vetter: 'Holländer-Metamorphosen', *Melos/NZM*, iv (1978), 206

J. Deathridge: 'Fragmente über Fragmentarisches: zur 'Lohengrin' – Kompositionsskizze', *Bayerische Staatsoper: Lohengrin – Programmheft zur Neuinszenierung* (Munich, 1978)

L. Finscher: 'Wagner der Opernkomponist: von der "Feen" zum "Rienzi" ', *Richard Wagner: von der Oper zum Musikdrama*, ed. S. Kunze (Berne and Munich, 1978), 25

R. Strohm: 'On the History of the Opera "Tannhäuser" ', *Festspielheft Tannhäuser* (Bayreuth, 1978)

I. Vetter: 'Der "Ahasverus des Ozeans" – musikalisch unerlöst? Der fliegende Holländer und seine Revisionen', *Festspielheft Holländer* (Bayreuth, 1979)

J. Deathridge: *An Introduction to 'The Flying Dutchman'* (London, 1982)

I. Vetter: *Der fliegende Holländer von Richard Wagner: Entstehung, Bearbeitung, Überlieferung* (diss., Technische Universität, Berlin, 1982)

C. Abbate: 'The Parisian "Venus" and the "Paris" Tannhäuser', *JAMS*, xxxvi (1983)

——: *The 'Parisian' Tannhäuser* (diss., Princeton U., 1984)

(*Der Ring des Nibelungen*)

G. B. Shaw: *The Perfect Wagnerite: a Commentary on the Niblung's Ring* (London, 1898, 4/1923/R1972)

A. Smolian: *Richard Wagner's Bühnenfestspiel Der Ring des Nibelungen: ein Vademecum* (Berlin, 1901)

C. Saint-Saëns: 'Bayreuth und der Ring des Nibelungen', *Die Musik*, i (1901–2), 751, 879

W. Golther: *Die sagengeschichtlichen Grundlagen der Ringdichtung Richard Wagners* (Berlin, 1902)

W. A. Ellis: 'Die verschiedenen Fassungen von "Siegfrieds Tod" ', *Die Musik*, iii (1903–4), 239, 315

R. Petsch: 'Der "Ring des Nibelungen" in seinen Beziehungen zur griechischen Tragödie und zur zeitgenössischen Philosophie', *Richard Wagner-Jb*, ii (1907), 284–330

E. Istel: 'Wie Wagner am "Ring" arbeitete: Mitteilungen über die Instrumentationsskizze des "Rheingold" und andere Manuskripte', *Die Musik*, x (1910–11), 67; Eng. trans., abridged, *MQ*, xix (1933), 38

W. Altmann: 'Zur Geschichte der Entstehung und Veröffentlichung von Wagners "Der Ring des Nibelungen" ', *AMz*, xxxviii (1911), 69, 101, 129, 157, 185, 217, 245

E. Kloss and H. Weber: *Richard Wagner über den Ring des Nibelungen: Aussprüche des Meisters über sein Werk in Schriften und Briefen* (Leipzig, 1913)

H. Wiessner: *Der Stabreimvers in Richard Wagners 'Ring des Nibelungen'* (Berlin, 1924/R1967)

L. A. Leroy: *Wagner's Music Drama of the Ring* (London, 1925)

W. Hapke: *Die musikalische Darstellung der Gebärde in Richard Wagners Ring des Nibelungen* (Leipzig, 1927)

O. Strobel: 'Die Originalpartitur von Richard Wagners "Rheingold" ', *Bayreuther Festspielführer 1928*, 47

——: 'Die Kompositionsskizzen zum "Ring des Nibelungen"; ein Blick in die Musikerwerkstatt Richard Wagners', *Bayreuther Festspielführer 1930*, 114

——: *Richard Wagner: Skizzen und Entwürfe zur Ring-Dichtung, mit der Dichtung 'Der junge Siegfried'* (Munich, 1930) [see also O. Strobel, *Die Musik*, xxv (1932–3), 336]

——: ' "Winterstürme wichen dem Wonnemond": zur Genesis von Siegmunds Lenzgesang', *Bayreuther Blätter*, liii (1930), 123

——: 'Aus Wagners Musikerwerkstatt: Betrachtungen über die Kompositionsskizzen zum "Ring des Nibelungen" ', *AMz*, lviii (1931), 463, 479, 495

——: 'Vom Werden der "Ring"-Dichtung: Authentisches zur Entstehungsgeschichte des Bühnenfestspiels', *Bayreuther Festspielführer 1931*, 77

A. Buesst: *Richard Wagner: The Nibelung's Ring* (London, 1932, 2/1952)

O. Strobel: 'Zur Entstehungsgeschichte der Götterdämmerung:

unbekannte Dokumente', *Die Musik*, xxv (1932–3), 336

R. Grisson: *Beiträge zur Auslegung von Richard Wagners 'Ring des Nibelungen'* (Leipzig, 1934)

E. Hutcheson: *A Musical Guide to the Richard Wagner Ring of the Nibelung* (New York, 1940/*R*1972)

H. Engel: 'Versuche einer Sinndeutung von Richard Wagners "Ring des Nibelungen" ', *Mf*, x (1957), 225

W. Serauky: 'Die Todesverkündigungsszene in Richard Wagners "Walküre" als musikalisch-geistige Achse des Werkes', *Mf*, xii (1959), 143

R. Donington: *Wagner's 'Ring' and its Symbols: the Music and the Myth* (London, 1963, rev., enlarged 3/1974)

C. von Westernhagen: 'Die Kompositions-Skizze zu "Siegfrieds Tod" aus dem Jahre 1850', *NZM*, Jg.124 (1963), 178

R. Bailey: 'Wagner's Musical Sketches for "Siegfrieds Tod"', *Studies in Music History: Essays for Oliver Strunk* (Princeton, 1968), 459–95

C. Dahlhaus: 'Formprinzipien in Wagners "Ring des Nibelungen" ', *Beiträge zur Geschichte der Oper*, ed. H. Becker (Regensburg, 1969), 95

D. Coren: *A Study of Richard Wagner's 'Siegfried'* (diss., U. of California, Berkeley, 1971)

R. Brinkmann: ' "Drei der Fragen stell' ich mir frei": zur Wanderer-Szene im I. Akt von Wagners "Siegfried" ', *Jb des Staatlichen Institut für Musikforschung Preussischer Kulturbesitz* (Berlin, 1972), 120–62

W. Breig: *Studien zur Entstehungsgeschichte von Wagners 'Ring des Nibelungen'* (diss. U. of Freiburg, 1973)

C. von Westernhagen: *Die Entstehung des 'Ring', dargestellt an den Kompositionsskizzen Richard Wagners* (Zurich, 1973; Eng. trans., 1976)

P. Nitsche: 'Klangfarbe und Form: das Walhallthema in Rheingold und Walküre', *Melos/NZM*, i (1975), 83

W. Breig and H. Fladt, eds.: *Dokumente zur Entstehungsgeschichte des Bühnenfestspiels Der Ring des Nibelungen*, R. Wagner: *Sämtliche Werke*, xxix/1 (Mainz, 1976)

J. Culshaw: *Reflections on Wagner's Ring* (London, 1976)

D. Coren: 'Inspiration and Calculation in the Genesis of Wagner's "Siegfried"', *Studies in Musicology in Honor of Otto E. Albrecht* (Kassel, 1977)

R. Bailey: 'The Structure of the "Ring" and Its Evolution', *19th Century Music*, i (1977–8), 48

J. Deathridge: 'Wagner's Sketches for the "Ring" ', *MT*, cxviii (1977), 383

J. M. Knapp: 'The Instrumentation Draft of Wagner's "Das

Rheingold" ', *JAMS*, xxx (1977), 272

R. Brinkmann: 'Mythos – Geschichte – Natur: Zeitkonstellationen im "Ring" ', *Richard Wagner: von der Oper zum Musikdrama*, ed. S. Kunze (Berne and Munich, 1978), 61

J. L. DiGaetani, ed.: *Penetrating Wagner's Ring: an Anthology* (Rutherford, Madison, Teaneck and London, 1978)

D. Cooke: *I Saw the World End* (London, 1979)

W. Kinderman: 'Dramatic Recapitulation in Wagner's "Götterdämmerung" ', *19th Century Music*, iv (1980–81), 101

L. J. Rather: *The Dream of Self-Destruction: Wagner's 'Ring' and the Modern World* (Louisiana, 1981)

D. Coren: 'The Texts of Wagner's "Der junge Siegfried" and "Siegfried" ', *19th Century Music*, vi (1982–3), 17

(*Tristan und Isolde*)

M. Kufferath: *Guide thématique et analyse de Tristan et Iseult* (Paris, 1894)

H. Porges: 'Tristan und Isolde', *Bayreuther Blätter*, xxv (1902), 186; xxvi (1903), 23, 241–70; ed. H. von Wolzogen (Leipzig, 1906)

W. Golther: 'Zur Entstehung von Richard Wagners Tristan', *Die Musik*, v (1905–6), 3

L. Lehmann: *Studie zu 'Tristan und Isolde'* (n.p., c1906)

A. Prüfer: 'Novalis Hymnen an die Nacht in ihren Beziehungen zu Wagners Tristan und Isolde', *Richard Wagner-Jb*, i (1906), 290

W. Golther: *Tristan und Isolde in den Dichtungen des Mittelalters und der neuen Zeit* (Leipzig, 1907)

K. Grunsky: 'Das Vorspiel und der erste Akt von "Tristan und Isolde" ', *Richard Wagner-Jb*, ii (1907), 207–84

E. Lindner: *Richard Wagner über Tristan und Isolde: Aussprüche des Meisters über sein Werk* (Leipzig, 1912)

E. Istel: 'Von Wagner angeordnete Striche und Änderungen in "Tristan und Isolde" ', *Die Musik*, xii (1912–13), 173

E. Kurth: *Romantische Harmonik und ihre Krise in Wagners 'Tristan'* (Berlin, 1920, 2/1923)

S. Anheisser: 'Das Vorspiel zu "Tristan und Isolde" und seine Motivik', *ZMw*, iii (1920–21), 257–304

H. F. Peyser: ' "Tristan", First-hand', *MQ*, xi (1925), 418

A. Bahr-Mildenburg: *Tristan und Isolde: Darstellung der Werke Richard Wagners aus dem Geiste der Dichtung und Musik: vollständige Regiebearbeitung sämtlicher Partien mit Notenbeispielen* (Leipzig, 1936)

O. Strobel: ' "Geschenke des Himmels": über die ältesten über-

Bibliography

lieferten "Tristan"-Themen und eine andere – unbekannte – Melodie Wagners', *Bayreuther Festspielführer 1938*, 157

G. Schünemann: 'Eine neue Tristan-Handschrift', *AMf*, iii (1938), 129, 137 [on a copy by Bülow]

H. Grunsky: ' "Tristan und Isolde": der symphonische Aufbau des dritten Aufzugs', *ZfM*, Jg.113 (1952), 390

J. Kerman: 'Opera as Symphonic Poem', *Opera as Drama* (New York, 1956), chap.7

V. Levi: *Tristano e Isotta di Riccardo Wagner* (Venice, 1958)

M. Vogel: *Der Tristan-Akkord und die Krise der modernen Harmonie-Lehre* (Düsseldorf, 1962)

H. Scharschuch: *Gesamtanalyse der Harmonik von Richard Wagners Musikdrama 'Tristan und Isolde': unter spezifischer Berücksichtigung der Sequenztechnik des Tristanstiles* (Regensburg, 1963)

H. Truscott: 'Wagner's "Tristan" and the Twentieth Century', *MR*, xxiv (1963), 75

E. Zuckermann: *The First Hundred Years of Tristan* (New York, 1964)

W. Wagner, ed.: *100 Jahre Tristan: 19 Essays* (Emsdetten, 1965)

W. J. Mitchell: 'The Tristan Prelude: Techniques and Structure', *Music Forum*, i (1967), 162–203

R. Bailey: *The Genesis of Tristan und Isolde, and a Study of Wagner's Sketches and Drafts for the First Act* (diss., Princeton U., 1969)

E. Voss: 'Wagners Striche im Tristan', *NZM*, Jg.132 (1971), 644

R. Jackson: 'Leitmotive and Form in the "Tristan" Prelude', *MR*, xxxvi (1975), 42

C. Dahlhaus: ' "Tristan"-Harmonik und Tonalität', *Melos/NZM*, iv (1978), 215

J. Deathridge: ' "Im übrigen darf ich wohl hoffen, dass Sie mich nicht eben gerade für einen Honorararbeiter halten . . .": Zur Entstehung der "Tristan"-Partitur', *Bayerische Staatsoper: Tristan Programmheft zur Neuinszenierung* (Munich, 1980), 42

E. Voss: 'Wagners "Tristan": "Die Liebe als furchtbare Qual" ', *Bayerische Staatsoper: Tristan Programmheft zur Neuinszenierung* (Munich, 1980), 50

P. Wapnewski: *Tristan der Held Richard Wagners* (Berlin, 1981)

C. Abbate: ' "Tristan" in the Composition of "Pelléas" ', *19th Century Music*, v (1981–2), 117

(*Die Meistersinger von Nürnberg*)

A. M. Bowen: *The Sources and Text of Wagner's 'Die Meistersinger von Nürnberg'* (Munich, 1897)

E. Thomas: *Die Instrumentation der Meistersinger von Nürnberg: ein Beitrag zur Instrumentationslehre* (Mannheim, 1899, 2/ ?1907)

J. Tiersot: *Etude sur les Maîtres-chanteurs de Nuremberg de Richard Wagner* (Paris, 1899)

R. Sternfeld: 'Hans Sachsens Schusterlied', *Die Musik*, i (1901– 2), 1869

H. Abert: 'Gedanken zu Richard Wagners "Die Meistersinger von Nürnberg" ', *Die Musik*, iv (1904–5), 254

E. Kloss: *Richard Wagner über die 'Meistersinger von Nürnberg': Aussprüche des Meisters über sein Werk* (Leipzig, 1910)

W. Altmann: 'Zur Geschichte der Entstehung und Veröffentlichung von Richard Wagners "Die Meistersinger von Nürnberg" ', *Richard Wagner-Jb*, v (1913), 87–137

K. Grunsky: 'Reim und musikalische Form in den Meistersingern', *Richard Wagner-Jb*, v (1913), 138–87

E. Mehler: 'Die Textvarianten der Meistersinger-Dichtung: Beiträge zur Textkritik des Werkes', *Richard Wagner-Jb*, v (1913), 187–233

G. Roethe: 'Zum dramatischen Aufbau der Wagnerschen Meistersinger', *Sitzungsberichte der Preussischen Akademie* (1919), no.37

F. Zademack: *Die Meistersinger von Nürnberg: Richard Wagners Dichtung und ihre Quellen* (Berlin, 1921)

H. Thompson: *Wagner and Wagenseil: a Source of Wagner's Opera 'Die Meistersinger'* (London, 1927)

O. Strobel: ' "Morgenlich leuchtend in rosigem Schein": wie Walthers Preislied entstand', *Bayreuther Festspielführer 1933*, 148

R. M. Rayner: *Wagner and 'Die Meistersinger'* (London, 1940)

W. Hess: ' "Die Meistersinger von Nürnberg": ihre dichter-ischmusikalische Gesamtform', *ZfM*, Jg.113 (1952), 394

W. E. Mcdonald: 'Words, Music, and Dramatic Development in "Die Meistersinger" ', *19th Century Music*, i (1977–8), 246

R. Brinkmann: 'Über das Kern- und Schlusswort der "Meistersinger" ', *Bayerische Staatsoper: Meistersinger Programmheft zur Neuinszenierung* (Munich, 1979), 82

E. Voss: 'Gedanken über "Meistersinger"-Dokumente', *Bayerische Staatsoper: Meistersinger Programmheft zur Neuinszenierung* (Munich, 1979), 76

——: 'Wagners "Meistersinger" als Oper des deutschen Bürgertums', *Rororo Opernbücher: Die Meistersinger von Nürnberg*, ed. A. Csampai and D. Holland (Reinbek bei Hamburg, 1981)

——: 'Die Entstehung der Meistersinger von Nürnberg: Geschichten und Geschichte', facs. edn. of 1862 lib (Mainz, 1983) [see also 'Autograph Facsimiles']

Bibliography

(*Parsifal*)

E. Hippeau: *'Parsifal' et l'opéra wagnérien* (Paris, 1883)

M. Kufferath: *Parsifal de Richard Wagner: légende, drame, partition* (Paris, 1890; Eng. trans., 1904)

E. Wechsler: *Die Sage vom heiligen Gral in ihrer Entwicklung bis auf Richard Wagners 'Parsifal'* (Halle, 1898)

A. Drews: 'Mozarts "Zauberflöte" und Wagners "Parsifal": eine Parallele', *Richard Wagner-Jb*, i (1906), 326–61

P. Sakolowski: 'Wagners erste Parsifal-Entwürfe', *Richard Wagner-Jb*, i (1906), 307

K. Grunsky: 'Die Rhythmik im Parsifal', *Richard Wagner-Jb*, iii (1908), 276–370

W. Golther: *Parsifal und der Gral in deutscher Sage des Mittelalters und der Neuzeit* (Leipzig, c1911)

A. Prüfer: 'Zur Entstehungsgeschichte des Bühnenweihfestspieles "Parsifal"', *Bayreuther Festspielführer 1911*, 152

W. Altmann: 'Zur Entstehungsgeschichte des "Parsifal"', *Richard Wagner-Jb*, iv (1912), 162

A. Heuss: 'Die Grundlagen der Parsifal-Dichtung', *Die Musik*, xii (1912–13), 206, 323

R. Petsch: 'Zur Quellenkunde des "Parsifal"', *Richard Wagner-Jb*, iv (1912), 138

H. von Wolzogen: 'Parsifal-Varianten: eine Übersicht', *Richard Wagner-Jb*, iv (1912), 168

E. Lindner: *Richard Wagner über 'Parsifal': Aussprüche des Meisters über sein Werk* (Leipzig, 1913)

C. Debussy: 'Richard Wagner', *Monsieur Croche antidilettante* (Paris, 1921, 2/1926; Eng. trans., 2/1962), chap.16

M. Unger: 'The Cradle of the Parsifal Legend', *MQ*, xviii (1932), 428

V. d'Indy: *Introduction à l'étude de Parsifal* (Paris, 1937)

T. W. Adorno: 'Zur Partitur des "Parsifal"', *Moments musicaux* (Frankfurt am Main, 1964), 52

M. Geck and E. Voss, eds.: *Dokumente zur Entstehung und ersten Aufführung des Bühnenweihfestspiels Parsifal*, R. Wagner: Sämtliche Werke, xxx (Mainz, 1970)

H.-J. Bauer: *Wagners Parsifal: Kriterien der Kompositionstechnik* (Munich, 1977)

S. Grossmann-Vendrey: *Bayreuth in der deutschen Presse, ii: Die Uraufführung des Parsifal* (Regensburg, 1977)

P. Wapnewski: 'Parzival und Parsifal oder Wolframs Held und Wagners Erlöser', *Richard Wagner: von der Oper zum Musikdrama*, ed. S. Kunze (Berne and Munich, 1978), 47

J. Chailley: *'Parsifal' de Richard Wagner: opéra initiatique* (Paris, 1979)

L. Beckett: *Richard Wagner: Parsifal* (Cambridge, 1981)
H. K. Metzger and R. Riehn, eds.: *Richard Wagner: Parsifal*, Musik-Konzepte, no.25 (Munich, 1982)
W. Seelig: 'Ambivalenz und Erlösung-Wagners "Parsifal": Zweifel und Glauben', *ÖMz*, xxxvii (1982), 307
B. Millington: 'Parsifal: Facing the Contradictions', *MT*, cxxiv (1983), 97

(*other works*)

R. M. Breithaupt: 'Richard Wagners Klaviermusik', *Die Musik*, iii (1903–4), 108
W. Kleefeld: 'Richard Wagner als Bearbeiter fremder Werke', *Die Musik*, iv (1904–5), 231, 326
K. Mey: 'Über Richard Wagners Huldigungschor an König Friedrich August II. von Sachsen 1844', *Die Musik*, v (1905–6), 327
——: 'Richard Wagners Webertrauermarsch', *Die Musik*, vi (1906–7), 331
E. Istel: 'Eine Doppelfuge von der Hand Wagners: nach dem ungedruckten Originalmanuskript mitgeteilt', *Die Musik*, xi (1911–12), 27
——: 'Ein unbekanntes Instrumentalwerk Wagners: auf Grund der handschriftlichen Partitur dargestellt', *Die Musik*, xii (1912–13), 152
H. W. von Waltershausen: *Das Siegfried-Idyll, oder die Rückkehr zur Natur* (Munich, 1920)
R. Sternfeld: 'Die erste Fassung von Wagners Faust-Ouvertüre', *Die Musik*, xv (1922–3), 659
O. Strobel: 'Das "Porazzi"-Thema: über eine unveröffentlichte Melodie Richard Wagners und deren seltsamer Werdegang', *Bayreuther Festspielführer 1934*, 183
G. Abraham: 'Wagner's String Quartet: an Essay in Musical Speculation', *MT*, lxxxvi (1945), 233
——: 'Wagner's Second Thoughts', *Slavonic and Romantic Music: Essays and Studies* (London, 1968), 294 [on rev. of *Faust* overture, *Der fliegende Holländer, Tannhäuser*]
W. S. Newman: 'Wagner's Sonatas', *Studies in Romanticism*, vii (1968), 129
E. Voss: 'Wagners fragmentarisches Orchesterwerk in e-moll: die früheste der erhaltenen Kompositionen?', *Mf*, xxiii (1970), 50
——: *Richard Wagner und die Instrumentalmusik: Wagners symphonischer Ehrgeiz* (Wilhelmshaven, 1977)
J. Deathridge: 'Richard Wagners Kompositionen zu Goethes "Faust"', *Jb der Bayerischen Staatsoper* (Munich, 1982), 90
E. Voss: *Richard Wagner: eine Faust-Ouvertüre*, Meisterwerke der Musik, xxxi (Munich, 1982)

Index

221

Index

223

Index

225